UNEXPLAINED

UNEXPLAINED

Supernatural Stories for Uncertain Times

RICHARD MACLEAN SMITH

SCEPTRE

Copyright © Richard MacLean Smith 2018

The right of Richard MacLean Smith to be identified as the
Author of the Work has been asserted by him in accordance
with the Copyright, Designs and Patents Act 1988.

A CIP catalogue record for this title is available from the British Library

Paperback ISBN 978 1 473 67116 4
eBook ISBN 978 1 473 67114 0

Typeset in Celeste by Hewer Text UK Ltd, Edinburgh
Printed and bound in Great Britain by Clays Ltd, Elcograf S.p.A.

Hodder & Stoughton policy is to use papers that are natural, renewable
and recyclable products and made from wood grown in sustainable
forests. The logging and manufacturing processes are expected to
conform to the environmental regulations of the country of origin.

Hodder & Stoughton Ltd
Carmelite House
50 Victoria Embankment
London EC4Y 0DZ

www.sceptrebooks.co.uk

For Donna, Boo and Scout

CONTENTS

INTRODUCTION

'Leave the door open for the unknown, the door into the dark. That's where the most important things came from, where you yourself came from, and where you will go.'

Rebecca Solnit – *A Field Guide to Getting Lost*

It's the evening of 4 December 1944, and at roughly 30,000ft above the border of Holland and Germany, twelve RAF Mosquito aircraft are leading a raid on the industrial harbour town of Karlsruhe. A short distance behind them, somewhere in the clouds below, are over 500 RAF bombers heading in the same direction. The Mosquitos form part of a unit known as the Pathfinders, whose job it is to fly at the head of a raid in order to mark the targets for a more effective run.

They do this by dropping a variety of multi-coloured flares: small pockets of light that float down on to the target below. One can only imagine the sight from the ground, watching as these soft-falling, colourful fireworks materialise out of the dark as if from nowhere, a weirdly beautiful precursor to the horror that would shortly follow.

On this night, inside the cockpit of Mosquito *O Oboe*, Captain Johnny Liddle holds the plane steady as he stares straight ahead into the night sky, while his navigator Albert Smith diligently plots a steady line towards their target under the dim green glow of the instrument panel.

For many of us it is impossible to imagine the heightened sense of fear and anxiety that Johnny and Albert would have felt as they drew nearer to their target destination; a familiar feeling for them both, especially Albert who was undertaking his ninetieth mission of the war. But even for a crew as battle-hardened as they were, one suspects it is something they never got used to.

'Alter course to one-six-four degrees,' Albert says through his oxygen mask.

'OK,' comes back the nasal reply.

Suddenly, there is a jolt.

Albert turns sharply to the left. Looking out of the window he sees something in the darkness, something that shouldn't be there: the black underbelly of another Mosquito aircraft. He can only watch in horror as the other plane ploughs right through their tail. There is a strange moment of calm as the drone of the engines continues and the plane seems to hold, but then comes a sickening, shuddering lurch as the aircraft starts to turn in on itself.

And now they are plummeting helplessly towards the ground.

Albert screams as he is thrown forwards, wrenched into the air and thumped to the floor of the plane. He grabs for the struts at the base of Johnny's seat as his legs twist above him and urine flows uncontrollably. Struggling to lift his head against the force of gravity, Albert can just make out Johnny wrestling with the joystick. But without the tail of the plane it is utterly futile, and the aircraft starts to spin violently out of control.

Johnny reaches up for the handle of the escape hatch and pulls down hard. In an instant, the warmth of the cockpit is replaced by the rushing of bitterly cold air. With the parachute already on his back, Johnny grabs hold of the joystick and unlocks his seatbelt. Immediately he is sucked towards the opening above. As he struggles to keep himself inside the plane, he tries desperately to reach out to Albert. For a moment he seems to hang in the air like a balloon being held by a child, just before they let it go. And then he is gone, into the darkness beyond.

Albert, now alone, with his legs still twisting above him, spots his parachute at the back of the cockpit strapped to the side. But any attempt to reach it and he'll be sucked straight out of the plane. In that moment, in the chaotic vortex of the spinning aircraft, Albert realises he is going to die. As the plane continues to fall, he pulls his head hard against the floor and closes his eyes. It will be quicker this way he thinks, and the thought of being sucked out into the darkness beyond terrifies him even more.

Then something flickers across his eyelids. He opens them to find a soft orange glow all around the cockpit.

The engine is now on fire.

Please God, let it come before I burn, he begs. But then, as suddenly as it had begun, his legs fall to the floor. It takes him a second to understand, but as Albert lifts his head he realises the plane is no longer spinning. What's more, he's been thrown right next to his parachute. In seconds he rips the chute from the side and, despite his trembling fingers, clips it to his harness before somehow managing to stand.

Above he sees only the darkness, the stuff of nightmares just a moment before, but now his only hope. He reaches for it but something pulls him back into the plane. This can't be happening. Then he realises: it's his helmet; it's still connected to the intercom cable. He rips it off and hauls himself up, pushing his head above the cockpit. But as the freezing wind lashes at his face, and he tries to kick off, his feet refuse to leave the floor. Finally, with one last desperate push, he is thrust into the air. And now he is falling, falling alone in the pitch-black sky.

On the ground, Pilot Johnny Liddle, after successfully bailing out of the aircraft, watches as the burning plane hits the deck. There is no sign of his navigator Albert in the sky above.

Two days later, at the home of Albert's parents, Albert Snr and Alice Smith, there is a dreaded knock at the door. It's the postman, bearing news that no parent wants to hear. As Albert Snr reads the telegram out loud, Alice struggles to contain herself. Although it isn't definitive, such telegrams rarely turn out well. The couple try to maintain hope, but it's hard to escape the creeping sense that their son will never be coming home. So it's with some surprise that they receive another telegram only a few days later. But this time it isn't from the war office: it's from their son. He is alive and recuperating well in hospital. A few weeks later he is finally returned home.

Although by no means unique for a time of war, it is nonetheless an incredible story and one I know particularly well because Albert was in fact my granddad. As you can imagine, it is a story that has been shared many times among the family. My granddad even went so far as to record his account of the incident in a book.[1]

I say it is a story I know well. In fact, it was only very recently that I discovered a piece of it is missing; missing from the book and missing from every account of this story I have heard since I was a child. A couple of years ago, when my dad was telling it again, he added something new. Shortly before the plane stopped spinning, for a brief moment, Albert saw a vision of an old woman he didn't recognise in the cockpit with him. When I asked why I'd never heard that part before, my dad explained that Albert had dismissed it as just a figment of his imagination. In the retelling of the story, this peculiar moment had gradually been erased because to include it meant opening the door to unwanted superstition. To be fair, this is my thinking too. It certainly adds a little more colour – not that the story needs any embellishment – but as my granddad had, I dismissed the vision of the elderly woman as nothing but a trick of the mind.

Then I found out something else. When Albert's mother received the news that her son was likely to have been killed in action, she was devastated. However, being Catholic, she retained the hope that he might now be in a better place. Seeking comfort, she paid a visit to a local medium. Perhaps she went with the genuine intention of trying to contact Albert from beyond the grave, or perhaps it was just her way of saying goodbye to her son.

When Alice entered the room, the medium knew immediately why she was there. Of course, it wouldn't take much to work out why a distraught middle-aged woman during the height of the Second World War would be paying a visit to a medium, and ordinarily you might expect the medium to commiserate the grief-stricken Alice and offer herself as a conduit to contact her recently deceased son. Only she didn't. Instead what she said was, 'You needn't worry, your son is not dead and he is being looked after by an elderly relative . . .'

Although the story about my granddad is relatively benign, for many, tales of strange and unexplained events of the supposed paranormal or supernatural will always hold a unique and often dark fascination. Not only do we enjoy revelling in the mystery, but we are fascinated by the questions that such stories consistently throw up – questions about our nature and the nature of the universe, perhaps even universes, around us. Writing this book, I began to think about when it was that my own fascination with such stories had begun. Much to my regret, I wasn't a voracious reader growing up. Maybe it was laziness or lack of imagination, but for me, the TV was my window of escape. Books seemed unwelcoming and aloof, quietly arranged in endless rows with their backs turned to me. They felt somehow inaccessible, requiring a guide or interpreter, some frame of reference to send me on my way (or the bravery to just take the plunge). And music in some ways felt much the same. I would eventually find my way to both, but with TV there was no such reticence. It didn't require me to awaken its words, or instinctively know where to look; it was already alive, waiting for me.

Everyone knew that, by day, TV was a succubus, a terminal parasite of regimented programming and strange, unnaturally enthused behaviour. Today daytime TV is characterised by the loud, brash brightness of a world that feels all too hyper-real. Growing up in the 80s and early 90s it was a vat of extreme normality by comparison; pastel in palate and populated with 'normal' people, rendered strangely artificial and Stepfordian in their ordinariness by the cameras; unutterably creepy to think about now, but to a child, just plain boring. There was magic to be found, of course: Saturday mornings with Cyril Sneer or the never-ending saga of *Dungeons & Dragons* (did I really see the one where they actually made it back home?). After school was Skips crisps, *Grange Hill*, *Round the Twist* and *Knightmare*. And, of course, *Neighbours*, always *Neighbours*.

But come night time, to this child at least, TV was a wholly different animal. It was a wild untamed thing, a place of unimagined topographies and netherworlds, a dangerous place. Being the spoilt child that I was, at some point I had convinced my parents to put a TV in my room, no doubt under a strict agreement of rationed hours that I had no intention of adhering to. And so it was that night, while the rest of the house was sound asleep, I switched it on. What greeted me was a strange and alien world, a world of unrestrained pop-culture, foreign voices, and if I was really lucky, *Moviedrome*. Presented by the riveting Alex Cox and later Mark Cousins, the weekly BBC2 series showcased an extraordinary programme of obscure cult films that offered up a world more real than anything I had known before. *Moviedrome* changed everything.

From that moment on, I would often lie awake in the dark as shapes and sounds emerged from behind the glass and crept into my room, things I couldn't possibly understand but that seemed oddly familiar at the same time. This wasn't the nightmare vision of Cronenberg's *Videodrome* or the *Infinite Jest* of Foster Wallace, however; I wasn't one of George Romero's zombies, slavishly hooked to the screen. I was the active participant. It was as if something deep inside had been roused from slumber, something primal and ancient, an Old One. And soon patterns would emerge, for it was in this fertile place between sleep and the screen, as I watched my dreams play out (or was it those images I would later dream?) that an appetite for the dark, the weird and eerie began to grow. Or, rather, awaken.

Moviedrome was the first gateway to the viscera of Horror and Science Fiction that I fell in love with. Films like *Assault on*

Precinct 13, *Solaris*, *Manhunter*, *The Fly* and *Society* were mind-blowing. These strange worlds would also be found elsewhere but somehow I uncovered them all: *Blade Runner*, *Suspiria*, *Blue Velvet*, *Hellraiser*, *They Live*, *La Planete Sauvage*, *Don't Look Now* . . . There would be many others but it was the ones with the dark, surreal qualities that left the deepest impression. And amongst them all, one, first broadcast in the UK at 9 p.m. on 23 October 1990, permeated the deepest. A peculiar offbeat soap opera soon to become the cultural phenomenon *Twin Peaks*. Age and experience would inevitably broaden my interests; bring a taste for nuance and subtlety. And yet so much of what fascinates me now is rooted in these first films and TV shows, and of course in time I would discover they had deep, timeless roots of their own.

As the cultural theorist Mark Fisher explains, the allure of the strange and the eerie has 'to do with the fascination for the outside, for that which lies beyond standard perception, cognition and experience'.[2] This, of course, can refer to the mundane as well as the fantastical but it is perhaps no more explicit than in our fascination with the potential for the supernatural and paranormal or the familiar otherness of dystopian science fiction. Simply, these films that I was watching – aside from being the most brilliant stories – were grappling with some of the biggest questions.

On the metaphysical and spiritual, for want of a better word, sides, my interest in these ideas begins with my fear of death and the existential crisis of cosmic insignificance. What draws me in is the tiny sliver of hope that somewhere in it all there will be something to convince me I need not fear the great infinite abyss. But conversely, since anything a bit more complicated was beyond me as a child, often the intrigue wasn't so much metaphysical or spiritual, but rather the horrors of cold, material reality, whatever reality was supposed to be.

As an atheist and rationalist, I've always been fascinated by the human imagination, the power of the subconscious and the nature of reality. Which is to say, the very basic, tangible fact that the world we see through the confines of our limited senses and our subjective social constructions and prejudices is in many ways not 'real', merely our own unique interpretation of it. It is this idea, explored through stories of the mysterious and the unexplained, that I find most invigorating.

Human concerns over the discrepancies between the worlds we experience and the world-as-it-truly-is are not novel by any stretch. We only have to look at the work of Parmenides or Plato's better-known cave allegory to reveal an ancient fascination with this ontological conundrum. But in recent times we have witnessed an explosion of science and pop-science books exploring these ideas, from physicist Carlo Rovelli's *Reality is Not What It Seems* and cosmologist Max Tegmark's *Our Mathematical Universe: My Quest for the Ultimate Nature of Reality* to the phenomenal success of books exploring counterintuitive thought, such as Malcolm Gladwell's *Blink* or Steven Levitt and Stephen Dubner's *Freakonomics*: all reveal to us hidden worlds beyond what we think we know.

You might say we are, for better or worse, the children of Heisenberg's uncertainty principle and post-modernist theory, uncovering a world where reality seems an ever-changing, many-splintered thing, a place where nothing is certain, not even immutable laws of physics. It is the arrogant preserve of every generation to think, as Max Tegmark puts it, 'that everything we know about is everything that exists'.[3] Yet, time and again, we are proven wrong. And as we continue to peer ever further into the far reaches of space, we see the universe enlarging as our own sense of place within it diminishes. Where once we considered Earth the centre of the solar system, whose sun revolved around it, it may transpire that the universe we live in is not even the only universe. And if we reject our solipsistic fallacies and accept there are likely to be other equally intelligent species out there, perhaps evolved differently to ourselves, who see the universe differently to us, it certainly begs the question: what is it exactly that we are perceiving? Which is not to reject truth or denigrate science or deny what we have discovered, but to wonder at what still remains to be found out. How naïve might our current perspectives look from the vantage point of five thousand years from now? Or five thousand million years from now? Because if there's one thing we can be certain of, they will change.

In my lifetime alone we have come to understand brain functions and the mechanism of genes in ways that could render any notion of free-will redundant; some of our finest minds have begun to question whether time, as we traditionally understand it, exists in any quantifiable way at all; the weirdness of quantum mechanics has led to predictions of an infinity of universes parallel to ours, in turn implying the possibility that everything that could ever happen not only *will* happen, but in fact already has; animals with which we share this extraordinary planet, much to our shame, are increasingly being revealed to be far more sophisticated and conscious than we once ever thought possible. And all the while the slow etherealisation of our lives into the digital sphere could be leading to the obsolescence of the physical form (if it hasn't already been done by the computer simulation we may in fact be living in!).

It is little wonder, then, that stories of the strange, supernatural and paranormal should be so alluring, stories that question the limits of our knowledge, consciousness and reality. Stories that play out in the places between what we think of as real and what is not. Such stories by definition, regardless of their veracity, serve as vital expressions of what intrigues and scares us but most of all, of what is unknown. And what makes the unexplained mystery different to the classic story structure of a Hollywood film is that it leaves us without closure, without the 'why'. It is this element that is so seductive because as a species, despite nature's best efforts to instruct us otherwise, we have a biological compulsion to find meaning. In 1994 social psychologist Arie Kruglanski coined the phrase 'cognitive closure', defining it as 'individuals' desire for a firm answer to a question and an aversion toward ambiguity.'[4] It is no coincidence then that horror stories and stories of mystery are often synonymous with the dark: a symbol for the unknown.

It is a clumsy reference perhaps, but for my granddad, even when he was falling from the sky in a burning plane, certain that he was going to die, there was something about being sucked into the unknowable space beyond that terrified him even more. And in a sense we are right to be afraid of the dark, the unknown. It is a basic primal reaction fundamental to our survival. In 2016, researchers from Brown University in the US discovered that even when we are sleeping, part of our brain remains vigilant, looking out for potential threats.[5]

But there is an important reason not to fear the dark. In his analysis of the archetypal story, Christopher Vogler, expanding on the work of mythologist Joseph Campbell, writes of a moment known as the Approach to the Innermost Cave. Fans of *Star Wars* might recognise it as the moment where Yoda tells Luke he must literally enter the cave to face his fears. But crucially, it is not the fear of the 'other' that scares him, but what his fear of the other will reveal about himself. Only when the hero, which is *you*, comes to terms with this will you be able to slay the dragon and emerge complete.

There may come a day, years from now, when all the many, many stars in our universe have flickered their last. And before that, as space continues to expand, light from even the closest galaxies will no longer be visible from Earth, as one by one all around the stars will go out. *This* is the dark that truly terrifies me, the dark from which there is no coming back. People often say we live in uncertain times but it has always been uncertain. We are, in a sense, always careering into the unknown, with no idea about where things will take us or what we truly know, or, indeed, to what extent we can really know anything. This is why it is as important as it has ever been that we don't retreat from the dark of the unknown, but instead embrace it while we still have the light to which we can return.

So what better way to explore all this than through the unexplained mystery – stories of bizarre and improbable events that test our fundamental beliefs and continue to evade our human need to understand and rationalise. In the pages to follow I have put together some of my favourite dark, strange and unsettling unexplained mysteries to get us on our way. So without further ado, let's take a step into the unknown . . .

Chapter One

RESURRECTED DREAMS

'She herself is a haunted house. She does not possess
herself; her ancestors sometimes come and peer out of the
windows of her eyes and that is very frightening.'

Angela Carter – 'The Lady of the House of Love'.

It could be argued that our ability to comprehend our own death
– and the fear of such an idea – is the very thing that makes us the
conscious, self-aware creatures that we consider ourselves to be;
that only in understanding our lives as something in opposition
to death do we develop a concept of the self. You might say that
death is the ultimate price of self-awareness. Despite the extent to
which humans believe in an afterlife in one form or another,[1] the
idea of death as a final end for us, and the ones we love, remains
the greatest of fears. We need only witness the ferocity with
which people will instinctively fight for their survival, to understand how potent this fear can be. This instinct, hardwired into
the brain's hypothalamus, suggests from a biological perspective
at least, that despite what we hope may await us after we die, our
bodies seem very reluctant for us to find out exactly what that
might be.

All stories, says Ernest Hemingway, will ultimately 'end in
death'.[2] What, then, of the stories we tell that go further?

The first law of thermodynamics dictates that the total
amount of energy in a closed system is constant; it can neither be
destroyed nor created, merely changing from one form to another.
If the universe is a closed system as many scientists believe, there

is little dispute as to what fate awaits the material of the body after death; its constituent parts broken down piece by piece, repurposed and reintegrated, never disturbing the scales of the universal totality of energy. Perhaps for the materialist, then, this is satisfaction enough that we, in some way or other, continue to exist long after our bodies have decomposed. However, the idea of where *we* go, 'we' being the slightly more abstract and intangible notion of the self, has proven an altogether more difficult beast to pin down. It is an unknown that calls into question the very nature of consciousness, and one that has been explored in stories told across every community and culture, from as far back as we know.

Death as an ancient Greek, provided you had received a burial, would be followed by the separation of your soul from your body, which would then be led by Hades to the entrance of the Underworld. From here your soul, taking the form of your 'living-world' self, would be ferried by Charon across the Acheron River where, under the watchful eye of Cerberus, the 'three-headed hound of Hades',[3] the Judges of the Underworld would decide your fate. For the virtuous, heroes and demigods, the golden Fields of Elysium would await; for those unlucky enough to be judged sufficiently undeserving, it would be to the unlit gloom of the Tartarus abyss that you would be dispatched.

For the ancient Egyptians, differing traditions offered a variety of afterlife scenarios. The most well-known is to be found in the Egyptian *Book of the Dead*, which details a horrifying and complex journey into Duat, the Egyptian underworld. Provided your soul was able to survive a treacherous gauntlet, chased by terrifying and grotesque entities, it would arrive at the Hall of Truth to face the judgement of Osiris, the god of the dead. If found to have lived a sufficiently virtuous life, your heart would be taken by Anubis, the god of embalming, and weighed against the goddess Ma'at's white ostrich feather of truth. If the heart was equal to or lighter than the feather, your soul would be granted access to the reed fields of Aaru, a paradisiacal and fertile land where, again in the guise of your once 'living' body, your soul would dwell for eternity. A heart heavier than the feather of truth would be thrown to and promptly gobbled up by the goddess and devourer of the dead, Ammit, condemning the soul to an eternal restlessness.[4]

In contemporary cultures influenced by the Abrahamic religions such as Islam, Judaism and Christianity, stories of the afterlife follow a similar theme, promoting a version of continued life consistent with our 'living' sense of self-image. Just as it was for the ancient Greeks and Egyptians, life becomes a test of moral courage, and where we end up subsequently being dependent on our actions with options invariably divided between some form of Heaven or Hell.

Followers of religions such as Hinduism, Sikhism and Buddhism, although by no means restricted to these, believe our lives to be but one moment in the process of Samsara: the repeating cycle of birth, life and death, also known as reincarnation. Much like the eschatology of other faiths, those that incorporate Samsara believe too in the karmic process of the life you lead dictating your fate in death, while also employing a dualist separation of body and soul. A fundamental difference is the complete rejection of a singular image of the body. Instead, Samsara dictates that the soul – your true *essence* – is the only consistency, while its body will take potentially infinite forms, as it is reborn ceaselessly into the material world. Release from the infinite cycle comes only to those souls who are able to become so transcendentally enlightened that they are liberated from the bondage of consciousness altogether and dissolved back into the great oneness of all things.

Buddhist teachings of Samsara have suggested that such a process could allow for the remembrance of previous lives, since all previous lives are considered different experiences of the same soul. Some believe this phenomenon, known as jatismara, although traditionally the preserve of the great Buddhist saints, can be unearthed through past-life regression – the technique of using hypnosis to recover these 'memories.' Although common in ancient India, it wasn't until the late 19th century, through the teachings of occultist Helena Blavatsky and the Theosophical Society that she co-founded in 1875, that the idea gained prominence in modern European society. Famous accounts such as those of Wisconsin housewife Virginia Tighe, who claimed to have lived as a 19th-century Irish woman named Bridey Murphy, helped to bring this controversial phenomenon into the mainstream. Many such accounts have been latterly dismissed as simple cases of false memories: recollections of names and places that have been subconsciously absorbed. However, there are a few cases that have not been so easy to dismiss, cases that have nothing to do with hypnotic regression.

In 2015, a young boy named Ryan from Muskogee in Oklahoma, who was ten at the time, hit the headlines with the claim that he could 'remember' the life of a man who had died fifty years previously. It had begun with nightmares suffered at the age of four where Ryan would wake up screaming that his chest was exploding. Soon he was dreaming of a life spent working in Hollywood in the 1930s and 1940s, a trip he had taken to Paris, that he had a sister and once lived on a street with the word 'Rock' in it, as well as the bizarre claim that he had had five wives. Ryan became so insistent that his mother, not quite sure what to do about it, took out some books on the golden era of Hollywood and brought them home for Ryan to look at. While perusing one of them Ryan yelled 'That's George!' pointing at an image taken from the 1932 movie *Night After Night*. 'And that guy's me,' he said, pointing to another man at the back of the picture.[5]

Growing increasingly unsettled by Ryan's proclamations, his parents enlisted the help of child psychologist Dr Jim Tucker from the University of Virginia whose Division of Perceptual Studies specialises in investigating cases of apparent reincarnation. With Dr Tucker's help the man that Ryan had pointed out in the picture was identified as Marty Martyn who had appeared in the movie as an extra. Incredibly the other man Ryan had pointed to was indeed called George; it was the actor George Raft. Neither man was listed under the image in the book. It was later discovered that Marty Martyn did indeed have a sister, had at one point visited Paris and incredibly had had five wives. Martyn was also found to have lived on Roxbury Drive. And that sensation of his heart exploding that had terrorised Ryan at four years old? Some might say it had something to do with the heart attack that killed Martyn at the age of sixty-one. Or at least, that's how old Ryan claimed Martyn was when he died. However, when Dr Tucker located his death certificate it listed his age at death as fifty-nine. It would be some time later when Dr Tucker found Marty Martyn listed in an old census report and was amazed to discover that the death certificate had incorrectly listed Martyn's birth by two years. He most likely had been sixty-one when he died after all.

The Division of Perceptual Studies at the University of Virginia was founded in 1967 by psychiatrist Dr Ian Stevenson. By the time of his retirement in 2002, Stevenson had logged over 2,500 cases of apparent reincarnation with varying degrees of credibility. One such case involved a young boy from Middlesbrough, England, whose story he would learn about after reading an article published in 1983 detailing the boy's extraordinary claims. It would prove to be one of the most compelling cases that Dr Stevenson would ever come across.

On the bitterly cold afternoon of 15 January 1942, with night beginning to fall, Captain E. S. Parks of the *SS Empire Bay* watches from the ship's bridge as all across the British Isles the lights go out. The sky shimmers like oil, its warm pinks bleeding into inky blue as the last of the sun's rays drop below the horizon. At 1700 hours the ship's engine gurgles and sputters before roaring into life, powering the vessel out of Hartlepool harbour as thick, black plumes of smoke are belched into the air. The bulk cargo ship is laden with 3,800 tons of coal and thirty-eight crew bound for London. Such journeys are among the most treacherous for the merchant navy as they seek to bring fuel to the capital to aid the British war effort, skulking close to the coast in small convoys in the hope that their limited company and the cover of darkness will keep them safe from the peril above.

It is shortly after 1715 when the *Empire* draws level with the *SS Corsea* and Captain Parks orders the anchor dropped while they wait for the final vessel of their convoy to catch them up. The crewmen wrap their Navy-issue jackets a little tighter, taking drags on Woodbines as the boat gently rocks and creaks on the ebbing tide, with all eyes turned nervously to the skies.

It's just gone 1730 when the looping wail of an air-raid siren comes twisting out of the dark from somewhere in the direction of Hartlepool.

'Action stations!' screams Parks.

Glowing embers are flicked overboard and hats hurriedly pulled on to heads as the crew scurry into position. Along the coastline, bulbous barrage balloons – vast inflatables designed to obstruct low-flying aircraft – are drifting up into the air as the men continue to scan the sky, craning their necks in manic desperation for any glimpse of incoming planes. Chief Steward John Cavanagh is perched behind the twin Lewis guns on the port side of the ship's bridge, his eyes fixed on Captain Parks, waiting for his signal, when he finally hears the dreaded, unmistakable hum of approaching aircraft.

'There!'

Cavanagh spins round, squinting into the distant darkness as his eyes work desperately to adjust to the gloom. Clouds and eye spots tease shapes in the sky that swiftly vanish into nothing until finally something solid materialises: a row of small spots twenty kilometres or so off the port beam, steadily growing in size as the engines' rumble grows ever louder. Soon the spots are longer and thinner, sprouting wings and tails. Cavanagh grips the gun tight and positions the planes in his sights. Then one breaks suddenly from the pack, the drone of its engine giving way to a piercing shriek as it plunges from the clouds. Cavanagh hopes for a moment that it might disappear into the water only to see it level out at the last instant before continuing on its path, straight towards them.

'Guns, hold fire!' yells Parks.

Cavanagh's fingers hover over the triggers as the aircraft, now less than 5 kilometres away, bears down upon them.

'Hold!'

Two kilometres . . .

'Hold!'

One kilometre . . .

'Fire!'

Cavanagh squeezes the triggers, releasing a thundering racket of arms as the plane roars overhead, swerving viciously to the aft before circling back round and heading off in the direction of the *Corsea*. Cavanagh watches with alarm as the plane reaches the second vessel, veering away at the last moment and releasing a single bomb that mercifully misses the ship and drops straight into the sea. Moments later the crew find their breath as the plane pulls up and away, heading inland towards the River Tees. A strange calm descends as the worst looks to be over. But then comes that sound again.

'Port side!' bellows Captain Parks.

Cavanagh swings the guns back round and there it is again, dropping out of the sky and heading straight for the *SS Empire Bay*. He fights to ignore the trembling in his fingers and steadies himself once more behind the sights.

'Hold your fire!'

And again it comes, closer, and closer, until finally it is so close that Cavanagh is sure he can see the pilot's eyes.

'Fire!'

A PAC rocket shoots out from the bridge with a fierce rasp as Cavanagh lets off another volley of fire pummelling into the underside of the wing as the plane rears up, appearing to miss the ship's funnel by inches. Cavanagh spins round just in time to see it swerve wildly again to the left before this time releasing five bombs from underneath its wings. For a moment they seem suspended above like soft clods of earth before ripping violently through the air. Cavanagh breaths a sigh of relief as he catches sight of four of them disappearing down the port side straight into the water.

But there were five.

A booming explosion reverberates from out of the starboard quarter as the boat is lifted from the sea. Flames and fountains spray up in unison. Cavanagh is thrown to the floor, his ears ringing from the chaos as the boat crashes back down. When he finally gets his bearings the ship appears to be holding and in the space beyond he can just make out the hulking silhouette of an aircraft heading towards the mouth of the Tees with a trail of thick, dark smoke spewing out of its engine.

Twenty miles inland on the outskirts of Billingham, a call has come through, reporting enemy aircraft spotted off the coast of Hartlepool. Leading aircraftman Walter Myers and his crew leap to their stations and begin manically pumping hydrogen into their defence balloons, standing back when they are done and watching together as 'Annie', the last of their set, makes its slow ascent into the sky, its limp tail flapping casually in the wind.

'Come on, if we don't get it up we'll be too late!'

Hands turn faster and faster on the winch, unspooling the cable until a final click locks it into place. A sudden gust of wind catches the tail, expanding the balloon to its full corpulent glory. The men make their way back to the station hut and have only just settled in when the ominous rumble of a choking engine is heard, drawing closer. Myers spots it first, coming in far too low and trailing huge clouds of black smoke. The rumble turns to a sickening, shrieking whine as the plane lurches suddenly to the right heading straight for the hut.

'He's going to machine-gun us!'

'No, look! The cable!'

The air itself seems to tear apart as the plane roars past, sending the men scattering for cover. A horrifying crunch and the winch-lorry lifts from the floor before clattering back down to the ground. The cable has sliced straight through the starboard wing, propelling it in the opposite direction. The rest of the plane jerks to the side and veers off towards the Middlesbrough docks before slamming into the ground just south of the Tees in a ball of fire.

An air-raid warden watches the drama unfolding from his back garden, tracking the plane until it disappears just metres from his home on to the train tracks behind the Dorman Long steelworks at the bottom of Clay Lane. After racing to the crash site as quickly as he can, he is immediately sent sprawling to the ground by the aircraft's ammunition exploding in every direction. When the popping stops, a fire too intense to attempt a rescue of the men trapped inside has engulfed the plane. It will be thirty minutes before firemen are able to extinguish the inferno.

Meanwhile, twenty miles up the coast, the crew of the SS *Empire Bay*, having all been successfully retrieved, watch huddled together from rescue boats as the ship's bow rises into the air before steadily sinking below the waves.

First light on Teesside reveals a monochrome landscape of industrial plants and wastelands, little changed from the evening's drama save for the smouldering pile of metal, 100ft of smashed rail track and a large hole in the ground measuring roughly 10ft deep and 12ft wide. In the distance beyond, the slag and coal heaps lie dotted with snow while the chimneys of the Dorman Long steelworks blow white clouds into the morning air. At the crash site, rescue workers, watched carefully by two men wrapped in thick woollen coats, pull three charred bodies from the wreckage; a fourth body is thought to have likely evaporated in the flames. The men presiding over the grisly scene have been sent by British intelligence to gather what they can from the German bomber. But with little of interest to be found, and the government keen to rebuild the track as soon as possible, the officers agree to wrap up the search that morning. Within days the remains of the aircraft are buried under a mound of earth and the track is reinstalled as if nothing had ever happened. The three bodies, identified by their dog tags as Feldwebel Joachim Lehnis,

Lieutenant Rudolf Matern and Oberfeldwebel Heinrich Richter, are taken to nearby Thornaby-on-Tees cemetery and laid to rest.

At the turn of the 19th century, Middlesbrough is little more than a farm located on the banks of the River Tees in the north-east of England, populated by roughly twenty-five people. But a wave of change is approaching that will soon turn this bucolic idyll into one of the country's most productive industrial powerhouses. As the spirit of enlightenment begins to permeate all aspects of British society, there comes a sudden synchronicity of vision with the means of production[6] igniting a fuse from which there will be no going back. From the bowels of the earth, the British Industrial Revolution erupts in an explosion of steam, fire and smoke; a time of extraordinary physical and philosophical upheaval built on ambition, greed and the blood and sweat of the men, women and children who rip it from the ground and smelt it in the factories. Soon, throughout the land, colossal cauldrons of industry are springing up wherever the raw ingredients are most abundant.

In the early 1820s, railway pioneer Joseph Pease gazes out over the banks of the Tees, scanning the river as it meanders towards the North Sea, seeing not the tranquillity of its placid waters, but rather a gateway to the world. By 1850, having bought that Middlesbrough farm in 1829, Pease brought coal-storage facilities and trains to the area, transforming the quaint hamlet into a bustling town with a population of over 7,000. Twenty years later after iron ore is discovered in the nearby town of Eston in the Cleveland Hills, Middlesbrough quickly establishes itself as a world leader in steel production and by the end of the century the population has grown to 90,000 and the town – widely referred to as Ironopolis – is producing a third of the nation's iron. Before long, with the increasingly expanding British Empire, Eston steel, 'like a strong and invincible serpent [is coiling] itself around the world'.[7] In the 1920s Arthur Doorman and Albert de Lande Long, better known as Dorman Long, purchase the Teesside ironworks and in 1932 will oversee the building of their most famous construction: the Sydney Harbour Bridge.

But a lot can change in fifty years. A combination of the reduced demand for steel and an ever-expanding pool of global competition leaves Middlesbrough's key industries floundering. By the early 1970s, the town once known as the 'infant Hercules' is struggling to stay afloat. 1972 is an especially chaotic year, characterised by strikes and stalemates between a Conservative government intent on consolidating what little profit there is left to be made and the workers' unions intent on protecting the interests of the people on whose backs that very profit had been raised. Throughout Middlesbrough, and many of the failing industrial towns of the Midlands and the North of England, many jobs are lost as companies seek to reduce expenditure in the hope of maintaining what are, by now, unrealistic profit margins. The government's disastrous efforts to combat falling employment ultimately results in unemployment figures passing a million for the first time since the 1930s.

It is during this turbulent period, on Friday 28 December 1972, that Carl Edon is born.

From the moment he arrives, Carl's mother Val senses there is something a little different about him. There are the physical differences first and foremost: both Carl's brother and sister have dark hair and brown eyes, whereas Carl's eyes are blue and his hair strawberry blond. Their skin was also a little darker and tanned easily, whereas Carl's is fair and pale. But there's something else too: the sense that Carl never quite seems able to relax. One night, shortly after Carl's second birthday, Val wakes to the sound of screaming coming from the other end of the house. Racing to Carl's room she finds the young boy sitting up, crying in his bed. As he struggles to get the words out, Val can just make out something about falling from the sky and a missing leg taken from his body before she is finally able to calm him down. Having settled, Carl explains the dream in more detail. He had been flying through the sky, he says, in some sort of plane. It had been on fire, and he couldn't get out and when it finally crashed he felt as if his leg had been taken away. Val hugs her sobbing son and rubs his leg to show him he hasn't lost it at all, reassuring him that it was only a dream and nothing to be worried about.

Despite her reassurances, Val and Jim, Carl's father, can't help but be disturbed by the strangeness of their son's nightmare, wondering how it is that a toddler can recount such vivid and chilling details. But Carl's peculiar visions are soon forgotten, disappearing into the background noise of the busy family home, until Val comes across Carl one morning a few months later, playing on his own with a toy aeroplane.

Carl notices his mother and looks up to greet her.

'I died before,' he says. 'My plane crashed straight through a window.'

Val stares in confusion at the boy, unsure what to say, before telling him to forget about the dream.

'But it wasn't a dream,' he says, turning back to play with his toy plane, 'it really happened.'

As the months go by, Val and Jim are surprised to find that not only does Carl refuse to forget the strange vision, he is beginning to 'remember' more.

'One of our engines ran out,' he would say, 'and after we crashed I opened a hatch to try and get out but one of my legs was gone and I bled to death.'

Although Jim and Val have little wish to indulge their young son's peculiar fantasy, they receive another shock when Carl becomes convinced that he had been a German pilot during the war and had crashed while on a bombing mission over England. One evening, Val sees Carl's birthmark – just below the groin on his right leg – afresh. Remembering what Carl had said about losing his leg in the dream, she asks him again which one it had been. The right one, he replies.

Throughout his early childhood, Val often finds Carl beavering away on join-the-dots or scribbling across the patterns of a colouring book, and soon he is drawing his own shapes and patterns.

One morning, Val notices he has been working on one particular picture for some time. Asking if she can take a look, Carl leans back with a smile as Val pulls the picture closer. She is amazed by how neat it looks – certainly not like the scribbles you would ordinarily expect from a five-year-old – yet she can't quite make out what the images are exactly. Carl calmly explains they are his airforce badges and points them out for her one by one. There's a badge with a bird, which Carl identifies as an eagle, its wings drawn laterally on the side. But before Carl can explain the next symbol, with a jolt Val realises what it is. It is a swastika.

Perhaps even more extraordinary is the picture that Jim finds in Carl's bedroom just after his son's sixth birthday. It, too, looks odd from a distance and it's only when Jim turns the picture round that he realises what it is: the cockpit of a plane complete with all the gauges and instruments, even the levers. Jim asks Carl if he drew the picture to which he replies yes, before pointing out the red foot pedal he'd detailed at the bottom, which he says was used to drop the bombs. The boy explains, nonplussed, that the picture is a Messerschmitt Bomber 101 just like the one he had flown in the war.

Despite Carl's increasingly detailed 'recollections', Jim is unconvinced. Clearly Carl is playing some kind of game; after all, he knew the Messerschmitt was a fighter plane not a bomber. Together with Val, he decides to test Carl a little more.

'So what uniform did you wear?' they ask, to which Carl replies without hesitation, 'grey trousers, tucked into knee-high leather boots and a black jacket.'

A few days later, Jim travels to the local library with Carl's pictures tucked under his arm. After being directed to the history section he proceeds to pull out whatever books he can find on the German air forces of the Second World War. Moments later, Jim is sitting with the books laid out in front of him in complete shock. It is all there. Everything from the picture of the cockpit, the badges, the description of the uniform: everything is exactly as Carl had described, even the plane. There had been a Messerschmitt

Bomber after all. It was a 110 but perhaps he had just misheard Carl when he said 101.

Some days later, the family are watching a war film when a character playing a German sergeant appears on the screen.

'The uniform's all wrong,' says Carl out of the blue, 'he's got the badge on the wrong side.'

Jim returns to the library the following day and sure enough, his son was right.

As Carl gets older he seems only to become more convinced of his other life. Of course, there are elements of his personality that are distinct and his own and he also enjoys many of the same things that any of the other local kids his age like: space hoppers, Middlesbrough FC, cartoons. But then there are the other quirks that catch Val a little off guard. Sometimes they are small things, like how particular Carl is about the clothes he wears for a child his age; how the collars always have to be pressed. Other times it's something else entirely, like when Carl is around seven years old, and his friend Michael is over for dinner. Carl launches into the story about how he had died once before during the Second World War. Val grows increasingly uncomfortable as Carl describes how he had bled to death and how he suspected he would die again before the age of twenty-five. He finishes by describing a man called Adolf Hitler then gets down from the table and starts goose-stepping round the kitchen. Michael doesn't stop laughing until Val quietly reminds them to finish up their food.

With Carl remaining convinced of this extraordinary past life it begins to impact on his time at school. A teacher during parents' evening asks Valerie and Jim if everything is all right at home.

'Why?' asks Val.

The teacher replies that she has noticed Carl becoming distracted in class.

'He has strange eyes,' she says. 'When I talk to him about anything, it's as if he is staring straight through me.'[8]

There is also Carl's peculiar habit of arriving at answers without fully understanding where the response has come from.

When asked to explain his reasoning he says only that there is no need to bother if he's already given the correct answer. Jim and Val can only smile and nod politely as they take it all in.

Over the next few years Carl continues to detail a vivid picture of a life lived somewhere else, in a time and place unrecognisable from the concrete streets and industry of 1970s Middlesbrough. Carl comes to the understanding that his name used to be Robert. He speaks of a quaint village tucked away amidst forested hills and explains how his father Fritz used to always make him laugh and how he taught him about all the flowers and trees of the local woodlands. 'Robert' couldn't remember his mother's name, however, only that she had been quite large with dark hair pulled tightly back in a bun, and that she wore spectacles.

'But I'm your mother,' Val would say whenever Carl got too carried away, her voice gently breaking.

'I know,' Carl would reply, 'but she's my mother too.'

According to Carl, in his past life as 'Robert' he would often have to do household chores, chopping up wood and bringing it home in a wheelbarrow or else face the wrath of his mother, bossing him about with her glasses perched on the end of her nose. When she wasn't ordering him to chop wood she would be standing by the stove making a soup, dark red in colour, like nothing Val has ever made. He had had brothers too who also fought in the war, including a younger brother who was apparently killed shortly after Robert had supposedly been killed.

It is strange when Carl thinks about it; the way the pictures come to him like he's watching clips from a television show, turning on and off for a few seconds at a time. Moments like Robert's apparent enlistment in the Luftwaffe. One minute he is a seven-year-old boy playing with toys in his bedroom, the next he is nineteen and living on a kind of camp with lots of small huts lined up in rows. One moment he is inside one of the huts, filled only with bunk beds, then he is outside watching grown-ups collecting water from a pump. Another time he'll find himself putting bandages on other grown-ups, as if playing at first-aid, or standing in a large hall, surrounded on all sides by rows and rows of men in uniform. In this hall is a framed picture of a man he recognises as Adolf Hitler. Together, he and the other grown-ups are stamping their feet and raising their arms above their heads in that way with the fingers together and all pointing forward. Valerie feels uneasy as Carl repeats the gesture for his mother. To hear that name spoken aloud by her young son, when it had never been mentioned in the home before, sends shivers down her spine.

One morning, an oddly subdued Carl tells his mother about a new dream from the night before. It was 1942 and he was 'Robert' again, who he now says was twenty-three years old, and he was sitting in what seemed like the cockpit of a plane. He couldn't say if he was flying it or not but it was shaking all over the place. The aircraft came down over some buildings when everything suddenly went black. When he woke again in the plane it was still falling with the buildings on the ground rushing up towards him. In that moment, Carl just knew he was going to die. When the plane finally crashed it must have gone through a window, he thought; there was glass everywhere. Afterwards he saw again that his leg had been cut off and he felt very sad but it was a different sadness than any time before. It wasn't for himself but someone else, someone 'Robert' had lost; a nineteen-year-old woman he wanted to marry, left behind in his village in Germany. Valerie listens in horror as Carl finishes the account by describing his 'final moments', bleeding to death alone in the plane.

The following year, a nine-year-old Carl is interviewed by Women's Own magazine after a local journalist had caught wind of his extraordinary claim and published a small piece in the local paper. Later that year the story even makes it as far as Germany when it is picked up in Berlin's Morgenpost. Inevitably with the exposure comes ridicule at school and within days of the articles appearing, Carl's classmates begin calling him Hitler and a Nazi, and throw their arms up in Nazi salutes whenever he walks by. Most days Carl returns home in tears from all the teasing. As the attention becomes increasingly unbearable, the young Carl decides on the only course of action he has available to him. He stops talking about it.

Unfortunately for Carl, this doesn't mean that interest in his case wanes. It is some time toward the end of 1983 when the *Women's Own* article finds its way to the desk of Professor Ian Stevenson in Virginia, USA. At the time the American–Canadian Stevenson was Carlson Professor of Psychiatry at the University of Virginia School of Medicine. A fascinating but controversial figure, for the previous twenty-five years he had dedicated himself to investigating the validity of so-called reincarnation cases, even establishing a specific department, the University's Division of Perceptual Studies, to better conduct his research. Despite much criticism from his peers, Stevenson's dogged research ultimately earned him begrudging respect in the psychiatric community, being described by a reviewer in the *Journal of the American Academy of Child & Adolescent Psychiatry* as a distinguished psychiatrist and scholar.[9]

Stevenson's interest in reincarnation stemmed initially from his fascination with how certain characteristic traits or unusual illnesses often seemed incompatible with environmental or hereditary influences, suggesting that perhaps there was a third type of influencer on character. Stevenson postulated that this might be the result of a type of memory transfer between individuals. One feature that occurred in many of Stevenson's case studies, of which there were hundreds, was the appearance of birthmarks or birth defects in places that held a deep significance to the alleged past life. For example, in *Reincarnation and Biology: A Contribution to the Etiology of Birthmarks and Birth Defects* (1997), Stevenson recounted the story of a young boy who became convinced that he had shot himself in a past life. The boy's recollections eventually led him to a woman whose brother had indeed shot himself in the throat. When Stevenson examined the boy he found a birthmark on his throat where the man's bullet was alleged to have entered. Stevenson suggested they check for an exit wound and sure enough when they pulled back the hair on top of his head they found a birthmark underneath.[10]

Stevenson is immediately fascinated by Carl's case, and in particular the birthmark on his right leg. Although Stevenson is unable to make the trip himself, early in the new year he sends UK associate Dr Nicholas McClean-Rice to interview Carl and his family. After analysing the various anecdotes and stories compiled by Dr McClean-Rice, Stevenson concludes that reincarnation was 'at least a plausible explanation for Carl's story'.[11]

By the age of thirteen, any lingering traits of 'Robert' the mysterious Luftwaffe pilot, whose memories Carl had seemingly found in his head, have all but vanished. Carl leaves school at sixteen to take up a job with British Rail preparing freight trains to deliver to the various industrial estates that line the banks of the River Tees. Five years later, now twenty-one-years old, Carl grants one final interview when Ian Stevenson, determined to analyse Carl's story for himself, travels personally to Middlesbrough to meet with him. Although the meeting proves disappointing for Stevenson, with Carl unable to offer any more insight into his apparent past life, Stevenson is pleased to find the young man happy and in love, having just moved in with his seventeen-year-old girlfriend. Twelve months later and the couple welcome their first child into the world. When Carl's proposal of marriage is accepted the following year, and now with a second baby on the way, it is as if his life has truly become his own and the spectre of the mysterious German pilot has finally been laid to rest.

In the summer of 1995 a heat wave sweeps across the United Kingdom that stretches throughout July and into August. On the evening of Wednesday 2 August the air is imbued with a heavy stillness when the officer on duty at Middlesbrough's South Bank police station caught the sound of a car screeching to a halt outside. They watch with some alarm as the hulking frame of a young man well over six feet tall pushes open the doors and steps into the waiting area, his clothes covered in blood.

'He got angry and came at me,' says the man who identifies himself as Gary Vinter.

Gary then explains he had been working the evening shift less than a mile away at the Grangetown signal box on Teesside when he and a colleague had got into an argument. He can't remember exactly what had happened, only that when it was over, his colleague was dead. Gary is immediately taken for questioning where he volunteers to draw a map for the police to locate the body. Moments later a squad car is despatched to the area, taking a left on to Tees Dock Road before heading towards the industrial scrublands beyond. Such locations can make you feel like you have stumbled upon the very edges of the world; landscapes of carved earth, slag heaps and silent smoking chimneys framed by small red and green lights that hang like stars on the silhouettes of cranes; the 'strange braidings'[12] of urban archaeology and, wherever they can get a hold, those more organic elements of the natural world fighting to take back what it can.

They almost miss it at first, so unassuming is the squat red-bricked building with the flat tarmac roof perched just off the road behind a short piece of rail track that branched out like frayed nerve endings into myriad warehouses and sidings spread out over the land. To its left is the small train preparers' cabin that Vinter had mentioned in his statement, where the fight had broken out. To the right, a huge electricity pylon towers overhead, marking the spot with its own confluence of energy that sprays out in multiple directions, stretching one way to the old Dorman Long steelworks still standing just behind and the other out to the distant dockyards. Giant haulage trucks rattle past in the dark as the officers exit their vehicle, catching the occasional chemical scent drifting through on the warm breeze.

A distant clanging can be heard as the officers cross the tracks and proceed into the small cabin on the left. The door gives a slight creak as they push it aside. Flashing their torches, they soon pick up the body of a man lying in a pool of blood on the cabin floor, the remains of a knife still protruding from his body. The man is Carl Edon. The full extent of the brutal attack will later come to light; Carl has been stabbed thirty-seven times with two knives. Vinter had grabbed the second after he had thrust the other with such intensity that it had broken in half. The autopsy reveals that Carl has been stabbed broadly across the entirety of his body, with most internal organs punctured. The pathologist's findings seem to contradict Vinter's initial claim that he acted in self-defence, a fact agreed by the jury at his trial. He is convicted of murder the following year.

When Carl's old school friend Michael first hears about his murder he is understandably shocked and upset. But within minutes he is ten-years-old again, giggling uncontrollably as Carl goose-steps round the kitchen recounting for the hundredth time the story about how he had once died young, bleeding to death. As for Carl's family – his fiancée and two baby daughters, his parents and brother and sister – the combined effect of his death and the manner in which it had occurred is catastrophic. But as the months go by, the Edons can't help but reminisce over Carl's early years and those peculiar visions that had plagued his childhood.

Then, in November 1997, something extraordinary comes to light.

It is the morning of 27 November when workers for the Northumbrian Water Board pull into the building site at the bottom of Clay Lane just east of South Bank station, barely a few miles down the track from the Grangetown signal box. The team, with instructions to install a sewage pipeline for a new business park due to be built nearby, have not been working long when one of the diggers hits something in the mud. With the digging halted, a couple of workers jump into the pit and start scraping away at the earth, finding a strangely mangled metallic structure underneath. Moments later, one of the men spots what looks like an old sack and opens it to find a bundle of pristine white silk stuffed inside. As he pulls the silk from the bag it soon becomes clear he is unfurling a parachute. The men look again at the hulk of metal in the ground and realise they have exposed some kind of aircraft.

Concerned that they might not only have a warplane on their hands, but also some unexploded ordnance, the Water Board immediately cease work and inform the Royal Engineers of their discovery. Within days a team of ordnance disposal experts from nearby RAF Wittering, working together with the Royal Engineers, set about excavating the wreckage. The plane is soon identified as a German Second World War plane known as a Dornier bomber that had belonged to a unit of the Luftwaffe based at the time at Schiphol airport in the Netherlands. A quick check of the records reveals the plane to have crashed on the evening of 15 January 1942 after taking a hit just off the coast and colliding with a barrage balloon on the outskirts of Hartlepool. As the engineers dig deeper into the vessel they find over five tons of wreckage including a number of machine guns, a wooden propeller and two further parachutes before coming across a fragment of bone.

From the records they ascertain that three of the crew, Joachim Lehnis, Rudolf Matern and Heinrich Richter had been recovered from the crash with a fourth body, that of Unteroffizier Hans Maneke thought to have been too badly destroyed to be removed. Digging a little further, the excavation team find a piece of battledress collar bearing the rank insignia for an Unteroffizier that appears to confirm the missing body is indeed that of Hans Maneke. However, when the team digs deeper they discover what appears to be a complete skeleton encased in the remains of a different uniform buried in what would have been the ventral gunner's position. The missing body wasn't Hans Maneke after all, but the plane's gunner Heinrich Richter. The section in which Richter's remains are found is a large bubble of glass at the base of the plane. As the aircraft crashed nose first, this bubble, which was effectively a spherical glass window, would have borne the brunt of the initial impact and been smashed to smithereens in the process, covering the occupant in thousands of tiny shards – similar to the way Carl had described the sensation of a shattering window in his dreams. Most peculiar of all, when the team pull the skeleton from the wreckage they discover it isn't quite as complete as they had first thought. The right leg is missing. It had been severed in the crash.

The author walking the train line from South
Bank station to Grangetown signal box.

News of the plane's rediscovery soon spreads throughout the town and the following year, Hans Maneke's gravesite at Thornaby Cemetery is named correctly and the additional remains of Heinrich Richter are laid to rest alongside his comrades. A moving ceremony takes place in October and is attended by the German Consul to Britain as well as a handful of the crew's descendants who are joined by twenty-two British ex-servicemen and over 200 members of the public. Together they watch as seventy-eight-year-old Heinz Mollenbrok, a former Dornier pilot of the same unit, who was shot down during the Battle of Britain, lays the first wreath on Richter's grave. He places another on a monument for the British airmen, representing the 55,000 members of RAF Bomber Command who, like Richter and his fellow crew members, had never made it back home. As the RAF military standards are lowered by the twenty-two ex-serviceman, and a bugler of the Cleveland Police begins the opening refrain of 'The Last Post', two other faces join at the back of the crowd: having read news of the plane's discovery in the paper, Valerie and Jim Edon have come to pay their respects to the German Second World War airman who lost his leg and died after being shot down over England.

Years later, after further investigative work, local Middlesbrough historian Bill Norman will eventually track down Heinrich Richter's family, publishing his findings in a book.[13] It transpired that Richter had been born in 1911 and was thirty at the time of his death. As Norman points out, regardless of what we may think of the cause for which he fought, Richter was undoubtedly a brave man having already flown sixty missions, earning the silver Frontflugspange as well as first- and second-class distinctions of the Iron Cross before his death in 1942. Norman also discovered that Richter had two brothers who were killed in the war as well: Kurt Richter, who perished while fighting in Russia in 1941, and Gerhard, who was killed in Romania in 1944. Although he never ascertained the name of Richter's mother he did discover that his father had been called Friedrich, a name frequently shortened to the more informal Fritz. One morning, Bill receives a letter from another relative of Heinrich Richter's containing a striking portrait photograph of the young airman shortly before he had been killed. When Val and Jim see the picture for the first time it is like seeing a ghost. There, staring back at them with his strong nose and chin, and that distinct shape of his brow, it is hard not to distinguish the face of their son, and on the collar of his jacket, they see also the insignia of eagles, just as Carl had depicted in his pictures all those years ago.

Whatever we believe about the possibility of reincarnation, there is little doubt that in a physiological sense, through the inheritance of genes, we are all in some way a reincarnation of those that have come before us. Although we may not inherit literal memories of the deceased, some fascinating new discoveries are

Evening Gazette

Tuesday, January 15 2002 · It's part of the family · Late Hour · 25p

The essential guide for your big day FREE inside

Teesside's premier holiday and leisure event FREE guide inside

Mac closes in on £6m striker PLUS Boro Cup latest – Sport

THE CHILLING CASE OF CARL EDON

IT'S GOT TO BE HIM
Carl's mum Val, above, with husband Jim

FACE TO FACE WITH THE PAST: Carl Edon, above, who claimed he was the reincarnation of a German airman and, above left, Luftwaffe gunner Heinrich Richter. Left, a Dornier bomber similar to that in which Richter was killed

60 YEARS AGO TODAY – read the story of the South Bank bomber crash: Page 2

When a Middlesbrough boy claimed he had been a World War Two Luftwaffe airman in a former life people shrugged and wondered... Now a startling new photograph adds an eerie twist to an amazing tale... Judge for yourself

Heinrich Richter and Carl Edon, Teeside, *Evening Gazette*, 15 January 2002

challenging our understanding of the way in which our lived experiences might biologically resurface long after we have gone. Prior to Charles Darwin's *The Origin of Species*, another naturalist by the name of Jean-Baptiste Lamarck had been causing a stir with a theory of his own. He suggested that an organism might pass characteristics to its offspring, not only through internal genetic mechanisms but also through external influences that it would have been affected by during its lifetime. Although the theory, known as Lamarckism, gained some traction at the time, it was soon eclipsed by Darwin's Theory of Evolution, before being widely discredited and falling out of fashion altogether. And so it was destined to remain.

However, a number of recent discoveries in the increasingly popular area of epigenetics have led to something of a Lamarckist comeback. Bearing similarities to the principles of Lamarckism, epigenetics is the study of how external and environmental factors can alter the functionality of genes without corrupting the base genetic code.[14] In 2013 neurobiologist Kerry Ressler and his research partner Brian Dias published a paper in leading medical journal *Nature* concerning the study of epigenetic inheritance in laboratory mice. What Ressler and Dias had discovered was that by conditioning a set of mice to associate a scent with a specific trauma, in this case a small electrical shock, that same fear would be passed down to at least two generations of their pups.[15] Taking this extraordinary discovery into account we might say that in some ways not only do we inherit our ancestors' physical traits, but quite possibly an instinctive sense of some of their lived experiences as well.

Being the unquantifiable negative space that it is, any concept of death in turn directly influences the shape of its opposite space: life. Very broadly speaking, if like the Ancient Egyptians, or followers of Abrahamic religions, you believe in an afterlife that rewards the morally virtuous, your lived life will most likely be dictated by these moral expectations – at least whatever you understand those morals to be. If you adopt religious teachings based on the principle of Samsara, the material self being continually replaced, ideally having no relevance to your true essence, life becomes a process of attempting to transcend this material prison in return for egoless bliss. For those who believe in neither, who maintain that *this* is all there is, the focus tends to be solely on how your actions in life will service you and the lives of others you come into contact with, in life alone. Looking at it in these schematic terms, it boils down to two seemingly fundamental and conflicting ideas: either our sense of identity is critically linked to our material body, in which case it dies with it; or it is not. As our lives become increasingly incorporated into the digital space, we may be discovering the tantalising prospect of a convergence of these two most polarising principles. If this convergence were to succeed, even for the most ardent antitheist or spiritual sceptic, its potential seems positively theological in scope.

If we maintain that our consciousness is wholly dependent on the material body – being something that is most likely to emerge via complex processes in the brain – we might also accept the possibility that a sufficiently sophisticated replication of a brain could allow for a mind to be held outside of the body it first emerged in. Although the information would most likely need to be stored somewhere, which in turn would require power to keep the mind 'alive', provided this was possible, might we one day be able to manufacture our own after-lives?

In 1965 pioneering mathematician Irving John Good speculated on the potential for artificially generated intelligence to one day eclipse the functionality of the human brain. It would do so in a moment of 'intelligence explosion' whereby a machine, on realising the extent of its intelligence, would suddenly understand how to build a machine with greater capabilities, that would in turn know how to construct an even more capable machine. This triggering of the sudden exponential growth of artificial intelligence is now commonly referred to as the technological singularity, and for many in the technology community, such as leading computer scientist and tech pioneer Ray Kurzweil, this moment of singularity is not a matter of if, but *when*.[16] Kurzweil has been making a name for himself since his time as a student at the Massachusetts Institute of Technology (MIT) where he pioneered the first text-to-speech technology and would later invent the world's first synthesiser to incorporate sampled instruments into its hardware. In 2012 Kurzweil was installed as Google's Director of Engineering to pursue development in machine learning and natural language understanding, and is one of the world's most revered futurists and a leading advocate of transhumanism – the belief that advancements in science and technology are fundamental to achieving the next significant evolutionary step for humankind.[17] Although for some the notion of singularity might be alarming, for Kurzweil its imminence is something to be celebrated – not least because he thinks it will ultimately hold the key to immortality (whether we want it or not). With an artificially generated super intelligence, Kurzweil predicts a biotechnological revolution that would enable us to upload our conscious minds either into virtual worlds or indestructible robotic bodies, which would allow us to live for however long the universe remains a stable place to inhabit (provided, of course, the new intelligence deems us necessary to have around): an 'after-life' of sorts, if we take that to mean an experience of consciousness after the death of our present bodies.

Such a notion would require a relinquishing of our bodies as a fundamental component of our sense of identity, the possibilities of which were explored to fascinating effect in a 2004 study conducted by scientists from University College London. In the experiment, subjects placed their left hand on a table while, with their right arm screened off from view, a substitute dummy arm with a rubber hand was laid out in place of their right. Incredibly when both 'hands' were stroked simultaneously subjects began to associate the rubber hand as their own. Additionally, when asked to point to their right hand with their left, subjects invariably pointed to the fake rubber hand. The effect is a consequence of how vision dominates the way in which the premotor cortex in the brain integrates sense information to recognise what constitutes our body.[18]

Although there would be some way to go yet, it poses interesting questions about the potential for realising entire other bodies either in a virtual, digital space or indeed in the physical, as exemplified in the 2009 film *Avatar*. In James Cameron's pioneering blockbuster, paralysed soldier Jake Sully is given the opportunity to 'drive' a fabricated shell of a species indigenous to the planet

Pandora known as the Na'vi. Jake's task is to integrate himself into the Na'vi community to better help the human colonisation of their planet, a task he performs so well that by the end he has achieved a complete transfusion with his new body. Such a notion, if it were one day realised, might finally deliver an answer to Theseus' Paradox. This ancient conundrum asks us to consider whether an object, in the original case King Theseus' ship, can be considered the same object if all of its component parts have at some point been completely replaced. In Jake Sully's case at least, the answer is, broadly speaking, yes.[19]

We are increasingly imparting pieces of ourselves into the digital realm, be that our visual memories or even just the small things we now deem unnecessary to have to keep in our heads, like phone numbers. As hellish as it may sound to some, it is surely only a matter of time before we are able to keep a 24-hour audio and visual record of our day-to-day experiences. We might even elect to store our emotional responses to these experiences somewhere digitally too. Future scenarios might see us being able to backup our individual conscious selves onto storage facilities that will allow us to be dropped into any number of post-body experiences after 'death'. Charlie Brooker's deeply touching and evocative *Black Mirror* episode 'San Junipero' explores such a possibility in its examination of a computer-generated after-life whereby our minds are given the opportunity to live in an idealised world of neon lights and beach glamour.

Why stop there? In the manner of Pierre Teilhard de Chardin's concept of the noosphere[20] might we then be able to fuse with the experiences of all those other digitally stored entities? Our selves becoming extant as one of a series of networked data points in an interconnected system, free to merge together into one vast single consciousness you might say; a fully mechanised system of universal oneness. Perhaps this networked digital space might one day encompass the entirety of the known universe, connected through all matter. It would be as if the universe had become self-aware. Then again, who's to say such a space wouldn't also fall into hierarchies similar to what we experience in our present material worlds; places locked off and only accessible to those with the requisite power and knowledge, controlled by gatekeepers like the five realms of Hades.

There is just one small problem. Newton's Second Law of Thermodynamics. It seems presently that even the digital heaven of San Junipero would likely have to come to an end since any such place would require a mechanism to store information, which in time would eventually succumb to heat death. As Newton's Second Law states, entropy – the level of disorder in a system – only increases. Much like the way an ice cube melts in hot water, as the universe continues to expand, all the heat, or energy, contained within is predicted to become so uniformly dispersed that processes which rely on the transference of energy to function will no longer be possible.

Whatever the truth of our potential to be reincarnated or recall the lives of others, or indeed to exist in a vast shared conscious space side by side with each other, one thing is for certain: we are all cosmically significant. Whether it be today, as the collection of matter that we call our 'selves', or tomorrow as a piece of stardust, for as long as the universe exists we will always be here making up a part of it, changing from one thing to another in a constant, balanced cycle.

Chapter Two

THE BOX

'Inorganic demons are parasitic by nature . . . [generating] their effects out of the human host, whether as an individual, an ethnicity, a society or an entire civilisation.'

Reza Negarestani – *Cyclonopedia:*
Complicity with Anonymous Materials

In March 2007, the much-celebrated writer and film director J. J. Abrams gave a TED talk entitled 'The Mystery Box' in which he outlined the notion of 'unseen mystery' as one of his fundamental principles of storytelling. In order to demonstrate the point, Abrams brought along a gift he'd received as a fourteen-year-old boy: Tannen's Magic Mystery Box. Though you couldn't be sure what was inside it, this brown cardboard box guaranteed you $50 of magic for only $15.

Only, Abrams had never opened it.

As he astutely realised, the real magic had nothing to do with what was actually in the box, but rather in the *wondering* of what might be. In the thirty-six years since the box had been gifted to him, it had come to symbolise something far more valuable than anything that could be inside. To Abrams, whose show *Lost* is widely considered one of the greatest TV mystery dramas of all time,[1] the box was a powerful reminder of the infinite potential of story and how mystery is the key to imagination.[2]

Before we go any further, let's try a little experiment:

A stranger approaches you in the street brandishing a suitcase.

They say to you, 'What I have in this suitcase will change your life. Do you want to know what it is?'

You want to know what's in the case, don't you? Would you ask them to open it, or not? Hold that thought . . .

The best mysteries are the boxes with lids that remain closed the longest, or, like a Chinese box, the ones that open to reveal another mystery inside. In the context of story at least, as the huge success of Abrams' enigmatic *Lost* demonstrates,[3] perhaps it's better not to open the box at all, since the revelation of what's inside rarely lives up to expectation. What I find most fascinating about Abrams' notion of 'unseen mystery' is not the tease of needing to know what's inside the box, but how withholding the truth of what is – like some sort of regenerative infinity loop – enables us to continually reimagine the possibilities.

The infinite possibility of story is not limited to the world of fiction. Some interpretations of quantum-mechanical theories, such as superposition and wave function collapse, first introduced by pioneering physicist Werner Heisenberg, suggest that sub-atomic particles, and by extension all matter, effectively exist as a set of infinite possibilities, becoming fixed only once 'observed' or measured.[4] It is a principle often associated with Erwin Schrödinger and his 1935 thought experiment Schrödinger's Cat, perhaps the most famous mystery box of them all.[5]

The experiment invites you to imagine a box, or steel chamber as Schrödinger has it, that contains a flask of poison and a hammer linked to a Geiger counter tracking the potential decay of a radio-active substance. A cat is placed inside the box, which is then sealed with no way for the observer to see what is occurring inside. If the counter records a single atom of decay from the radioactive substance, the hammer will fall and release the poison, killing the unfortunate moggy.[6] However, as we can't see inside the box, it could be said that, regardless of what has happened, the cat exists in a state of superposition, being simultaneously alive and dead at the same time. Only when we look inside the box, in other words empirically measure what has occurred, does the cat's actual state become known.

It is an idea with quite extraordinary implications, even horrifying perhaps: the notion of the material world as something unfixed and indeterminate, only settling into place once it has been observed. After all, is there any knowing who or what might constitute the observer? Indeed, if we allow ourselves to stretch the analogy further, wouldn't the true horror be in discovering that having opened the box, it wasn't *us* who was observing the cat but the cat who was observing *us*?

So we're back with the stranger in the street brandishing their mysterious suitcase. Did you decide to open it? You did? Notice that I never said anything about it changing your life for the better . . .

'All of the events that I am about to set forth in this listing are accurate and may be verified . . . with the copies of hospital records and sworn affidavits that I am including as part of the sale . . .'[7]

Posted in June 2003 by a then thirty-eight-year-old Kevin Mannis, a furniture and antique seller from Portland, Oregon, this certainly wasn't your average eBay listing. Then again, the article in question was not your typical eBay item. This was something else entirely . . .

In September 2001, Kevin Mannis is the owner of Addy's Market, a small used-and-restored furniture business he set up earlier in the year. His primary area of expertise is recovery and restoration, but what he enjoys more than anything is the hunt for new and interesting pieces to work with. On weekends it's common to find Kevin cruising round the Portland suburbs, visiting yard sales and personal property auctions much like the one he is approaching now.

Parking his pick-up in front of a modest 60s low-rise, Kevin finds the usual group of curious onlookers and amateur collectors poking round the bits and pieces stacked up on the lawn. A cursory glance reveals most of the items to be quite dated, suggesting to Kevin that their last owner has recently passed away. Although a little morbid, it's this kind of sale that Kevin relishes, since it's often when people die that the most interesting items become available; peculiar objects kept and treasured for years, once loaded with personal meaning, now stripped of all but their original purpose.

After purchasing Lot #29, a good mix of household furniture, it's only when Kevin is loading the items on to his truck that he notices one particular piece for the first time: a peculiar little cabinet unlike anything else in the sale. Roughly a foot wide and just over 16 inches tall, it's made from a richly coloured, if slightly scuffed, mahogany, and adorned on the front with two bunches of grapes shaped from brass. Kevin recognises it as a wine cabinet common in Jewish households, often used as a ceremonial piece due to the prevalence of wine in Jewish ritual practice.

'I see you bought the dybbuk box.'

Kevin turns to find a young woman standing behind him.

'Dybbuk box?' he asks.

The box, the woman explains, was one of only three items that her grandmother Havela brought to America when she arrived from Europe after the Second World War, along with the sewing box and a steamer trunk. Havela was born in Poland where she'd lived before the German Army's invasion of 1939, after which she was sent to a concentration camp where she lost contact with her entire family. Later she managed to escape and made her way to Spain, where it is thought she purchased the strange box. Havela would never see any of her family again, but thanks to the sanctuary offered by the United States, she was able to build a new life, a new home and a new family, passing away at the age of 103.

Moved by her story, Kevin no longer sees the item as just a piece for him to sell, but as something with great history and weight. Without hesitation, he offers it back to the woman. Her response is unexpected: 'No, I don't want anything to do with it. Please, it's yours now.'

Alarmed by her response he asks, 'Why is it called a dybbuk box?'

The woman tells him that ever since she can remember, her grandmother kept the box in her sewing room, closed and out of the reach of small prying hands. Whenever she had asked what was in it, her grandmother would spit through her fingers three times and say it was a dybbuk, insisting the cabinet should never be opened under any circumstances.

As for what a dybbuk is exactly, the woman isn't able to say.

'Do you want to open it with me?' Kevin jokes.

The woman's response is an emphatic no.

Kevin looks back to the quaint little box. 'Are you sure you don't want to keep it?' he asks.

'You bought it, we don't want it,' she says, turning away and walking off towards the house, leaving a bemused Kevin to finish loading the rest of the goods before driving back to Addy's Market.

Having arrived back at the shop, Kevin takes the new purchases down to the basement for logging later that afternoon. With a few more errands to run, he heads out again, leaving his assistant Jane in charge until his return. With business a little slow on the shop floor, Jane takes the opportunity to make a start on the new items. As she descends into the cold darkness of the basement, she feels a profound sense of unease. Moments later, almost without realising, she finds herself staring at the funny-looking cabinet with two bunches of metal grapes on its doors; that sense of unease now unmistakable as the feeling of being watched.

A ringing phone snaps her out of it. Running back up to the shop floor Jane picks it up but when she answers there is no voice at the other end. The next moment, she hears a loud crash coming from below.

'Hello?' says Jane, stepping down into the basement.

Moving further in, she sees with some relief the cause of the disturbance: a phosphorescent light bulb has blown, scattering milky white glass across the floor.

Jane grabs a brush and cleans up the mess but as the pieces of glass rattle and scuff against the floor and the bristles of the brush swish over the surface, Jane hears something else. She stops for a moment and strains to listen.

It sounds like somebody is whispering to her.

It's quiet at first, like tiny licks of wind whipping at her ears, getting louder until she can almost pick out whole words, all undercut by a dark tone of malice.

SMASH!

Another light bulb blows, raining glass all over the floor, plunging the basement into darkness. Jane drops the brush and runs straight for the exit, but the basement gate has somehow swung shut and locked itself. She pulls at the bars screaming for help.

Kevin is a few blocks away when he picks up the phone to find a frantic Jane on the other end. *There's someone here*, she keeps saying, *someone's smashing the place up*. Before Kevin can make any sense of it, the line goes dead. He hurriedly returns to the shop but finds it completely silent with no light coming from the floor below, and when he calls out for Jane, he gets no response. Grabbing a flashlight from under the counter he races down to the basement but finds the gate locked shut. Fumbling for the keys he hurriedly unlocks it and pushes it open.

Kevin flicks the light switch, but the room remains dark. After turning on the torch and taking a step forward, he is hit by an unexpected and pungent odour, sickly-sweet like cat urine, as glass cracks under his feet. Directing the torch around he is shocked to find that every light bulb has blown out. The torch beam catches something crouched on the floor at the far end of the room. Kevin freezes for a moment as it begins to stand.

'Fuck you,' says Jane, pushing past him, before heading up the stairs and out of the shop.

A stunned Kevin is still standing in the dark when he hears the shop's bell ring, followed by the slamming of the front door.

Jane never returns to work at Addy's Market, convinced that Kevin has played a hideous prank on her. For Kevin's part, he could be forgiven for thinking Jane herself might have had something to do with it. Certainly it doesn't occur to either of them that perhaps a small mahogany cabinet could be to blame.

A month later, Kevin finally gets round to fixing up the wine cabinet, having decided it would make the perfect present for his mother Ida's upcoming birthday. Pulling it out from the back of the basement, he places it on his worktop and is just about to unlock the clasp when he remembers the warning of the seller's grandmother: *never open it*. With a shrug, he flicks back the clip and pulls open the doors.

As he does, something unexpected occurs. A small drawer at the bottom opens simultaneously, revealing two old pennies and two locks of hair. Kevin pulls the drawer open further and the doors follow suit, as if the box itself were offering its contents to him. Looking inside the cabinet, Kevin is confused. On the inner side of the door he finds a cup and brackets for holding wine bottles as he had anticipated, but what he hadn't expected to find were further bizarre objects left inside.

He starts with the pieces in the drawer, taking out the two US wheat pennies first, one from 1925 and the other from 1928. Next, he takes out the wine cup that appears to be made of gold, and places it on the side next to the pennies. In the main box he finds a dried rosebud and a ghoulish-looking cast-iron candlestick with four octopus-like feet curling around the base. He picks up the strands of hair and examines them closely. One lock is curly, tangled and reddish blonde in colour, the other much darker, almost black and very straight. Both are undoubtedly human.

Kevin also finds an oddly shaped granite statue with the Hebraic *Shalom*, meaning 'peace', engraved in copper on its front – it is like nothing he has seen before. With all the pieces removed, Kevin has just started rubbing lemon oil gently into the wood when he notices something else written in Hebrew across the back of the cabinet. Unable to read it, however, he finishes the oiling, returns the items and carefully closes its doors.

A few days later, Ida arrives at Addy's Market to find Kevin waiting for her with his newly restored gift.

'Happy Birthday Mom,' he says, 'What do you think?'

Ida smiles politely, not quite sure what to make of it as Kevin places it on a table, before heading downstairs to finish off a few small jobs before they can go for lunch.

Ida takes a seat, feeling a small breeze rush through the shop. She looks up to find to her astonishment that the doors of the box have opened. Rising from her chair, she places her hand over it, only to be gripped by an extraordinary feeling of power, as if she has been plugged into the mains. In a panic, she tries to pull away, but something fixes her to the spot. Slowly, the left side of her mouth begins to sag.

Kevin returns to find his mother completely unresponsive with tears streaming down her face. After being rushed to hospital she is discovered to have suffered a stroke resulting in the partial paralysis of her left side and a loss of speech. Once settled on a ward, with her son sitting next to her, she picks up a pen and scribbles the words NO GIFT on a piece of paper and shows it to him. He rubs her hand and reassures her he has indeed bought her one, but Ida becomes agitated, shaking her head. She scribbles furiously again and turns the pad around to reveal the words: HATE GIFT.

With his mother unwilling to keep the present, Kevin offers it first to his sister, who returns it a week later complaining that the doors won't stay shut, and then to his brother and his wife who also return it days later upset by the strange urine-like odour it exudes. Kevin takes it back to the shop where a middle-aged couple take a shine to it and duly take it off his hands only to return it the following day. Kevin finds it waiting for him on the doorstep of the shop with an odd note taped to it that reads, 'This box has an old darkness about it.' In the end he decides to take it home and keep it for himself.

The first night with the cabinet in his house, Kevin dreams that he is walking through an enchanting autumnal scene alongside an old friend. But as they walk through the burnt orange and browns of a forest pathway, something begins to shift out of place.

He turns to his friend, whose face is morphing and twisting into a grotesque mask until it is replaced entirely by the gruesome features of an almost inhuman-looking elderly lady, her dark sunken eyes exuding what he takes to be a deep, primordial and unfathomable evil.

Suddenly she sets upon him with startling ferocity, beating and tearing at his skin.

Kevin wakes with a scream, dripping in sweat as his heart thumps audibly in his chest. When he looks down he sees that his body is covered in welts and bruises. Not long after, he becomes convinced that something is stalking the house, sometimes catching black wispy shapes that retreat into the shadows when he looks up. Afraid of what others might think, Kevin keeps these nightmares and visions to himself for the next eighteen months.

One morning over breakfast, Kevin's sister, who is visiting for the weekend along with their brother and his wife, complains of a hellish nightmare she had the previous night involving a fearsome elderly lady. Kevin's sister-in-law stops eating and looks nervously at the others. She had the exact same dream too. In fact, all four of them had had it, and not for the first time. Together they realise their nightmares had occurred whenever each of them had been looking after the dybbuk box. Despite Kevin's unwillingness to believe a Jewish wine cabinet has anything to do with it, he decides to put it away in a storage space behind the house for some peace of mind until he can get to grips with what's going on.

That night, through the fogginess of sleep, Kevin hears a distant siren and wakes to find the smoke alarm in the storage unit going off. He races to the unit but finds no fire, only the potent stench of cat urine. After returning to bed, he wakes again at 4.30 a.m. with the sensation of someone's breath on his neck, recoiling in horror at the sight of a large humanoid shadow disappearing into the hallway. Kevin has had enough.

Kevin isn't religious or superstitious in the slightest, so to think this harmless box might have some kind of spiritual power is complete anathema to him. But how many of us, despite inner certainty and our better judgement, will still avoid walking under a ladder or feel a little tightening of the chest when a black cat walks across our path? The easiest solution for Kevin is to throw the box away or burn it, but he can't shake the thought: *what if?* What if the box was cursed? What if destroying it would unleash the curse indefinitely upon himself and all his loved ones? Would he want to carry that burden for the rest of his life?

Just over 2,000 miles away in Kirksville, Missouri, twenty-year-old students Brian and Ioseph are browsing the aisles of their local grocery store when Ioseph mentions a curious box he has seen for sale on eBay. The pair are students of Truman State University and share an apartment close to their campus.

Less than an hour later, they are sitting in front of Brian's laptop pouring over a listing titled 'Dibbuk Box' that has been put up by a user called nw-net-trade. It begins:

'All of the events that I am about to set forth in this listing are accurate . . .'

The listing goes on to enumerate every detail of the owner's terrifying experiences since purchasing the item. Sadly for Ioseph, Brian doesn't quite share his enthusiasm for the piece and is reluctant to invite it into his life, and without Brian, Ioseph isn't sure he can justify the current $100 asking price. But the more he tries to forget about it, the more he can't seem to let it go, in thrall to the idea that it might truly be haunted. A few days later, alone in his room, Ioseph logs on to find the following addition to the listing:

'June 14th at 5:21:

For those of you wanting to know if I am still experiencing anything out of the ordinary, I thought everything was OK until I got home on Friday – the 13th of June – and found that the fish in my fresh water aquarium – all 10 – were dead.'[8]

It's too good to resist. Ioseph selects the bidding box, types in a number and clicks the mouse.

Just over a week later Brian returns home to find the apartment reeking of urine. He follows the scent into the living room where he is surprised to find the same box he and Ioseph had been looking at online now sitting for real, right in front of him. When Ioseph returns a few hours later he takes it to his bedroom and jokes with Brian to listen out in case anything strange happens.

The night passes without incident.

Brian works a part-time job at his University's Museum of Osteopathic Medicine. Every Monday, the department, led by director Jason Haxton, would hold a team meeting to set their goals for the week and give the team the chance to catch up after the weekend. Usually Brian would remain silent for these sessions, choosing just to listen to the contributions of others. But this week he finally has something of his own to offer.

'We bought a haunted box,' he says.

As the words settle over the group, there are a few raised eyebrows and nervous smiles but Jason, whose special area of interest is the 'spiritual context of ancient art pieces',[9] is especially intrigued. He offers to examine the box to get a proper look himself, but Brian is unsure, offering only to let him know if there's any peculiar activity.

There isn't long to wait.

It starts with the lights. Just like they had in Kevin's shop, bulbs suddenly pop or blow entirely, even when newly replaced. The urine-like smell that the boys had assumed to be coming from the wood disappears, only to reappear in different parts of the apartment. Brian's laptop crashes inexplicably due to a critical failure of the hard drive, and despite attempts to fix it, the damage is found to be unknown and irreparable.

Ioseph decides to do some further research into just what exactly it is that he has bought. What he finds terrifies him. Although spelt with an 'i' by Kevin in his eBay listing,[10] a dybbuk is a demon of Jewish folklore, often used in stories to scare little children. Only it isn't just an old bedtime story, as Ioseph discovers, but a 'misplaced spirit that can neither rise to Heaven nor descend into Hell ... An Evil Spirit,' that will attach itself to an unsuspecting victim, like a parasite, 'cause(ing) mental illness, rage and changes of personality'.[11]

The clinging torment of the dybbuk, as depicted by
Ephraim Moses Lilien in *Dybbuk* (1908).

Ioseph also observes that it is more Hebraic text that is carved into the back of the box. A Jewish prayer that translates as:

'Hear O Israel, the Lord is our God, the Lord is one. Blessed is the name of His honoured kingdom forever.'

It is a common and well-known prayer. The sort of prayer, perhaps, that one might say when fearful for their life, or just before they die.

After six weeks of the strange phenomena, Iosef and Brian's four other flatmates return from their summer break, apprehensive at the thought of sharing the flat with the apparently haunted box. Word gets out around campus and for a short time, their apartment becomes a popular hangout for the brave and curious – but events soon take an ominous turn.

Two of the flatmates begin to suffer from itchy and irritated eyes. Another contracts bronchitis and Ioseph breaks his finger. Most complain of listlessness, as if something is draining them of energy. When one flatmate's car breaks down, a check under the bonnet reveals a handful of dead mice. A few days later, a biblical infestation of gnats appears in the room the box is being kept in.

At first, Ioseph is determined not to give in to superstition. '*It's merely coincidental*,' he says to himself; '*a series of completely unexceptional events given an illusory supernatural context through the presence of the box*.'[12] But outwardly, cracks begin to show. His behaviour becomes increasingly erratic and Brian and the other flatmates start noticing it. Ioseph's certainty weakens.

After the Thanksgiving holiday, the flatmates return to the apartment, relieved, and a little perplexed, to find that Ioseph has left, taking the box with him. Like a turning of the tide, the strange events immediately appear to stop: the smell of urine clears up, there are no more inexplicable electrical shortages and the bugs seem to have gone.

At the museum Brian's stories have become a constant source of fascination for Jason, so it's greatly disappointing when the student has to leave his job at the end of the summer to focus on his studies. Months later, Jason spots him in the audience at a lecture he's presenting. Afterwards, he makes an approach, hoping to hear more about the cabinet, but is dismayed to learn that Ioseph moved out weeks before and Brian hasn't seen him or the box since. Jason is gripped by an eerie and profound sense of loss, as if the ring from Rivendell has just slipped from his grasp.

Six weeks later, Jason receives word from Brian that Ioseph has decided to sell the box.

Reluctant to tell his wife Lori for fear that she won't want anything to do with it, Jason turns to his colleague Michael for some advice. Michael is a friend but also a keen performer of stage magic in his spare time. Intrigued by the idea of building an act around a 'haunted' artefact, Michael's offer to go in on the purchase convinces Jason to buy it.

In early February 2004, Jason logs in to eBay under his handle agetron and finds item number 3701347648, otherwise known as the selling page for the 'Dibbuk Haunted Jewish Wine Cabinet Box'.

As Jason reads, he feels a surge of excitement. Everything Brian had described, including Kevin's story from the original listing, is here. And there is more:

'Around October 6th, I started feeling bad, with trouble sleeping. This problem has persisted through today.

I've started seeing things, sort of like large vertical dark blurs in my peripheral vision.

Most disturbingly, last Tuesday (1-27-2004), my hair began to fall out. Today (Friday) it's about half gone. I'm in my early twenties, and I just got a clean blood test back from the doctor's. Maybe it's stress related, I don't know.'[12]

The description reads more like a distress beacon than an auction listing and it is clear that the last few months for Ioseph, who for unknown reasons decided to move back home to live with his parents, have become increasingly dark and bizarre. Jason scans back to the top of the page, reading the original listing, finding those fateful words from the original owner, 'You bought it . . . We don't want it!'[13]

For a moment Jason's fingers hesitate over the keys before he types his opening bid of $0.99. He takes a long breath and clicks the bid button, knowing that whatever happens next, he will forever be part of the box's mythology. For the next few minutes Jason sits transfixed; his face lit up by the dim glow of the computer screen, stealthily upping his bid as the auction clock ticks down until it finally reaches zero. Jason leans back from the screen and exhales deeply as the sound of approaching footsteps from outside his door is followed by the arrival of a very tense-looking Michael.

'Tell me you're agetron?' he says.

Jason smiles.

'I am.'

Ioseph had originally bought the box for $140, and in the end Jason has to stump up $280 to secure it. But there's a snag. When Jason emails Ioseph to arrange delivery, it seems that the box's owner has vanished into thin air. After several unanswered emails, Jason tries contacting Ioseph's parents, but neither have any knowledge of their son's association with the box.

Jason eventually receives a call from Brian who is now in charge of completing the sale because Ioseph, in a fit of desperation, had begged him to take the box away. The following Tuesday, a bleary-eyed and distracted-looking Brian arrives at Jason's office with a large cardboard container. Any other day, Jason might have noticed the desperation on Brian's face, or maybe wondered at his eagerness to leave the building immediately after dropping the package off without pausing to say goodbye – but today, Jason only has eyes for the box. Peeling the cardboard back to reveal the bubble-wrapped curio inside, he feels almost euphoric. It's a piece well-suited to its new environment, he thinks, surrounded by gruesome tools for primitive brain surgery, dissected human nervous systems and wallets made from human skin.[14]

Having agreed not to open the package until Michael is free, Jason has to resist until 8 p.m. before his friend is able join him. In the eerie silence of his deserted and dimly-lit office, he eases the box from its container. Having unpacked it, Jason slips on a pair of white examination gloves and runs his hand over the top before taking the drawer handle and pulling. As the drawer opens, the two front doors follow suit, swinging open to reveal the hidden treasures inside and releasing a pungent scent into the air.

One by one, they place the various items on a length of blue velvet which Michael has bought specially for the occasion. Jason bathes the box in black light, as you might do if looking for blood at a crime scene, but the box gives nothing away save for a small spot of candle wax. Then Michael notices something interesting: the letter N written on the inside-right edge. Jason wonders if it has a ritual purpose, signifying the need to have that side of the box facing north. Or maybe, he thinks, it isn't N at all but the

Hebrew Aleph, the very first letter of existence – the first point of the Alpha and the Omega – its numerical value of 111 symbolising the divine, spiritual and physical.[15] They find the same symbol again marked into the gold cup. Only it isn't gold, as Kevin had assumed, but rather brass with a silver plating that has all but worn away over the past eighty years or so since it was made. Going by the box's modern design and style of the hinges, Jason judges it to have been put together around the 50s or 60s, but looking at the pieces spread out before him on the cloth – the pennies, the bulbous candlestick, the two locks of hair and the strange granite statue – he is unable to say quite what it was used for. Certainly none of the items have any traditional supernatural or occult connections. Whatever this is, it is unlike anything he has ever seen before.

With Michael taking a closer look at the pieces, Jason slowly removes one of the gloves and places his bare hand on top of the box – but hurriedly pulls it back. *Peculiar*, he thinks. This time he closes his eyes and once more feels the top of it, getting the same sensation again. It is as though the wood is moving, rippling like water, vibrating even, as if it were alive. Unseen by Michael, Jason recoils, letting out a stifled cry as a sharp and searing pain grips him inside before moving up into his stomach. They finish by taking some pictures before calling it a night, returning the items to the box and packing it away.

That night, back at home, Jason's eyelids flicker and pulsate with the REM twitch of deep sleep. In his mind a dark and disturbing set of images are playing out. Faces morphing from one into another, hideously disfigured, bleeding and wounded, and amidst it all, the recurring image of a ghoulish elderly woman with dark sunken eyes. He wakes in the dark, sweating and short of breath, his wife Lori lying sound asleep beside him. He closes his eyes again and soon finds himself in a small department store, this time with a different, benign, elderly woman pleading with him and pointing at an empty box just about the size of the Dibbuk Box.

The next morning, after splashing his face with cold water from the sink, Jason is shocked to find both of his eyes are red-raw and bloodshot. A few days later the irritation hasn't cleared and he is now plagued by a dull metallic taste in his mouth, dominating everything he eats. He chokes on the smallest sips of water and worst of all, can't fight the continual feeling that something is lodged inside his throat.

Jason's doctor suggests he might be suffering from dysgeusia, a distortion of taste that can be caused by any number of illnesses. But Jason isn't convinced. That might explain the now-consistent taste in his mouth but it doesn't account for his irritated eyes or his difficulty swallowing, not to mention the mysterious stomach cramps. The evidence seems clear: he has been poisoned.

After assessing a variety of substances, the methodical Jason finds ammonia to be the perfect candidate for his symptoms. Aside from the issues he is suffering from, exposure to ammonia can result in hallucinations as well as sensing the smell of urine. Finally, all the stories from the previous owners begin to make sense. When Jason tests the items, however, everything comes back completely clean. Whatever is happening to him has nothing to do with poison.

Meanwhile, strange things have started occurring at the museum. Light bulbs are blowing, popping and exploding, all over the office. Jason's deteriorating health hasn't gone unnoticed either. Brian, now back working at the museum, approaches him first. It's clear to him that whatever had latched on to Ioseph has now focused its attention on his boss. The other staff, irrevocably spooked, plead with their colleague to take his box home.

The only problem is Jason's wife Lori. Having heard about the cabinet from Michael's partner Erin, she has made it abundantly clear that her husband is not to bring the thing anywhere near the family. With Michael unwilling to take it off his hands, and Jason unwilling to part with it, he makes the decision to *secretly* bring it home. He can only hope that if something has indeed 'attached' itself to him, it will leave his family alone. It is a decision he will soon come to regret.

It starts with unusual fluctuations in temperature. Entire parts of the house become so cold that the family can see their own breath, even in the height of summer. Jason's nightmares grow even more intense and terrifying, but now it isn't only when he's asleep that he sees things. One evening he and his thirteen-year-old son are watching television together in the lounge when they witness a strange billowing mass, like a black fire, crawling up the wall.

The following day, an agitated Jason makes a call to Steve Maass, president of the Long Island Paranormal Research Group. When he first bought the box, Jason hadn't realised the vast interest it would generate online. Tens of thousands of people across the world had watched as he won his bid, and many had contacted him later on, eager to hear of any strange happenings. Steve had been one of the first enthusiasts to get in touch and had impressed with his sincerity and extensive knowledge of similar artefacts. Steve listens patiently as Jason recounts the series of events of the last few weeks before giving his chilling verdict. One way or another, he unleashed something when he opened the box and now it's in the house with his family.

Steve suggests Jason carry out an appeasement ritual taken from Chapter XXII of a 15th-century book of spells known as *The Key of Solomon*. The ritual asks for a sacrifice to be made to the demonic spirit. Later that evening, the rational, unflappable Midwesterner stands alone in the pitch dark of his garage holding the two cuttings of hair from the box, hoping they will make a sufficient offering. He writes a promise to make better gifts in future on a strip of paper and ties it all together around a pine twig. Lighting a match, he holds it underneath until the bundle catches fire. As it burns, he repeats his promise: 'better gifts shall come from me.' After the flames have died out, Jason steps from the dark of the garage into the clear night air as if he were surfacing from under water. That night, no grotesque old ladies haunt his dreams and over the next few weeks his ailments will all but vanish. With the appeasement ritual appearing to have worked, Jason returns his focus to finding out more about the haunted artefact. However, despite consulting a number of experts, from Rabbis to historians, Jason discovers little more than what he already knows. The man he needs is Kevin.

Jason is able to trace Kevin to Portland through the original eBay listing and with a work trip to the city coming up he doubles his efforts to find him. He discovers one 'Mannis' listed in the phone book and calls the number, which turns out to be that of Kevin's sister. However, she is unwilling to give out her brother's details and wants nothing to do with Jason's quest to find him. Undeterred, he turns to the Internet and through a genealogy site discovers Kevin had a grandmother called Ethel who had died some years previously. Enlisting the help of a researcher, Jason finds a contact for another relative of Ethel's who reveals some intriguing information: Kevin's grandmother was a Russian-Jewish immigrant who arrived in the States some time at the beginning of the 1900s and died around the age of 103 – similar to the alleged original owner of the box, who Kevin claimed was a Jewish émigré from Europe. Ethel also had a fascination with Jewish mysticism and Kishuf – a form of Judaic magic.

The relative is convinced Ethel was the inspiration for the box and that Kevin has faked the whole thing. The admission leaves Jason deflated until something extraordinary occurs a few days later when the same relative sends Jason a photograph of Ethel by email. When Jason opens the attachment, staring back at him is the elderly woman he has seen in his dreams, standing in the department store pointing to the empty box. Ethel, it turns out, had also owned a department store.

When Jason travels to Portland in June, he has almost given up on speaking to Kevin entirely when he makes one final effort to locate him. Looking through local courthouse records he finds a phone number. Later that night he makes the call from his hotel room and a woman answers the phone. She assures him that nobody by the name of Kevin lives there but Jason isn't convinced.

'Tell him,' he says, 'I've got a hundred and fifty dollars if he can just call me at the hotel.'

The voice on the other end says she will see what she can do before hanging up.

With midnight approaching, the hotel phone finally rings. Kevin had got the message. The pair meet the following day and Jason proceeds to fill Kevin in on how the Dibbuk Box has been affecting his life and what he's done to stop it. He explains, much to Kevin's surprise, that the box has become somewhat of an Internet sensation, racking up over 140,000 hits to date on its original eBay listing. For Kevin's part, the last year hadn't been going too well. What hadn't been mentioned in his eBay listing, as he explains to Jason, was that not only had his mother had a stroke the day she touched the box, but on the same day the FBI had inexplicably raided his store. A number of agents and police officers had descended on Addy's Market, bizarrely confiscating all electrical items with a memory chip inside. Months later, the articles were returned to Kevin with no explanation for the raid and no arrests being made. When his landlord got wind of the incident, Kevin was asked to close down the business and he had been struggling to find work ever since.

Thankfully, after he got rid of the box, his mother had made a significant recovery from her stroke, but something of the box had remained: those strange visions and dreams had never truly left him. Jason is concerned by the story of the police raid, which sounds completely fantastical, but he can't argue with the strange visions since he knows them only too well. That afternoon Kevin takes Jason to see Addy's Market, his old store, and the Jewish cemetery where the box's original owner is apparently buried. They make an attempt to find the house where Kevin had first purchased the item but by then the day has got away from them. With Jason due to fly back that evening, Kevin promises to do his best to track the original owner's family down.

The next few months in the Haxton household are mercifully event free until one late-September morning when Jason finds a small brown mouse rotting away under his car seat. A few days later, Jason and his children come home from school to find the house reeking of excrement. The water from one of the toilets has been completely sucked away, leaving a clear channel to the city's sewer system. Jason is told in no uncertain terms by an engineer from the Public Water and Sewer Works that such a level of suction was impossible. It is then that he catches a glimpse of his bloodshot eyes in the mirror and notices the hives have broken out once again over his body. When he coughs, his mouth is filled with that familiar repellent metallic taste – or is it blood? Jason feels, with a terrible certainty, that the thing is back.

Clearly Steve's appeasement spell, if it had worked at all, is beginning to wear off. Like Kevin, Jason is hesitant to merely sell the box, or destroy it, fearing that something more substantial was needed to rid him of its curse. This time he seeks the advice of his friend Tracey, a devoted follower of Wiccan magic who had also contacted him early on with offers to help.

He awakes early the next morning. Careful not to disturb his wife and children, he picks up the Dibbuk Box from the spare room and carries it to the property next door, an apartment that he and his wife had bought earlier in the year that was still being renovated. In the basement is a small door leading to a pitch-black crawl space that expands into a hidden room. Jason, also carrying a collection of herbs and a purple candle as per Tracey's instructions, pushes the box through the crawl space and into the other room.

Switching on the flashlight he illuminates the makeshift altar he constructed earlier from plywood and cinder blocks and slides the box beside it, placing the candle on the other side. Taking sea salt from his bag of herbs, he draws a square with a circle inside on the top of the altar, followed by a cross, to form the four points of the compass. Dry basil is sprinkled into the four corners, sage in the middle and the candle placed on top. The torch is switched off.

Bathed in darkness, Jason composes himself for a moment before striking the match and lighting the candle. In the dim light, he burns the dried sage above the altar and waves it around three times in a circular motion. As he makes these movements and inhales the scented smoke, he solemnly utters the words as instructed by Tracey:

> 'Beloved Hekate, defender of the weak,
> protector of those who fear the might of the wicked,
> for whom each step into the dark is filled with dread,
> I pray to you, I ask your favour. Hekate,
> who knows well of all things we mortals most fear,
> who knows well how best to drive away all ill,
> I ask your blessing. Goddess, preserve my home
> and my family from evil, guard us well
> against all that would do us harm. Goddess, hold back
> the dangers of the dark, grant me wisdom and courage
> that I may face my fears and my foes with open eyes.'[16]

The flame of the candle flares as Jason moves it to the side and places the box on to the altar over the basil, salt and sage whilst whispering the vital words, 'you will be contained, you will be contained, you will be contained.' A gust of wind blows through the basement, then all becomes still. Jason crawls out of the room, looking one last time at the box before nailing the little door shut.

After completing a ritual bath of herbs and salt water, Jason returns to the basement for the second part of the spell. Lit by two candles, this time he pours the salt in a circle around himself. Careful not to exit the space he has drawn, he lights more sticks of sage and circles the salt perimeter three times, invoking the Goddess Hekate once again. Using a burnt stick of sage, he writes on a piece of paper the banishing words 'All blocks are now removed,' wraps the paper around the sage and lights the bundle.[17] Once it has burned out, he makes another three circular movements with one of the candles, closes his eyes and blows out the flame.

Jason returns to his house for a second ritual bath. Stepping into the hot herb-scented water and allowing the peppery basil fragrance to flow into his lungs, Jason immediately feels lighter. But as he lets his body sink down, a searing pain grips his stomach. In agony he heaves himself out of the tub and falls to the floor. Now on his hands and knees, he begins to retch. The pain, growing in intensity, is moving from his stomach and up into his throat. Jason begins to choke and struggle for air. Then, as if wrenched out from within him, a final heave ejects a dark 'mucus-like slime'[18] from his mouth. The pain gone at last, Jason slumps back against the bathtub, exhausted.

Inspired by the materials used to build the Ark of the Covenant as detailed in the biblical book of Exodus,[19] Jason has the box formally interred, binding it in a gold-plated ark made of acacia wood, because one can never be too careful. Since the ritual, Jason

The Dibbuk Box encased in the ark Jason had made especially.

has not suffered any more terrifying occurrences, but the question of the Dibbuk Box's provenance still remains.

It has been a few months since Kevin promised Jason that he would track down Havela's family and his silence on the matter has become more suspicious by the day. It hasn't escaped Jason's attention that their failure to locate the original point of sale that summer afternoon in Portland was more than a little convenient. In fact, Jason is beginning to question Kevin's entire account when he finally gets in touch. What he has to say is more than worth the wait.

According to Kevin, he had tracked the family down through the auctioneering company that handled the sale and driven out to see them at the first opportunity. After ringing on the front door, he was met by the familiar face of a former classmate who was also, as it happened, another granddaughter of Havela's, the original owner of the cabinet. She knew of the box, although it soon became evident that it was just a joke to her. Even as Kevin relayed the events of the last few years, he could see he was wasting his time and turned to leave. This was when another voice called him back.

'It chose you,' she said.

Kevin turned to find a frail, elderly woman in the doorway beside his old classmate. She was pointing a lean skeletal finger towards him.

'Who chose me?' replied Kevin.

'The dybbuks from the demonic side,' she said.

Havela's granddaughter introduced the woman as her aunt, Sophie, and together they invited Kevin inside. As the granddaughter made tea, Kevin and Sophie pulled up chairs on a patio in the back garden and after a moment of quiet, Sophie turned to Kevin and apologised profusely for everything from the events of the Second World War to obscure and damaging stock market fluctuations, alongside most other atrocities that had occurred in the last seventy years. *They* were sorry for all of it.

As Sophie had continued to explain to Kevin, it had all started with a séance held many years ago. It was Havela's idea, born from the daily anti-Semitic terrors confronting Polish Jews in the late 1930s. Terrors that grew darker and more monstrous with each passing day and had at some point resulted in the death of Havela's children and husband.[20] Determined to fight back, Havela had invited a number of friends to her home one night, including Sophie's mother. When the women arrived, they found a table laid out, covered by a cloth bearing the words 'Yes' and 'No', as well as the digits 0–9 and all the letters of the alphabet. Havela then explained that she had called them all there in the hope of summoning spirits that might protect them and their community from the ever-encroaching dangers of fascism.

That night the women succeeded in summoning forth a number of spirits, of indeterminate place and form. Over the following few weeks, the friends continued to meet and seek guidance from these same spirits, but it wasn't long before they began to fear what they had beckoned into their world. The spirits were growing restless, demanding to be unleashed so that they might better serve their purpose, but something in their tone alarmed the women.

They hatched a plan to banish them for good.

In the early hours of 9 November 1938, Havela and her friends sat around the table one final time. Sitting on the Ouija cloth was a small wooden box that looked distinctly like a Jewish wine cabinet, which they planned to lure the spirits into and keep locked inside forever; but something went wrong and the spirits escaped. It was Sophie's mother's belief that this night had led to every subsequent misery to befall humanity ever since. According to Sophie, the original box had been destroyed during the war. The box bought by Kevin had been made by Havela sometime later in Portland in an attempt to recapture the maleficent entities.

After listening to Kevin speak, Jason isn't quite sure what to think. It is an incredible story, and he can't argue with the reality of his own horrific experiences. However, much like the way he feels about Kevin's story, something doesn't add up for Jason. One thing in particular hasn't sat right with him: Kevin's insistence that a completely unexplained FBI raid had occurred the exact same day his mother was shown the box, and subsequently suffered a stroke.

One morning, after doing some research, Jason comes across an old article in the *Portland Oregonian News*. On 8 July 1998, the paper reported on a series of police stings that had taken place across Portland the week before. At the time, as detailed in the article, a number of small stores in the area had been running a racket selling stolen items. One of these stores was Addy's Market, before it had been bought and run by Kevin. Could the raid Kevin described have been genuine after all, a follow-up operation perhaps?

If this unlikely story were true, why not the rest of it? Certainly, stranger things have happened . . .

Having already watched some videos of him online, Jason comes across on Skype exactly as I had expected him to: bright, affable, engaging and full of what I now know to be a distinct ever-welcoming midwestern charm. In short, he's everything you would expect from a curator of an osteopathic museum of an academic institution. We talk for almost two hours as he is sat in his office, surrounded by a number of wholesome family portraits. I soon get the impression that Jason isn't somebody easily sucked in by superstition, and that his open-minded interest in the box is rooted in genuine curiosity rather than any sensationalist obsession with the paranormal. Which, of course, only makes his testimony more astounding.

I had originally come across the story of the Dibbuk Box after watching Sam Raimi's *The Possession*. Surprised to learn that the film was based on a true story, I soon found myself online trawling through Jason's website.[21] A few days later, as I was deep into reading his book, *The Dibbuk Box*, it was fair to say I had become a little obsessed. As often with such stories, the first thing that struck me about his tale was the number of people involved who claimed to have suffered similar horrors, with little to gain from sharing their experiences. It hadn't escaped my attention that

Kevin sold his box on eBay, the perfect platform if you wanted to concoct a wild and seductive story to pique interest in an otherwise un-extraordinary item. Yet Jason had made similar claims, and I had no reason to doubt his integrity. As he notes in his book, he is more than happy to admit that the box might have no genuine supernatural properties, but he did experience something that was, at times, terrifying; something that, as claimed by others who came into contact with the box, had a tangible physiological effect on him.

One Wednesday night in June 1962, a slew of US news outlets reported a curious outbreak afflicting the workers of a textile mill in the town of Strongsville, Ohio. In total, sixty-two people had been struck down by a mystery illness caused by apparent insect bites. As one worker recounted, '. . . the small insect attacks the skin, the bites leave a wound similar to a gnat bite. In about twenty minutes the victim is struck with severe nausea.'[22]

Yet no insect, or other cause for the incident, was ever found. According to sociologist Alan C. Kerchoff, the reason for this was that there *was* no insect. Instead, it is his belief that the ailments were due to the effect of Mass Psychogenic Illness (MPI). What differentiates MPI from the broader and better-known phenomena of mass hysteria is that MPI results in genuine physical symptoms, an effect shared with another peculiar phenomenon now being taken increasingly seriously by the medical community.

Physician Walter Kennedy first coined the term 'nocebo' in 1961, drawing on Harvard researcher Walter Cannon's 1940s studies regarding the power of suggestibility in the practice of voodoo. A nocebo is a 'harmless substance or treatment that when taken by or administered to a patient is associated with harmful side effects . . . due to negative expectations or the psychological condition of the patient.'[23] A counterpoint to the more commonly known placebo effect, nocebo demonstrates how the power of the psyche alone can cause negative effects on the body if it can be sufficiently convinced that it is coming under harm.

One extraordinary example of the nocebo effect was demonstrated in a 2017 study led by Dr Peter Sever of Imperial College London, which examined the apparent negative side effects of taking statins – a drug frequently prescribed to the over-50s that improves heart function by reducing lipoprotein cholesterol. Statins have come under increasing scrutiny from healthcare professionals concerned that they have been too widely dispensed, considering the number of users who have reported alarming side effects after taking them.

What Dr Sever's study revealed was that these side effects, which mostly involve muscle-related aches and pains, were indeed real, only they weren't to do with the drug. According to his findings, patients only suffered from the side effects when they already had negative expectations of taking the medicine. Essentially, their symptoms had been completely imagined into being. Crucially, Sever notes:

> This is not a case of people making up symptoms, or that the symptoms are 'all in their heads'. Patients can experience very real pain as a result of the nocebo effect and the expectation that drugs will cause harm . . . What our study shows is that it's precisely the expectation of harm that is likely causing the increase in muscle pain and weakness, rather than the drugs themselves causing them.[24]

It's important to note that just because we might be able to imagine negative biological symptoms into being it doesn't mean we might equally be able to imagine negative physiological issues away, like cancerous cells for example, but the question remains: if the body is capable of inflicting physical harm on itself due to an illusory danger, what might the limits of self-affliction be? Could it be that all the ailments affecting the various owners of the Dibbuk Box, the hallucinations, red stinging eyes, the burns and choking fits, were, in a sense, the result of a spirit after all: the spirit of mind? What if the belief alone in a malevolent spirit, catalysed by the box's mythology, its indistinct connections to Jewish mysticism and a deep cultural fear of the demonic, led to Jason, Ioseph and Kevin bringing something into being that truly did endanger them? A fanciful notion perhaps, yet do we not spend most of our daily lives continually affected by illusory and abstract ideas that have physical, real-world consequences?

The term hyperstition was coined in the 1990s by a group of philosophers known as the Cybernetic Culture Research Unit (of which more in Chapter Nine). Distinct from superstition, which implies a false belief, hyperstitions, although broadly much more complex,[25] are essentially beliefs that, like an occult thought-form – or egregore – can 'by their very existence as ideas function causally to bring about their own reality.'[26] Once a hyperstition is collectively accepted as a fixed reality, we can become trapped by it since we no longer have 'real' truths from which to draw on, only the truth as we 'know' it to be. More profoundly, they demonstrate how our entire lives can be dictated by systems that exist only because we believe them to exist.

Consider for example the way the stock market works, or the abstract and relative nature of something's 'worth' in general. We can argue that when stock is first floated on a financial market there is an initial transaction of 'real' money, which the company whose shares are being floated receives. For the individual or company that has bought those shares, however, they now possess something that has no intrinsic value. It is essentially an illusion of worth – the value will increase or decrease depending on demand but what drives that demand is often little more than faith in the future success of the company. If you want to sell a share for hard cash you can actually spend, it requires others to also believe in the illusion of its worth. Essentially, the entire existence of the stock market, this hyperstition that underpins much of the global economy, only survives as long as other people are willing to keep believing in it. If tomorrow everybody decided they no longer thought it was real, the shares in circulation – since they are no longer financially linked to the company they were originally floated by (unless the company has purchased its own stock) – would effectively vanish without any immediately visible impact on the bank account of the business they nominally represent.

Or, in other words, if enough people are willing to believe in a world that allows for ancient demonic entities, and, having fostered that belief, speculate too that such a box exists that houses one of those entities, regardless of what *you* believe, you may want to think twice about opening it . . .

As I ended my Skype call with Jason, he generously offered me a place to stay should I ever want to visit. Once again I was struck by the integrity and openness of this kind stranger, and it's still an offer I sincerely hope to take up one day. But as I thanked him, an unsettling thought came over me. For whatever this meant, I was now a part of the Dibbuk Box's story and I couldn't help but feel a little unsettled. Because whether the box does indeed hold an unfathomable demonic entity, or if it was cynically constructed to dupe gullible punters, in one way or another it has been brought into existence. Real or not, the haunting possibilities of this inanimate box filled with inanimate things have been conjured into our shared imaginative space. And if I am a part of that story, having now read it, so too are you . . .

The next day I was struck by a pungent smell that seemed to pervade every room of our flat. It was unmistakable. Cat urine. We do live with cats but neither of them had ever peed inside and neither had sprayed, since they were neutered. I grew increasingly alarmed when the smell followed me out of the flat on my way to work and up to the top deck of the 243 bus. For a moment I felt gripped by something, the sense of being on a psychological ledge that if I allowed myself to, I could easily tip off from. By now, the smell had become unbearable, and judging from the reluctance of fellow passengers to sit next to me and the steady domino cascade of windows being opened around the deck, it was clear that I wasn't the only one who could smell it. I sniffed my clothes but couldn't smell the sweet, acrid odour on myself. Then I picked up my bag and brought it to my nose. It absolutely reeked.

Returning to the flat in the dark later that evening was admittedly an unsettling experience. All the more so when an unrecognisable shape shot out from the living room into the kitchen, followed by a clattering sound at the back door. The smell of urine was now more pungent than ever.

Switching on the light, I found the culprit: a large black stray cat, trapped inside by a malfunctioning cat flap.

Chapter Three

OUT OF THE TREES
AND ON INTO DARK

'We have found a strange footprint on the shores of the unknown'

Arthur Eddington – *Space, Time and Gravitation*

Throughout the history of humankind we have recorded stories of strange apparitions in the sky, of gods and monsters from above that either threaten or protect us. From a contemporary perspective, peeling back the religious and superstitious elements we might recognise many of these stories as tales of Unidentified Flying Objects. The term 'flying saucers', as they were known before 'UFO' was more widely adopted in the 1950s,[1] is thought to originate from a newspaper article written in 1878 detailing the account of Texan farmer John Martin. It was while out working on his farm one morning that Martin was alleged to have seen a large saucer-like object travelling through the sky with 'wonderful speed'.[2] It wouldn't be until the summer of 1947, however, that 'flying saucers' really caught the public imagination. In July of that year, an American recreational pilot named Kenneth Arnold claimed to have been followed by nine 'saucer like' objects while flying his plane over Mt Rainier in Washington State. In a world still deeply traumatised by the Second World War, the United States Air Force were unwilling to take any chances and swiftly set about establishing two things: what exactly these strange objects were and, more importantly, to what extent they posed a threat to national security.

On investigation, Arnold's story proved of little military concern, but the ensuing publicity led to an unprecedented influx of claims from hundreds of others eager to share their own experiences. Although the Air Force was happy to ignore the civilian reports, it proved a little harder to dismiss reports that had come from their own trained personnel. In response, in 1948 the USAF recruited Josef Allen Hynek to act as scientific consultant on a newly established project called Operation Sign. The purpose of the project was to collate information on all suspected UFO sightings in order to conduct rational scientific investigations with the aim of providing credible explanations for each account. For Hynek, a Doctor of Physics and Astronomy from Ohio State University, and a committed man of science, the opportunity to dispel the emerging myths of little green men was too good to turn down.

For the first few years, the task proved fairly easy; then Hynek noticed a pattern creeping into his work. Although the majority of cases were fanciful and easily dismissed, for every twenty claims he received, there would be at least one that was impossible to explain, claims he termed 'Unknowns'. Hynek also realised that in spite of Operation Sign's initial intentions, the project had rarely followed his own strict principles of scientific method: that every case should be approached with complete disinterest and without bias. It became clear that even if a UFO were to land on the road in front of his superiors, they would have refused to believe it. It soon dawned on Hynek that his job had not been to *investigate* the UFO reports, but to debunk them.

In 1949, Operation Sign was renamed Operation Grudge, before becoming Project Blue Book in 1952. Fans of David Lynch and Mark Frost's *Twin Peaks* may be familiar with Blue Book through the characters Major Garland Briggs and Windom Earle, who are revealed to have worked together at the top-secret organisation. As the storyline goes, it was radio operators working for Project Blue Book who first intercepted the strange signals emanating from the woods outside of *Twin Peaks*, later uncovered as the sight of a trans-dimensional realm known as the Black Lodge. In reality, or at least as far as we know, the real Blue Book never uncovered anything quite so profound, but the existence of such a programme in the first place suggests that the world's greatest superpower, and military might, took the idea of UFOs very seriously indeed. By the time Hynek died in 1983 at the age of seventy-five, he was convinced that the UFO phenomenon was real, believing there to be sufficient evidence to suggest that both extra-terrestrial and extra-dimensional intelligence could be responsible for a significant number of UFO sightings.[3]

The United Kingdom has experienced its fair share of 'UFO' sightings over the years, one of the most well known being the Howden Moor incident as I have previously explored on my podcast.[4] For true enthusiasts of the British UFO experience however, there is one story that stands out above all others, which took place in the county of Suffolk over the course of three extraordinary days in December 1980.

Located on the east coast of England, Suffolk is a haunting and enigmatic land with a rich and eerie history. A landscape of pale fens and country gardens[5] it was home to the infamous zealot and self-anointed Witchfinder General, Matthew Hopkins, whose ghost is said to roam the surrounding countryside; and to composer Benjamin Britten whose work was regularly inspired by its bucolic mystery. Since the early 20th century it has also been synonymous with strange, secret military experiments.

Located on the Suffolk coast, Orford Ness is a ten-mile shingle spit separated from the mainland by the River Alde-Ore. Purchased in 1913 by the British War Department, this quiet and genteel slip of the British Isles would for the next seventy years act as a primary testing ground for the nation's war apparatus from the durability of armour and parachutes to the ballistics of bullets and bombs. In the 1930s, a team of scientists led by pioneering Scottish physicist Robert Watson Watt moved on to the Ness, as it is known locally, to develop a radical new defence system for the British military that would later become known as radar.

During the Second World War, like a more boisterous version of Bletchley Park, the spit teemed with personnel in white coats and tweed, plotting and calculating behind vast concrete screens as one projectile after another was hurled at its target. With the atomic age came the construction of two peculiar concrete pagodas, designed to withstand the impact of high-explosive testing. Below the pagodas, laboratories were sunk into the ground, into which nuclear-bomb casings were lowered and experimented on. Despite continuing rumours to the contrary, the British Ministry of Defence maintains that it was only the integrity of the casing that was ever tested on the island, not the fissile material.

In 1993, the National Trust acquired Orford Ness from the Ministry of Defence and having been cleared of (most) of its unexploded ordnance, it continues to enchant as both nature reserve and an affecting and eerily desolate testament to its carefully shrouded past; those bizarre pagodas still standing, like the architectural apocrypha of a long-since-lost and indecipherable civilisation.

Located just ten miles inland from the Ness, deep within the thick pine forests of Rendlesham and Woodbridge, lie two ominously empty aircraft bases roughly five miles apart, each surrounded by high perimeter fencing. They were the twin air bases of RAF Woodbridge and RAF Bentwaters, constructed in 1943 to assist damaged warplanes on their return from bombing raids over Europe. With the onset of the Cold War, the British Air Ministry saw fit to loan the bases to the US Air Force to be used as staging posts for their fighter jets. By 1980, the bases were home to 81st Tactical Fighter Wing, and it is here that our story begins, one freezing cold evening in December . . .

'Look at that, in the treeline over there. You ever see anything like that before?'

Sergeant Bud Steffens pulls up the jeep, switches off the engine and kills the lights. Darkness floods the car as Airman First Class John Burroughs scans the clear night sky. As his eyes adjust, a multitude of stars emerge from the inky black around the gibbous moon hanging bright and high to the left.

'Look there!' says Steffens again.

Burroughs follows Steffens' outstretched finger towards a peculiar light that appears to be hovering somewhere in the distance above the pines of nearby Rendlesham Forest. It being Christmas Day, with the clock fast approaching midnight and with no late flights scheduled, things have been especially quiet on the base tonight, nowhere more so than out here at the far east perimeter. Burroughs squints to get a better look, his hand clutching the M16 rifle by the side of his legs.

'What is that?'

As the pair look closer they can see there are in fact two lights flashing red and blue, one on top of the other roughly a mile or so due east of the gate. As Security Police for the 81st, tonight it's John and Bud's responsibility to patrol RAF Woodbridge, looking out for any errant personnel or anyone else who might find themselves venturing a little too close to the perimeter fence. This also being 1980 and the height of the Cold War, the sudden appearance of unexpected lights in the night sky is serious cause for concern.

Despite Steffens' superiority, having only recently transferred here from the States it falls to twenty-year-old Burroughs to make the judgement call that whatever this is, it certainly isn't part of the usual landscape.

'What should we do?' asks Steffens.

'There's something out there,' says Burroughs, opening the door, letting in a rush of freezing cold air. 'I say we check it out.'

Before Steffens can argue, Burroughs leaps out of the truck, closing the door behind him. Steffens hesitates for a moment before turning the engine, catching Burroughs in the headlights as he bends down to unlock the gate, his breath swirling in thick clouds. Moments later they're cruising down the east gate road skirting the edge of the forest, keeping their eyes trained on the peculiar lights in the sky that now appear to be dropping into the trees. At the end of the road Steffens takes a sharp right then, after barely 50 metres, pulls up at the top of a logging track that leads deeper into the forest.

As they peer through the trees, the two guards can clearly see the slim trunks of Corsica pines lit up from behind by what must be the source of the light. Burroughs gives Steffens a shrug before cautiously opening the door and stepping out into the cold. Immediately he is struck by a bizarre sensation of static, as if the air were electrified around him. Taking a step forward he feels the hairs stand up on the back of his neck and a strange fuzzy sensation dragging across his skin. Looking up with alarm, he sees the distant light growing stronger. Not only is it moving, it's coming straight for them. Realising they have no clearance to be outside the wire and are in no legitimate position to call for backup, in a fit of panic Burroughs jumps back into the jeep and the pair speed back to the gate to phone it in.

At 2400 hours in the Bentwaters Mess Hall, Staff Sergeant Jim Penniston has just sat down to eat his breakfast before starting the night shift, when his radio crackles into life.

'Be advised, we have a report of a UFO, requesting 10/12 to Central Security Control.'

Penniston stares for a moment at his eggs.

'I'm sorry, can you repeat that?'

The straight-laced Midwesterner does not take kindly to practical jokes. With seven years of service under his belt, the six-foot-three, twenty-six-year-old Penniston is Senior Security Officer at Bentwaters and Woodbridge with the primary responsibility for protecting the bases' instruments of war.

Despite his suspicions, an irritated Penniston has no choice but to contact Central Security immediately. Connecting with Staff Sergeant Coffey on the CSC desk, Penniston is surprised by the urgency in his voice, even more so when Coffey orders him to grab his co-rider and proceed with haste to the east gate at RAF Woodbridge. Unusually, Coffey refuses to brief Penniston over the phone, telling him all will be explained when he gets there. Leaving his eggs untouched, Penniston races from the mess, radioing for his shift partner, Airman First Class Edward Cabansag to meet him at their jeep.

After tearing across the tarmac, Penniston and Cabansag arrive at the gate minutes later to find a shaken Burroughs and Steffens waiting for them. As Jim is about to ask them what's going on, he catches sight of it too: a peculiar diffused light glowing orange, red and blue coming from inside the nearby forest. Having handled more than thirty air-crash incidents, Jim can recognise the strange coloured light of a chemical burn anywhere.

'Shit, did you see it come down?'

'It didn't crash,' says Steffens.

'It didn't crash?'

'No, it landed.'

Penniston stares dumbstruck out into the distance.

'And you didn't hear a sound?'

'Nope.'

Penniston pauses and looks again at the light, noticing for the first time that it is actually coming from three separate sources; one white, one red and one blue. The red light is blinking. Penniston orders Cabansag to wait with Burroughs and Steffens while he calls lead flight chief, Master Sergeant Chandler, from the guard shack.

Chandler confirms there were no flight operations scheduled that evening and suspects a possible light aircraft might have strayed off the path and crashed into the trees. Penniston waits for the chief to check with Bentwaters Air Traffic Control, all the while keeping check on Burroughs, Steffens and Cabansag who continue to stare out towards the lights that are still clearly visible. When the flight chief returns on the line he informs an increasingly anxious Penniston that something had indeed been picked up on radar only fifteen minutes previously: an unidentified aircraft two miles off the coast, heading inland in a south-easterly direction before disappearing below radar coverage about five miles east of the Woodbridge runway. It wasn't only the tower at RAF Bentwaters that picked it up. Heathrow Air Traffic Control, nearby RAF Bawdsey as well as Eastern Radar at RAF Watton, the UK's primary Cold War Radar for the south-east, had all apparently tracked it.

Chandler advises Penniston to take two men and set up a cordon, then wait for fire and medical personnel to catch them up. He also agrees to head out and join them as soon as he can.

'And Sergeant Penniston?' says Chandler.

'Yes Sir?'

'Proceed with caution,' he says, before hanging up.

Returning to the gate, Penniston asks for a volunteer to accompany him and Cabansag into the forest. Steffens shifts uneasily but before he can say anything Burroughs pipes up, requesting permission to join.

For legal reasons, no personnel are permitted to take guns off the premises and with no idea what they might be facing, it is with some reluctance that the three men are forced to relinquish their rifles to Steffens before piling into the jeep and driving off towards the strange lights. Steffens, now alone at the back gate, scans the perimeter nervously as the red taillights of the jeep disappear down the east gate road, turning off into darkness at the bottom.

The three men in the jeep keep their eyes fixed firmly on the lights as Burroughs directs Penniston to the forest road and on into the thick of the trees. Up ahead, lit by the headlights, a thin track of frozen mud stretches out under a carpet of browning pine needles. To their left there is only the darkness behind the trees but to their right, the refracted soft rays of the strange light coming from some place deeper inside the forest. As they draw closer, Cabansag eyes Burroughs, his face pressed against the back window, in the rear-view mirror. Nineteen-year-old Cabansag is a brand-new recruit to the base having transferred only two days ago, and he is starting to worry this might be some kind of initiation ritual.

The men hold on tightly as the jeep rocks and bumps violently over the increasingly rugged track. With the path ahead beginning to narrow, Penniston brings the vehicle to a skidding halt then clicks on the radio, unleashing a loud burst of static.

'Delta 7, Golf 14,' he says, relaying their position back to Master Sergeant Chandler.

A garbled voice comes back on the receiver, barely audible through some interference. With no way of knowing if their message has been received, Penniston makes the decision to press ahead regardless, on foot. As they step out of the truck Burroughs recognises the same sensation as before, as if the air is electrified. Cabansag and Penniston feel it too. Having anticipated a crash site, they are surprised to find it strangely quiet, with no smell of burning fuel. Unperturbed, Penniston grabs a camera from the back of the truck as well as three flashlights and the two-way radios, handing one of each to Burroughs and Cabansag.

Penniston shines his flashlight into the trees and, with Cabansag bringing up the rear, proceeds to lead the men into the forest with a cautious urgency. The distant sound of Chandler's jeep heading into the forest is followed by the crackle of their radios bursting into life. They strain to hear the words as Chandler's voice battles again against intermittent bursts of interference. Sensing the signal weakening as they get further away, Penniston advises Cabansag to stay put to keep the line open as he and Burroughs carry on towards the lights.

Having reached a small field of saplings, Burroughs and Penniston now have a clearer view of the lights and watch them with confusion as they appear to be receding away from them in a zigzag pattern, backing deeper into the forest. Penniston attempts to inform Cabansag but his radio crackles in response, Cabansag's voice – if that is what he's picking up – lost in the white noise.

Penniston clicks off the radio and looks to Burroughs in frustration. For that moment, as they prepare to move further in, all is silent, until suddenly a horrific cascade of high-pitch screams, almost human, rear-up from out of the forest, startling the two men. The screams are accompanied by the sound of things in the darkness ahead, rushing through the trees. Penniston and Burroughs brace for contact when a vast flock of birds shoots out from the canopy above. The pair watch with terror as the birds, silhouetted against the moonlit sky, flap away noisily into the night. Taking a moment to collect themselves, they continue forward through the next line of trees noticing for the first time that the lights have settled, becoming less diffuse, more solid. As they press on something is beginning to take shape in a small clearing ahead.

'What the Hell's that?' asks Penniston.

At the edge of the forest road, Cabansag has joined Chandler by the vehicles and the pair grow increasingly agitated. The strange lights are long gone and it's been almost forty-five minutes since they lost contact with Penniston and Burroughs. Chandler is on the verge of sending for a search party when two small lights and the sound of cracking twigs alert them to something coming out of the woods. There is great relief when Penniston and Burroughs finally step from out of the trees, bewildered and shocked to be informed by Chandler that it has gone 3.45 a.m., despite both their watches showing the time to be closer to 3 a.m. Penniston explains that they had come across some type of aircraft deep in the forest. After approaching it, the vehicle lifted into the air and headed off towards the coast. They got pictures, says Penniston, holding out his camera. While Chandler tries to decide on the next steps, a call comes in from Flight Security Officer Lt. Buran ordering the men back to base immediately.

Penniston and Burroughs barely say a word as Cabansag drives them back to Bentwaters. After signing in their weapons and taking Penniston's camera to be developed at the onsite photo lab, the pair head to the Shift Commander's office for debriefing. Moments later, opposite a doubtful Capt. Mike Varrano and Deputy Squadron Commander Major Drury, the tired but resolute Penniston and Burroughs stand side by side as they proceed to give their startling account of what exactly they had seen that morning.

Penniston explained that, after breaking through to a small clearing, they had discovered a triangular-shaped object that appeared to be made of light. When they stepped towards it a flash of white shot from the top of the object, sending them both sprawling to the ground. When the light receded, sensing there was no danger, Penniston had got up and helped Burroughs to his feet, ordering him to remain on the edge of the clearing while he attempted to get a closer look at the peculiar object. As he drew near, he could feel static in the air and a growing sense of nausea, his movements seeming to slow down as if being held back by invisible strings. Turning, he saw Burroughs standing inside a beam of light coming from somewhere above. He called out to him but got no response. Shielding his eyes, he looked back towards the object and it was then that he was able to see it clearly for the first time. It looked like some sort of craft floating just above the ground, shaped like a squat pyramid, about 3 metres high with a triangular base. At its top was a pure white light, while underneath a swirl of red, blue and yellow was projected out on to the ground.

Still unable to get Burroughs's attention, he decided to take some photos with his camera after which he plucked up the courage to touch the craft, which was smooth with no rivets or joins anywhere. Up close it appeared to be made from black glass that was somehow illuminated both from inside the vessel and within the material itself. He also discovered a row of etched markings at the base, clear and distinct but like nothing he had ever seen before. They seemed to him like hieroglyphics; six precise geometric shapes about 3 inches high. He had just reached out to touch it again, almost certain he had seen something moving inside, when another flare of light was followed by the silent lifting of the object into the air. Alarmed but utterly transfixed, he continued to watch as it moved slowly from side to side, manoeuvring its way out of the small clearing before rising finally above the treetops.

When it was roughly 200 feet in the air, it shot off into the night sky, heading back towards the coast.

'That was when I grabbed him,' Burroughs cuts in, 'and pulled him out of the clearing. We chased the lights for a short time together,' he continues, 'before losing them completely. Burroughs isn't able to remember what he was doing exactly when Penniston was examining the craft, only that afterwards they had chased it then returned to the clearing to find broken branches at the top of the trees and three small indentations in the hard frozen ground. They made the shape of a triangle, each side roughly 3 metres long. That was when they headed back to Chandler and Cabansag.

After some deliberation, a dumbfounded Drury orders the pair to lead him out to the alleged 'landing site' so he can take a look for himself. At first light, the three of them along with Capt. Verrano and Master Sergeant Ray Gulyas, who is requested to take more photos, make their way back into the forest.

They trek for almost half an hour, going round in circles as Drury's patience wears thin, until Burroughs suddenly yells for them to stop.

'There!' he says, pointing to a clearing up ahead.

The area is a small patch of land at the eastern edge of the forest, revealed in daylight to be only twenty or so yards from a large open field belonging to Green Farm in the nearby hamlet of Capel St Andrew. Burroughs points out the three indentations in the ground and the men immediately get to work inspecting the area, putting post markers by the shallow holes and measuring their distance from each other. Drury thanks Burroughs and Penniston for their time and discharges the pair, suggesting they take a few days off to rest.

Less than an hour later Police Constable Brian Creswell, dispatched from a nearby Ipswich police station, joins Drury's team in the forest – it was a legal requirement that the US Air Force inform British authorities of any operations taking place outside of the base. One police officer had already been sent to the site after a call was received at 04:11 from RAF Bentwaters letting them know that a team had been dispatched from the base to investigate the possible sighting of a UFO. PC David King arrived shortly after Burroughs and Penniston had first left the area but found the place deserted with no hint of anything untoward. King didn't witness any lights other then the bright intermittent light of the Orford Ness lighthouse located some five miles due east.

Now it was PC Cresswell's turn to take a look: he stands in the middle of the clearing looking up to the narrow gap in the trees and back to the floor.

'So you're telling me a UFO landed right here, without making any sound, then flew away, straight up in the air?'

Drury can only shrug his shoulders.

'Well I'm not putting that in my report,' says Cresswell.

Turning his attention to the three markings on the ground, Cresswell is less than impressed, believing them to be nothing more than the work of burrowing forest animals. Cresswell makes a few notes in his book before heading back to his station.

The author standing at the 'landing site' in
Rendlesham Forest, October 2017 .

*   *   *

A few hours earlier, just after 0500, Deputy Base Commander Lieutenant Colonel Charles Halt reports for duty at the Law Enforcement offices. On arrival he finds the Duty Desk Officer laughing to himself.

'You'll never guess what happened last night,' he says as Halt approaches the front desk. 'Seems like Burroughs and Penniston have been out chasing UFOs.'

Forty-one-year-old Halt, who had transferred to Bentwaters earlier that year, is a sixteen-year veteran of the US Air Force, having previously worked at the Pentagon and also serving in Vietnam. Assuming it is all some kind of practical joke, Halt insists nonetheless that something be put in the duty log, proposing that they use the more rational term 'unexplained lights' rather than 'UFO'.

After learning more later that morning about the experience of Burroughs and Penniston from Base Commander Colonel Conrad, Halt returns to the duty log to update his earlier note, only to find that it has been removed. Halt also discovers that a second security log has also disappeared along with the original incident report. Back at Central Security Control, Staff Sergeant Coffey is also asked to hand over his log.

The next day, as John Burroughs tosses about in his bed, something is creeping into his dreams. Letting out a stifled cry he bolts upright gasping for breath, his body drenched in sweat. For reasons he can't discern he is overwhelmed with the absolute conviction that the peculiar object is about to return imminently.

Later that evening, the senior women and men of 81st's Combat Support Group and their partners are gathered at Woody's bar on RAF Woodbridge for their annual awards dinner. The event is in many ways an unofficial Christmas celebration and a chance for the hardworking service personnel, so many stationed away from their families for months on end, to enjoy themselves. Halt is just walking to the bar to fetch a drink when he catches sight of Lt. Bruce Englund approaching from the back of the room with a look of grave concern on his face.

'Sir,' says Englund quietly as he anxiously scans the room, 'it's back.'

'What's back?'

'The UFO, Sir.'

Realising Englund is serious, Halt orders him to wait by the door while he informs Col. Conrad. Both have grown tired of the increasingly elaborate rumours swirling round the base and although reluctant to leave the party, Halt knows this is his chance to put an end to them once and for all. With Conrad set to make a speech later that evening, it is left to Halt to leave the party and make an immediate investigation.

Shortly after midnight, a jeep speeds across the Woodbridge runway heading straight for the east gate. Inside are Lt. Col. Halt, accompanied by Lt. Englund as well as flight chief Master Sergeant Bobby Ball and chief officer of disaster preparedness Sergeant Monroe Nevels clutching his Nikon camera as well as an AN/PDR-27 Geiger counter to measure any residual radiation that an unknown craft might have left behind.

As they turn on to the forest road, a peculiar series of light bursts are shooting from out of the trees 150 metres or so away, as if someone was taking photos. But when the team make it to the bottom of the road, they soon discover the source. Halt had issued a request to have some light-alls set up to help with the search, large industrial spotlights on wheeled platforms. They're simple devices powered by petrol and generators but, bizarrely, none of them appear to be working. More irritating to Halt, the area is swarming with USAF personnel hoping for a glimpse of the mysterious lights. Fearing a public relations disaster, Halt, shouting over the din of the generators, orders the area cleared save for a small number of personnel to help with the light-alls. As most of them return to base, more devices are eventually brought down but something very strange appears to be going on. No matter what they do, none of the lights will work.

Halt demands that further replacements be sent out, but when the officer tries to make the call the radio also refuses to work, as if something was trying to jam the signal. It isn't only his radio; all the radios in the vicinity are malfunctioning. There were no strange lights in the sky when Halt and his team arrived at the forest but Halt is soon led to a shaken Sergeant Bustinza, whose earlier sighting of them had set the whole evening in motion. Halt can't help but feel sceptical as he listens patiently to Bustinza's report detailing scatterings of rainbow-coloured lights above the trees and blue orbs flying through the air. A strong wind whips through the makeshift camp as Halt, clutching on to his hat, thanks Bustinza for the information and gathers Englund, Nevels and Ball at the edge of the forest before leading them into the trees.

Now out of the wind, a relative calm descends as the men push on behind the light of their torches. The incessant chugging of the light-all generators recedes into the background, replaced by the gentle cracking of pine needles underfoot and before long they are deep inside the forest.

As the team move in further, Halt leads the way, speaking quietly into a Dictaphone to keep track of their observations. At the rear, Lt. Nevels flicks the switch on the Geiger counter to the five-tenths scale of millirems p/hr, a unit of measurement for gamma- and X-ray exposure named after Wilhelm Röntgen who discovered radiation. Nevels slowly unclasps the probe and begins a scan of the surrounding area. Moving steadily through the trees the team soon arrive at the original 'landing site'. Halt flashes his torch across the ground, picking out the posts left behind by Maj. Drury and Capt. Verrano marking the three indentations and is surprised at how small they are. Nevels moves the counter over one of them, watching as the needle bobs around the middle of the scale.

'I'm reading about third, fourth mark,' says Nevels to the group.[6]

'OK, we're still comfortably safe here,' confirms Halt with some relief.

The team move over to the second indentation.

'Nope,' says Nevels as he fails to pick up anything on the counter.

Nevels then points the probe towards the third mark and looks up in surprise.

'I'm getting some residual.'

Halt shines his torch on to the meter as it flicks up to the top of the scale.

'Definitely giving a little pulse!'

'Hey,' says Englund finding what looks like some scorch marks on the ground. 'This looks like an area that could be a blast, in the centre of the triangle.'

Nevels moves across to Englund and directs the probe to the floor. To their astonishment, the device springs to life. With a sudden burst of clicks the needle shoots up to the top of the scale, forcing Nevels to switch it up one.

'Just jumped up towards seven tenths!' says Englund.

Shining his torch to the trees, Englund then notices a peculiar set of abrasions about 4 inches wide carved into the trunks and all facing towards the clearing.

'They're all at the same height,' notices Ball.

As the men quietly examine the puzzling marks a sudden burst of static from Ball's radio breaks the silence.

Unable to shake the weird sense that something was going to happen that evening, the off-duty Burroughs had made his way back to the forest, astonished to find a team of airmen already camped out on the edge. Burroughs's request to join the search is radioed over to Ball but Halt refuses permission to let him come out. A disappointed Burroughs has no choice but to hang by the perimeter with the remaining personnel as they try to stay warm, keeping their eyes peeled for any activity in the sky above.

Back in the forest, the men are still examining the abrasions on the trees.

'Hey, check this out,' says Ball excitedly to Englund as he hands him a starlight night-vision scope. Englund puts the scope to his eye and peers through the viewfinder at the eerie green world now revealed before him. Ball holds the torchlight over the trunk then clicks it off.

'Do you see it?' asks Ball.

'Sir?' says Englund, handing the scope to Halt.

'OK, shine the light on it again, Bob,' says Englund.

Bob holds the torch up again to the tree then takes it away.

'This is strange,' says Halt.

They do the same for each of the indentations and each time they get the same increase in light, suggesting a possible heat source.

'Heat, or some form of energy?' says Halt as he turns his attention to the forest canopy.

He shines his flashlight high up into the branches and sees something else peculiar. A number of branches have been snapped off about 15 to 20 feet up. Moving the light to the base of the trees he is astonished to find the freshly broken branches littering the floor, as if something had recently dropped into the clearing.

A strange cry startles the men.

'Did you hear that?'

It sounds like stirring forest animals, disturbed by something unseen in the distance. When the noise dies down, the men catch sight of it.

'Look there, a light!'

Englund rushes to the edge of the clearing.

'Wait a minute, slow down,' says Halt, racing to join him.

'Straight ahead, between the trees. There it is again!'

'I see it too! What is it?' says Halt in astonishment.

From out of the dark a small red light has appeared due east, half a mile from the clearing. Halt turns to the others and orders the flashlights to be switched off. After losing it for a moment, the men spot it again hanging just over the farm at the other side of a nearby field. With the light reflecting so strongly against the windows of the farmhouse, the whole building looks as though it is on fire.

'See if you can get the scope on it,' asks Halt as he leads the men into the field.

Englund, who has now taken possession of the Geiger counter, is picking up stronger and stronger readings as he points it towards the light source.

'I think that's coming from something other than the ground,' he says, listening to the clicks as he stares out at the light in the distance.

The men, having moved some 200 metres from the 'landing site', watch in amazement as the strange orb now flashing yellow and red moves ever closer towards them. As it draws nearer, the men notice bright pieces seem to be falling off it, as if it were shedding some kind of molten metal.

'There is no doubt about it, this is weird!' exclaims Halt uneasily.

Then, from the left, a second light appears.

'Keep your flashlights off,' demands Halt. 'There's something very strange . . .'

'Sir, it just moved to the right!' gasps Englund.

The orb is now less than 200 metres away from them and moving swiftly from side to side. As Halt continues to stare at it, he has the distinct feeling that it is looking directly at them, as if it were the pupil of an eye. Taking a look through the starlight scope, Halt just has time to make out a dark spot at the centre of it before it becomes too bright to look at through the viewfinder. The men continue to look on aghast when moments later, the object splits into five separate orbs of light, shooting off in different directions. As the orbs move away, the men give chase through the field.

It is just gone 0200 hours when the team move past the farmer's house, splashing down into a small creek before continuing into the second field behind the house. The Geiger counter clicks incessantly as Halt does his best to get it all down on tape.

'At about ten degrees, horizon, directly north we've got two strange objects, er, half-moon shape, dancing about, with coloured lights on 'em. About five to ten miles out, maybe less,' he says breathlessly.

A sudden strobe of light flashes out from one of the objects and moments later another object appears directly to the south.

'This one's moving away from us,' says Halt.

'Moving out fast,' continues Nevels.

'They're both heading north. Hey, here he comes from the south, he's coming toward us now!' says Halt.

Seconds later the orb is upon them. The men freeze in utter confusion as it shoots down a thin beam of light no more than ten feet from their boots, almost as if it were preparing a laser-guided weapon.

'This is unreal,' laughs Halt.

As quickly as it had appeared the beam switches off and the orb moves away. For the next thirty minutes the men watch in stunned silence as three further objects appear in the sky, and then with alarm as one of the objects moves into position above Woodbridge base before beaming another mysterious light down to the ground. Unable to get a clear signal back to HQ, and freezing in their creek-soaked clothes, at 0400 hours Halt orders the men to return back to Bentwaters.

Later, as a soft orange dawn breaks, Halt attends a debriefing led by Base Commander Col. Conrad. He hands over his taped commentary for the record and provides a full account of the morning's events to the best of his knowledge. A further debrief is held on Monday morning with senior staff reportedly agreeing that no report of the previous nights' events be made to the public relations office and that all records be kept in the strictest of secrecy. On 13 January at the advice of Donald Moreland, the British Liaison Officer, Halt types up a memo to send to the British Ministry of Defence detailing further the peculiar events of 26 to 28 December. The memo is never answered. A few days later when Jim Penniston visits the base processing lab to collect the photographs from the morning of 26 December, he is informed that the film has been completely ruined. Sergeant Monroe Nevels is equally disappointed when he attempts to develop his own photographs from the morning of 28 December only to find all his images are blurred beyond recognition.

It will eventually transpire that the USAF personnel were not the only witnesses to the peculiar events of those nights; a number of witnesses from across the South of England come forward detailing strange lights in the sky and bright glowing trails falling from the heavens. For two years the US Air Force deny any incident had ever taken place until a Freedom of Information request led by an organisation known as Citizens Against UFO Secrecy results in the release of 'The Halt Memo'. As well as acknowledging the events of 26 December, Halt's memo gives a startling account of what his team witnessed in the early hours of 28 December, including a report of numerous objects that 'moved rapidly in sharp, angular movements ... display(ing) red, green and blue lights'. Lt. Col. Charles Halt will continue to serve with the USAF until his retirement in 1991, having achieved the full rank of Colonel. To this day he stands by everything detailed in his memo.

The author standing in the shadows of Orfordness
Lighthouse, which some have suggested as the source
of the original mysterious lights in the sky.

*   *   *

Humans have long speculated about the existence of extra-terrestrial life; Lucian of Samosata's 2nd-century novel, *True History*, being one particularly early recorded example, features battles between the people of the sun and the people of the moon.[7] It wasn't until the 20th century, however, that we started to seriously consider what the statistical likelihood of finding such life would be. In 1961, astronomer and physicist Dr Frank Drake devised an equation to estimate the number of communicative extra-terrestrial civilisations that might exist in the Milky Way galaxy alone. The Drake Equation takes into account a number of variables such as the rate of star formation, the average number of planets that orbit stars and which fraction of those planets might actually host sophisticated life. Although the equation was intended only as a point of discussion, many critics were quick to argue that attempts to estimate such a number would involve too big a margin of error to ever be reliable.

A recent paper published in 2016 by astrobiologists Adam Frank of the University of Rochester and Woodruff Sullivan of the University of Washington offers an interesting new approach to the question. Rather than trying to estimate the possible number of other sentient civilisations in our galaxy, they ask what the odds are that the human race might be the only one. Their answer equates to roughly a 1 in 60 billion chance.[8] When you consider that the Milky Way is thought to be only one of 2 trillion galaxies in the known, observable universe, going on Rochester and Sullivan's calculations not only is it highly likely that other sophisticated civilisations exist out there, but it is entirely plausible that some may already have flourished and died out millions of times over before our own came into existence.

In 1950 physicist Enrico Fermi was visiting Los Alamos National Laboratory, the American research centre for the development of nuclear weapons, when he sat down for lunch with fellow nuclear scientists Emil Konopinski, Edward Teller and Herbert York. A flippant conversation had arisen on the subject of little green men and how likely it would be that we would one day see a flying saucer that could travel faster than the speed of light. As the men batted statistics back and forth, discussing the possibility of alien civilisations, Fermi suddenly exclaimed, 'Then where is everybody?' In what is now known as the Fermi paradox, the physicist went on to question why, in spite of the statistical likelihood that other sentient species exist in our universe, have we not seen any evidence of them.[9] Although many would point to incidences such as the Rendlesham Forest 'sightings' as clear evidence that we have in fact seen them, there are few in the academic world who would agree.

One simple answer would be the fact that we haven't been looking for very long, and our methods might not be particularly sophisticated. The scientific endeavour of searching for alien life, often referred to as the search for extraterrestrial intelligence, or SETI, relies predominantly on the use of radio telescopes to listen out for irregular radio waves as evidence of alien life. With radio waves having only been proved to exist in 1887, thanks largely to the work of physicists Heinrich Hertz and James Clerk Maxwell, it wouldn't be until Frank Drake's 1960 Ozma project began, that we took seriously the possibility that other civilisations might in fact be trying to contact us, and may have been doing so for quite some time. The project, named after Princess Ozma – the ruler of L. Frank Baum's fictional land of Oz – required a team of astronomers to listen out for potential radio wave-based communications from distant planets and is widely considered the birth of the modern SETI movement, inspiring many others to pick up the mantle. In the almost sixty years since, there has been little concrete evidence to suggest Earth isn't alone in housing intelligent life, but two recent discoveries, detailed below, have captured the imaginations of the SETI community, leading many to believe more than ever that contact with others is an inevitability.

The first involves a public engagement project called Planet Hunters, set up in 2010 by world-renowned astronomer Professor Debra Fischer of Yale University. Planet Hunters sought to enlist a huge resource of amateur astronomers and SETI enthusiasts across the globe to assist NASA's Kepler mission in their hunt for new worlds. Currently, the best-known method for discovering a planet is the 'transit technique'. It is not presently possible to observe the silhouette of a planet outside our solar system, as it transitions around a star, so instead, the star's light is monitored for any dip or fluctuations in its output that would suggest something large enough to be a planet has moved across it. We can tell from the length of the dip in the star's light how big the transit's radius is: the longer the dip, the bigger the transit, the more likely it's a planet.[10]

In May 2009, NASA picked up an unusual signal coming from the star KIC 8462852, located roughly 1,280 light years away in the constellation of Cygnus. But it was only when Planet Hunters began analysing the data that the peculiar signal was brought to the attention of the Kepler team. What they discovered was unlike anything they had ever encountered before. The signal seemed to suggest that something gigantic had passed in front of the star, causing its light to dim for days as opposed to the few hours that would normally be expected. Unlike a planet, the object appeared not to be symmetrical either. In February 2013, the transit caused the star's light to dip for a hundred days, with measurements suggesting that whatever the object was, it had a surface area one thousand times the size of Earth.

According to astronomer Professor Tabetha Boyajian, who is leading the study on KIC 8462852, now often referred to as Tabby's Star in her honour, theories for the cause of such a massive dip range from two planets in the process of collision while orbiting the star to an abundance of comets moving over the sun in an unusual elliptical orbit. Although Boyajian's hunch was that one such natural explanation would prove to be correct, some suggested we were in fact observing an unfathomably large alien megastructure known as a Dyson Sphere. Physicist Freeman Dyson first proposed the theoretical structure after coming across the idea in Olaf Stapledon's novel *Star Maker* published in 1937. Dyson suggested that a civilisation that had grown unmanageably large might utilise such a device to more efficiently distribute energy from a sun. The device would be made from a suitable material that could harvest and store the solar energy, and constructed either partially or completely around the star capturing the power output for later use. Despite the logistical improbability of building something so vast, it certainly isn't beyond the realms of possibility, since, after all, such realms may simply be beyond our present limits of comprehension. In early 2018 it was reported that the unusual dimming of Tabby's Star was most likely due to a large dust cloud, the result of an as yet unknown catastrophic event, though some SETI enthusiasts continue to hope that it might still prove to be alien architecture.[11]

The second most recent intriguing discovery for SETI observers was announced in February 2017 during a live press conference held by NASA. A team of astronomers, led by Michael Gillon from the University of Liege in Belgium had discovered a peculiar solar system located roughly 40 light years from Earth. At the heart of the system was a star relatively small in size and of low luminosity, known as an ultra-cool dwarf star, which appeared to be orbited by two Earth-sized planets. It was first spotted in 2016 by astronomers using the Trappist Telescope in Chile, so was named Trappist-1. In the months that followed, the team, working with NASA's Spitzer telescope, made what was described by Spitzer Center manager Sean Carey as the 'most exciting discovery' in the history of the department.[12]

What the astronomers had uncovered was not two Earth-sized planets, but seven. Furthermore, three of the planets were found to be occupying the crucial 'Goldilocks Zone', an area of orbit necessary for the potential for water to pool on a planet's surface. This was the first time that so many theoretically Earth-like planets had been found surrounding one single star and virtually on our doorstep. The masses and radii of these specific planets marked them out as the best ever discovered to warrant further investigation for life, or at the very least a habitable ecosystem that could one day be explored. In the words of NASA's associate administrator of the science mission directorate, Thomas Zurbuchen, 'What we have in this story is a major step forward towards answering one of the questions that is at the heart of so many of our philosophies . . . and that is, are we alone?'[13]

In a 2016 interview with *The Sunday Times*, physicist Brian Cox gave one startling proposition as to why we haven't yet discovered evidence of intelligent alien civilisations. Could it be, he suggested, that sufficiently sophisticated life forms were simply incapable of surviving their own scientific advancement long enough to achieve intergalactic communication?[14]

Interestingly, Ufologists have frequently suggested a link between UFO sightings and development sites of weapons of mass destruction. In 1992 the I-Team, a group of investigative journalists working for KLAS-TV in Nevada received a number of files from the US Department of Energy through a Freedom of Information request, revealing a litany of UFO sightings over major nuclear weapons facilities stretching back to the 1940s from Los Alamos to the Hanford Site in Washington State,[15] which in 1943 became home to the world's first plutonium reactor.

The Rendlesham Forest incident is no different.

We might never discover exactly what happened over Rendlesham that peculiar December weekend in 1980 and in the passing years as more 'witnesses' have continued to emerge so too have their reports grown increasingly elaborate, only to obfuscate further the true facts from fiction. What seems little in dispute is that a very deliberate effort to hide all knowledge of the event was adopted by the United States Air Force and the British Ministry of Defence, which some believe was an attempt to heavily guard a particular secret. The official line is that RAF Woodbridge and RAF Bentwaters were merely staging posts for the Cold War, allowing the US Air Force to house, repair and refuel fighter planes before they continued on their way. It is now thought that the twin airbases, unbeknownst to the British public, were home to a stockpile of nuclear weapons larger than anywhere else in Europe at the time.

It is fanciful and naïve no doubt, but I like to imagine that if such sightings were extraterrestrial in origin, far from being dangerous their purpose might in fact have been benign, an effort from a wiser, more advanced species to save us from ourselves.

But what if they don't come in peace?

I think of how things might be if the shoe were on the other foot, if it were us travelling through the galaxy on the hunt for planets to explore.

I imagine a team of explorers from Earth coming across a new and wondrous planet, home to a previously unknown species of comparably intelligent life forms. Having crawled from the liquids of their oceans to the shores, and later evolved from arboreal dwellers, these life forms had become sufficiently advanced to develop a sense of community with an awareness of each other and their mutual shared interests. Then they discover a gruesome act of violence that's beyond the necessity for survival: the ability to kill, not in defence or out of desperate necessity, but purely for self-gain. For years the spectre of this act haunts all attempts at diplomacy, leaving some to strike out on their own. Wandering off into the great lands stretched out before them, the intrepid tribes eventually settle down again into similar communities of shared interests.

In these new groups, hierarchies emerge based on threat and fear, and an instinct for self-preservation, and soon the communities begin to isolate themselves further from each other, separated by their different ways, learning new, distinct, wonderful things but forgetting other, older, wonderful things in the process. Now so stubbornly separate, they forget the substance that united them all in the first place. Some learn there is value in the places where others reside and an endless cycle of war, death and destruction begins, each cycle bringing new and more sophisticated ways with which to destroy each other. Until one day there is such a tool that can destroy millions in an instant. So it continues, over and over, until slowly, with almost nothing left to fight for, it stops. As if by some impossible miracle, those that emerge from the rubble *remember*. The weapons are destroyed, new understandings are forged and a peace arrives. For thousands of years the life forms live without war, free to finally interrogate the shackles of their unhappiness. So they live on, finally in harmony.

Many years later a spacecraft descends from the stars, landing on the outskirts of a placid lakeside community. The new arrivals emerge from their vessel and are greeted warmly by the planet's inhabitants. The aliens announce themselves as 'human beings' from the planet 'Earth' and are relieved to find their new hosts don't wish them any harm. On the contrary, they invite the human beings into their homes and together they rejoice in each other's company, sharing what food and wisdom they have.

Back on the ship, the aliens from 'Earth' will laugh at how primitive and backward this new species are, with not even sticks to defend themselves. They have nothing to teach us, they decide. And when gold, oil and coltan are discovered, a decision is made.

The other life forms didn't stand a chance.

Chapter Four

LOOK ME IN THE I

'. . . such things take place in an instanf, in an eyeblink.
This can only be because they have been rehearsed by us
already, over and over, in silence and darkness; in such
silence, such darkness, that we are ignorant of them
ourselves. Blind but sure-footed, we step forward as if into
a remembered dance.'

Margaret Atwood – *The Blind Assassin*

Humans often take for granted that *we* are ultimately responsible
for our actions. That the choices we make are governed by nothing but our own free will. After all, to question free will is to question not only moral responsibility but also the very notion of the
self, since if we are relieved of our conscious agency, then who, or
what, exactly are we? If we take a Newtonian deterministic view
of the universe, accepting the universe as a place in which every
event is caused by a pre-existing set of conditions resulting in pre-
determined actions, we would have to concede that free will in the
strictest sense is an impossibility; 'Our acts,' as John Gray notes in
Straw Dogs, would be nothing but 'end points in long sequences
of unconscious responses.'[1]

In 1980, a series of pioneering experiments led by neuroscien-
tist Benjamin Libet stretched the validity of free will even
further. In Libet's study, participants – linked up to an electroencephalogram (EEG)[2] machine – were required to carry out a
simple function such as pressing a button or flexing a wrist
while at the same time making a note of when they first felt the

urge to carry out the action. After comparing the participants' perception of when they decided to act, with the actual brain function instigating the act, Libet and his team discovered that these seemingly voluntary choices were being initiated up to 0.35 seconds before the subjects were aware of them.[3] The implications of Libet's findings have been fiercely debated with some suggesting that the minimal delay is just a period of latency between our brain 'seeing' a stimulus and our actual conscious understanding of it. This was challenged significantly in 2008 after a series of similar experiments, conducted by a team of scientists led by Professor John-Dylan Haynes at the Max Plank institute in Germany, revealed that decisions could actually occur in the brain as much as seven seconds before we become aware of them.[4]

To think of free will as little more than a useful illusion is unnerving to say the least, and although we might yet come to accept this as merely a quirk of life, for others the implication speaks of something else entirely, something far more sinister.

After all, if we aren't in control of our minds, then who, or what, is?

To travel upstream along the placid waters of the River Main as it breaks from the mighty Rhine is to enter an enchanted world of ancient forests, colourful wedding-cake towns and neatly turreted castles lifted straight from the manuscripts of the Brothers Grimm (it's of little surprise to learn that the pair were born in Hanau, one of the first towns you encounter heading east out of Frankfurt). Following the river south into Bavaria, you soon find yourself cutting through the Odenwald mountain ranges to the west and the vast forests of the low-lying Spessart hills to the east. It is from these ancient mountains, with woods of oak, beech and fir, that tales such as *Snow White* and *Hansel and Gretel* are thought to have originated, before being compiled and eventually published as *Grimms' Fairy Tales* in 1812.

Travelling deeper into these mythical lands, you might discover a place where four roads meet; a place where, had you stumbled upon it one dark night centuries ago, you may have witnessed a young doctor by the name of Faustus drawing mystical circles in the earth and speaking incantations into the wind. Perhaps you would have watched in secret as the young man's chants were drowned in a cacophony of inhuman sound, whilst strange and monstrous apparitions threatened to emerge. If you hadn't already succumbed to fear and made a hasty retreat, you might have seen one such apparition take shape: a demon and servant of Lucifer by the name of Mephistopheles, as told in the legendary tale of *Doctor Faustus*.

Southwest of the Spessart lies a pretty hamlet of colourful stucco and half-timber houses with neat terracotta roofs. Known as Klingenberg, the town has weathered many storms throughout the years, with some bringing destruction, like the troops of King Louis XIV of France who razed Klingenberg Castle to the ground in 1680, while others left seeds that later took root, blossoming through the ages, like the many surrounding vineyards that provide much of the town's trade; a legacy of Roman settlers from more than 2,000 years ago.

In 1952 Klingenberg, with its modest population of 3,000, is part of Western Germany, a nation newly forged from the ashes of the most destructive war the world has ever known. The old flags of red and white with their black crooked symbols that flew from the municipal buildings only a few years before have been taken down and replaced by simple black, red and yellow stripes. It is in this town, one Sunday morning in September, that Anna and Josef Michel celebrate the birth of their first child together. Twenty-four years later, that same child will be dead; the result, some have said, of the most terrifying and convincing case of demonic possession ever recorded.

In 1948, 200 miles to the east of Klingenberg, in the district of Leiblfing, twenty-eight-year-old Anna Fürg is in a desperate state.

The recent birth of her child Martha, born out of wedlock, has brought disgrace on her and her devout Catholic parents. Terrified that their daughter will no longer be able to marry, Anna's parents spy an opportunity when they are introduced to a young man named Josef, recently arrived in town on business. With the help of the Diocese of Würzburg and, it is rumoured, a few hundred Deutschmarks, the Fürgs gift their daughter to the young man. Josef and Anna, shrouded in a black veil as a symbol of her disgrace, are married the following year. Despite their inauspicious beginnings, the couple are happy together and soon settle down in Klingenberg where Josef, now the head of his family's sawmill business, builds them a house on a quiet street overlooking Klingenberg cemetery; a modest two-storey home, with cream stucco walls and a high peaked roof reminiscent of the steep vineyard terraces that slope up behind it before disappearing into the foreboding Spessart trees.

Josef loves Anna's daughter Martha as his own, but it is nothing compared to what he feels when his and Anna's first child together arrives on a warm September morning. Born on the Lord's Day, it is only fitting that she should be named Anneliese, meaning 'God is bountiful', and she is as beautiful a baby as any parent could wish for. She is joined soon after by sisters Gertrude Maria and Barbara, and together the four sweet children are a blessing on the pious and devoted Anna and Josef.

In 1956, a tumour is discovered in eight-year-old Martha's kidney, requiring immediate surgery. It is a delicate and dangerous operation that will ultimately cost Martha her life. To the avowedly Catholic family it seems a particularly unfathomable tragedy: an innocent so cruelly and suddenly snatched from them. But part of Anna has always known this day would come. Martha had come into the world a literal embodiment of sin upon God's earth, and Anna had failed to compensate for it. It is clear to her that Martha's premature death is God's inevitable revenge. Nevertheless, it is with great sorrow that Martha is laid to rest in the cemetery next to the house, albeit hidden away at the back, in grounds set aside for suicides and the illegitimate.

Convinced now of what she must do, Anna determines to make Anneliese her vessel. Never will her daughter be without the rosary or be absent from mass, as they fight to win back God's trust. When Anneliese contracts measles, followed by the mumps and scarlet fever, Anna fears her efforts have once again been in vain, but together they pray and soon her ailments subside, and she becomes a healthy, happy child once more. In the autumn of 1958, a six-year-old Anneliese takes her first communion. As Anna and Josef watch proudly while she eats of the body and sips of the blood, it is with the feeling of a great weight being lifted. The arrival of another baby girl in December, christened Roswitha, comes like a reward for all their efforts.

In 1965, aged twelve, Anneliese graduates to the Dalberg Gymnasium in Aschaffenburg. It is only a ten-minute train ride from her home, but those ten minutes spent gazing at the passing hills and bright yellow fields are a freedom she has never before known. There are new friends to be made, like Maria with whom Anneliese regularly laughs and jokes on their daily commute, and over the next few years there are other changes; changes inside that Anneliese struggles to reconcile with the demands of the scriptures. Though she desires to learn dance at the local ballroom like her sisters, Anna forbids it. Her place is at mass to give thanks to the Mother of God, her mother reminds her, and to show penance for all those less fortunate than herself. Some nights Anneliese will even take to sleeping on the floor as a sign of contrition, but in spite of it all, something is stirring.

In the summer of 1968, Anneliese and Maria are working together in class when Maria notices something amiss.

'Anneliese?' There is no reply.

'Anneliese?'

It is as if she has fallen asleep in her chair.

'*Ist alles in ordnung?*' asks Maria: 'Is everything okay?'

'*Oh, ja, naturlich,*' says Anneliese, turning back to her work as if nothing had happened.

That night she wakes with a start, unable to breathe, eyes wide in horror. She cries for help but no words come out. Her limbs are rigid, while something strong and invisible seems to be pinning her down to the bed. When she is finally released a warm dampness is spreading out from underneath her.

Keeping the events of that night to herself, the incident is all but forgotten until a year later when it happens again, only this time, her screams of terror are heard throughout the house. The next morning, disturbed by the night's events, Anna accompanies her daughter to see neurologist Dr Siegfried Lüthy. The clipped and urbane Lüthy finds little wrong with Anneliese but suggests an EEG test in the hope of shedding some light on the cause of her peculiar seizures. Two days later, a nervous Anneliese sits in an examination room surrounded by the quiet hum of machinery as a series of small electrodes connected to wires are stuck to her head. At the flick of a switch a feed of paper is cranked through a printer, while a row of crooked metal arms makes sharp lines of colour across the page. Anna squeezes her daughter's hand with relief as Lüthy regards the EEG briefly before revealing there is nothing to be concerned about. A few weeks later, however, Anneliese is struck down with tonsillitis, followed by bouts of pleurisy and pneumonia. In February 1969, having also contracted tuberculosis, a devastated Anneliese is taken out of school and sent for treatment at Hochgebirgsklinik Sanatorium.

The sanatorium, located on the edge of Mittelberg on the southern border of Western Germany and Austria, is nestled a thousand feet high in the Allgäu at the northern tip of the Alps. The rarefied air and majestic views of the Füseen Mountains should be the perfect tonic for Anneliese's lungs, but there is no shaking the sense of foreboding on her arrival as she looks up at the isolated monolithic building with the dark evergreen firs looming behind it. As Anneliese is led to her dormitory, each step through its sterile iodic corridor brings another pallid face to look her up and down, but the familiar chirrup of teenagers soon puts her at ease. When she enters the dorm, the girls inside are quick to welcome her into their makeshift commune.

As spring turns to summer, Anneliese is making good progress until one night a throat-ripping scream wakes the girls, and sends nurses sprinting down the halls to her dorm. Only a few catch the faint whiff of ammonia, but all see Anneliese shaking with terror. After being calmed, she is moved to a clean bed, but is too scared to sleep. The next morning's check-up finds nothing wrong.

In the dorm a few weeks later, Anneliese sits alone in the gloaming as the last of the day's light fractures in a burst of golden orange from behind the distant mountain peaks. Closing her eyes, she picks up her rosary, and starts to pray.

'Hail Mary, full of grace. The Lord is with thee . . .'

She is still sitting in her chair, speaking to herself when the girls find her.

'Anneliese?'

'. . . blessed is the fruit of thy womb . . .'

'Anneliese?'

'. . . now and at the hour of our death . . .'

The girls look on with unease as an unresponsive Anneliese continues to stare vacantly out of the window; her trembling hands held up in front of her face, stiff and rigid like claws. A moment later she snaps out of the trance and turns to the girls in silence, her eyes like two black discs and an odd beatific smile playing about her lips.

In June, after another EEG reveals a slight anomaly in the pattern of her brainwaves, Anneliese is diagnosed with grand mal epilepsy and prescribed a course of anti-convulsant pills. A week later, alone in her room, she is again staring out the window as she passes the rosary beads between her fingers when something strange begins to take shape above the mountain peaks. First she sees the misshapen nose, then the oddly twisted ears, followed by a hideous mouth of gnashing teeth and a pair of eyes staring directly at her. She tries to turn away but something is stopping her. Finally, she is released, running in terror to the back of the room screaming to be left alone.

One afternoon, when asked if she has been suffering any further issues during her time at the hospital, Anneliese says no, fearful of what they might do if she tells the truth. She is given a clean bill of health and after nearly six months in the sanatorium returns home. Later, she takes a moment sitting alone in the quiet of her bedroom to feel over her old things; the prayer book with the wild flowers pressed inside, her badly neglected diary and the framed picture of Jesus on her wall. Elsewhere in the house, her sisters are speaking amongst themselves with concern; something isn't quite right with Anneliese they say.

She seems . . . different.

Over the next few years, Anneliese continues to excel at school and, barring a few minor seizures, appears to be returning to a semblance of normality. In truth, she knew it would only be a matter of time before it came for her again.

It started in the spring of 1973 with a gentle knocking on her door in the middle of the night, with no one there when she opened it. After another fruitless visit to the doctor, Anneliese's sister Barbara asks her mother what the visit was about this time.

'Nothing,' replies Anna. 'She's just imagining noises at night.'

'But Mama,' says Barbara, 'I have heard them too.'

In fact, all of her sisters have been hearing it; the soft banging coming from somewhere in the house. Sometimes it is in the walls; sometimes it comes from under the floorboards, and sometimes from the inside of Anneliese's wardrobe.

One night, unbeknownst to the rest of the family, a now twenty-year-old Anneliese awakes in the dark to find a voice is speaking to her.

'Join us in Hell forever,' it rasps, over and over again.

Josef, alerted by his daughter's anguished cries, finds Anneliese writhing in terror with her hands clasped over her ears, begging it to stop.

Later that summer, Josef takes Anneliese on a pilgrimage to Italy to visit the garden of Rosa Quattrini-Buzzini, a recently venerated shrine in the village of San Damiano. When Anneliese nears the garden she is crippled by a searing pain in her feet as if they were on fire and when she next looks up, is horrified to find the faces of the other pilgrims have turned into wide mouths of sharp gnashing teeth.

On the coach ride back to Klingenberg, Anneliese rips an icon medallion from the neck of Thea Hein, a friend and neighbour who had organised the trip. Josef apologises profusely for her behaviour and shepherds her back to their seats trying his best to keep his daughter calm while the rest of the passengers whisper and stare.

A few days later, Anneliese is back in Dr Lüthy's office.

'The Devil is in me.'

Lüthy shifts uncomfortably in his chair and looks to Anna.

'What do you mean?' he asks.

'He has been speaking to me through them.'

'Who are *they*?'

'Demons.'

'And these are the ones whose faces you have seen?'

'Yes.'

'And how do you recognise this as the Devil?'

Anneliese looks to her mother but is unable to reply, realising Lüthy will never understand.

It is the last time she will mention anything to so-called doctors about gruesome faces or tormenting voices.

It is September 1973 when Father Ernst Anton Alt first learns about Anneliese's case. The tall and sharply bearded Alt, although relatively young at thirty-five, is considered deeply thoughtful and intelligent by his peers and listens with great concern as Father Karl Roth recounts the meeting he has just attended concerning a possible case of demonic molestation. Before Roth can say more, a strange feeling comes over Father Alt. Much to Roth's amazement, Alt proceeds to describe Anneliese and her family's situation in complete detail, as if he had attended the meeting himself. Two days later Father Alt consults with another colleague, Father Eduard Herrmann, who had also been contacted by the desperate family. When Herrmann hands Alt two letters he received from Anna and Josef documenting the case, Alt is overcome by a strange nausea. Disturbed by this turn of events, he wastes little time in arranging to speak with the family.

'I am looking for people who believe me,' Anneliese tells him when they meet for the first time.

It is strange for Alt to see the young woman, now twenty-one, so lucid and determined, albeit a little pale, considering everything he has heard so far. But after an hour of examination, Father Alt and Father Roth suspect that Anneliese is indeed in the grip of a terrifying possession. Not wanting to cause any alarm, the pair keep the judgement to themselves and agree to a period of observation before they decide what to do next. In the meantime, Anneliese is to keep living her life as she has always done.

Anneliese gains entry on to the University of Würzburg's teacher-training course and in November, galvanised by regular consultations with Father Alt, she moves to Würzburg to begin her studies. After moving into the University's stark five-storey dormitory known as the Ferdinandeum, she spends the next few months attending lectures and making new friends. There are ups and downs, with Anneliese sometimes staying entire days in her room, too lethargic to even speak to anyone. But on one of her better nights, she is dragged to a dance at the dormitory. As euphoric rock and roll shimmers from the speakers, a young man with soft, pale skin and dark, wavy hair watches from the edge of the hall as Anneliese dances blissfully under the smoky haze and dimmed lights. He introduces himself as Peter. She likes his eyes and his gentle self-assurance, and something about him puts her immediately at ease. They agree to meet up again and in the days that follow Peter grows ever more fond of the enigmatic young woman from Klingenberg.

One morning, Anneliese enters the local church to make confession but when she tries to speak, the words stick in her throat. Before long, the seizures and headaches have returned. Over the next year, she struggles with her various ailments, making visits to Father Alt whenever they threaten to overwhelm her. On one occasion, Josef delivers a deeply despondent and oddly distracted Anneliese, home for the holidays, to Alt's office. A moment later she kneels on the ground with her head bowed as Alt brings his arms forward.

'May the Lord bless you and keep you,' he begins.

When he is finished, he makes the sign of the cross and watches in astonishment as, like a flower turning to the sun, a newly bright and alert Anneliese is revealed before him in place of the dour and vacant young woman of only moments ago. It is a clear sign to Anneliese that only the church can save her now. Alt, however, insists that she check in regularly with the University physician, who sets her up with yet another course of pills.

Throughout it all Peter, falling ever more in love, supports Anneliese however he can but she is often saddened by the way her condition leaves her so lethargic and numb, unable to reciprocate his love. With things becoming strained she feels she has little choice but to trust him with what she has suspected all along: that something monstrous is trying to take over her mind. Peter is shocked at first but seeing the sincerity in her eyes, promises to be there for her whenever she needs him.

In her second year, Anneliese, now with her own room, gradually withdraws from her old social circle and finds new, more religiously committed friends like Maria K and Anna to share her prayer sessions with. After Alt's latest intervention the seizures seem to have all but cleared up and by early 1975 the voices and faces have been banished.

In late spring, Anneliese's grandmother, a much loved and calming influence, passes away at home in Klingenberg. With Barbara now living in Sulzbach and Gertrude working in Spain, Anneliese can't help but feel that something is shifting away from her. A few days later, her friends Anna and Maria are talking loudly in Anneliese's room, but when Anneliese yells for them to stop, they merely look at her in confusion. They hadn't been talking at all. One evening not long after, having torn down a picture of Christ from her wall and ripped apart her rosary beads, Anneliese runs to the church to pray, but no matter how hard she tries to enter, her legs will not carry her across the threshold. That night the terrors come again as she tries in vain to fight the voices condemning her to Hell.

The next morning, Anneliese calls Father Alt in a fit of desperation. Once he has arrived, he kneels with the terrified young woman by her bed, and together they begin to pray as tears stream down her face, 'I believe in God, the Father Almighty, Creator of Heaven . . .' Moments later Alt watches in horror as an unearthly scream is ripped from Anneliese's throat. Anna stands at the door with her hand over her mouth.

'Has she taken her pills?' asks Father Alt as Anneliese screams in anguish.

'Yes, yes! I saw her take them.'

'Get Peter now!' says Father Alt.

Next, Alt makes the sign of the cross and quickly and quietly utters the Solemn Blessing. Anneliese's breaths begin to slow until she is finally stilled. After a moment of calm, Alt collects himself before placing his hand on her head.

'I, Father Ernst Alt, minister of Christ and the Church, in the name of Jesus Christ, command you, unclean spirit, if you lie hidden in the body of this woman created by God.'

Father Alt feels a movement under his hand. Slowly Anneliese lifts her head to reveal an unrecognisably hideous face twisted in anger. Soon her body is contorting and writhing under Alt's hand as he struggles to compose himself and continue with the words. Anneliese grabs at her rosary and rips it to shreds, before throwing it across the room. When Anna arrives with Peter, Anneliese turns directly to him and in a rough, guttural voice, screams 'Get out!' She is eventually calmed and gently ushered to sleep, but those present are left in no doubt as to what they have witnessed.

That summer, as Anneliese drifts between a complete lack of sense and her lucid self, she and Peter agree that whenever she stiffens up or disappears into a trance, he should look her in the eye to see if she is still present. If she moves them, he will know that it is her inside.

In mid July, with Anneliese having returned home, Father Roth receives a phone call at his office and is surprised to find the trembling voice of Josef Michel on the other end of the line. Having been unable to get hold of Father Alt, Josef begs Roth to help as his daughter's terrifying screams can be heard in the background. When Roth arrives at the house a few hours later, he is overwhelmed by a foul stench as if something putrid has just been set on fire. Josef leads him through to the kitchen where the smell intensifies. Anneliese stands stiff in the middle of the room as if in a deep trance. Without warning she runs towards Roth who only has time to stumble backwards before she stops sudden and rigid no more than a metre away. She regards his face for a moment before flinging herself back towards the other side of the room.

Roth presents his crucifix, which sends Anneliese into a fit of rage.

'Stop it! You are tormenting me!' she shrieks, grabbing a bottle of holy water from San Damiano and hurling it to the floor.

Feeling out of his depth, Roth promises to inform Father Alt before swiftly taking his leave.

Together Roth and Alt take their findings to Bishop Stangl who finally grants permission to attempt a small exorcism. On Sunday 3 August, at the Michels' home, a now twenty-three-year-old Anneliese sits patiently before the two priests as Alt pulls a small black book from his case containing the exorcism prayers of Pope Leo XIII and kneels down before her.

'Most glorious Prince of the Heavenly Armies, Saint Michael the Archangel . . .'

Anneliese's eyes draw closed. Slowly her head begins to loll while her body starts to twist. What starts as a moan grows steadily to a full-on growl.

'. . . defend us in our battle against principalities and powers . . .' continues Alt.

'Stop, it's burning my arms!' she shrieks.

The priest continues, '. . . against the rulers of this world of darkness, against the spirits of wickedness in the high places.'

Without warning Anneliese flings forward trying to knock the prayer book from Alt's grasp but is restrained by Josef and Anna. Alt and Roth have seen enough.

While the family wait for the church to decide what to do next, Josef and Anna struggle to keep the worst of it at bay with prayers and the rosary, but nothing seems to work. One morning Anna finds Anneliese in her bedroom gasping for air, as an invisible force appears to be shoving her face down against the floor. But any attempt to pull her up or straighten her out results only in a terrifying choking fit that Josef can't bear to watch. As quickly as the fits begin they can just as quickly stop, leaving Anneliese in bizarre catatonic states. When the hot summer days reach their peak, she tears at her clothes and runs naked through the house in a desperate attempt to cool down. At night, having moved into the attic, she can be heard running about the room, accompanied by an endless slew of blood-curdling screams. One morning Anna finds Anneliese staring at a spider as it makes its way across the floor. Before she has time to intervene the young woman has put it in her mouth, swallowing it whole. She senses clouds of flies amassing around her while strange distorted creatures scuttle about in the shadows and all religious iconography is torn from the walls or smashed to pieces.

At one point, with Father Alt on holiday, Jesuit priest and exorcism specialist Father Rodewyk is sent for. He arrives to find Anneliese lying on the kitchen floor in a trance with small open wounds on her hands and feet that Anna claims appeared one morning without reason. After shepherding Anneliese to the sofa, Rodewyk confirms to Anna and Josef that a force of immense evil has possessed their daughter.

Rodewyk takes hold of Anneliese's hands and in a clear, assertive voice he asks, 'What is your name?'

Her head lolls to the side.

'I am Judas,' she replies in a low unfamiliar tone.

Moments later Anneliese opens her eyes and looks at Rodewyk as if for the first time.

The church agrees unanimously to proceed with a full exorcism before it is too late but with Father Alt now living 100 kilometres away in Ettleben and unable to commit fully to the task, it falls to the much-respected Father Arnold Renz of the Salvation monastery in Rück-Schippach, to lead the ritual. At 4 p.m. on 24 September, Renz arrives at the Michel household to begin the blessed Exorcism Rite of the Rituale Romanum.

Anna and Josef have prepared a room upstairs at the back, lest the sound of Anneliese's screams draw any more concern from the neighbours. Renz enters the room to find Anneliese waiting patiently for him on a wooden chair. Seated around her are Anna and Josef, her sisters Barbara and Roswitha, and the ever-dependable Peter who has stuck with Anneliese through it all. Thea Hein and her husband complete the congregation. To the left is a makeshift altar laid with white, embroidered cloth, on which is placed a crucifix bearing a statue of Christ along with framed pictures of the Virgin Mary, the Archangel Michael, Father Pio of San Damiano and the Sacred Heart of Jesus.

The group watch in anxious silence as Father Renz, in his white and black robes, lays his briefcase on a side table and removes the purple stole before placing it solemnly around his shoulders. Next he takes out a vial of holy water and relics of Pope Pius X, St Vincent and fragments of the cross. With great trepidation Renz shares a solemn look with Alt before turning back to Anneliese. Holding his Bible in one hand, Renz makes the sign of the cross with the other then takes the vial of holy water and flicks it lightly over the nervous congregation. When he comes to Anneliese, the touch of the water causes her to jerk and growl in pain. Roswitha's eyes widen in horror as Barbara squeezes her hand. After a brief pause, Renz drops down to his knees.

'Lord, have mercy.'

'Lord have mercy,' they murmur in reply.

As Renz proceeds with the Litany of the Saints, a strange moan escapes Anneliese's mouth as her body becomes more and more restless.

'St Luke, St Mark . . .'

Anneliese thrusts forward, her legs kicking out violently. Herr Hein rushes towards her and together with Peter and Josef they force the young woman back down into her seat. She growls, thrashing wildly as the three men struggle to hold her down, her teeth gnashing as she tries to bite their skin.

'I command you,' continues Renz, 'unclean spirit, whoever you are, along with all your minions now attacking this servant of God . . .'

A monstrous scream erupts from deep in Anneliese's throat.

'Stop with that shit!' she cries.

Anna gasps, struggling to hold back the tears as all in the room stare in terrified amazement.

Renz places his hand on Anneliese's head as she continues to growl and squirm.

'They shall lay their hands upon the sick and all will be well with them . . .'

Another flick of holy water has Anneliese howling again in pain.

'Put that shit away!' she yells.

Unable to keep her safely on the chair any longer, Peter and Josef help Anneliese on to a small couch at the back of the room.

Emboldened by the Father's words, the congregation break into gentle song.

'*Gloria Patri, et Filio, et Spiritui Sancto,*' they sing.

Anneliese cries out at the sound of every word, as if they are being carried to her on waves of fire.

After sixteen hours, Renz brings the session to an end. Anneliese implores him to continue, but Renz is wary of pushing too hard and insists they finish for the night, realising that a long road lies ahead.

Over the next month Father Renz and the others will gather eight times in that little room at the back of the house, occasionally breaking for tea and cake during the more exhausting sessions. Sometimes Anneliese becomes so enraged they bind her hands and feet to protect her from herself. Those who attempt to restrain her complain of a great weight pushing down on them whenever they draw near. Often Anneliese will return to her normal self, her mind lucid and clear, only to be taken over again by the dark spirits and their wretched voices. Alt tests Anneliese by switching languages, questioning the voices in Dutch or Latin but each time the voices seem to understand. During one session she again develops the four wounds on each of her hands and feet; the marks of the stigmata according to Renz.

After weeks of interrogation, Anneliese's tormentors finally reveal their names as Nero, Cain, Lucifer, Hitler and Judas.

One afternoon, Father Alt is telling the family about a disgraced priest by the name of Valentin Fleischmann who ran Alt's parish back in the 16th century, when Anneliese lets out a terrible scream. They watch in horror as her body twitches and her face shifts into strange shapes as if something is trying to come through, and a sixth demon announces itself. It is Fleischmann. Father Alt is astonished when the voice later recounts how it had once killed a man and battered a woman in details that could only have been gleaned from the archives of his Ettleben parish.

In the days between sessions, Anneliese, incredibly, is able to study for her end of term exams. Other times her mother finds her staring off into space whilst simultaneously kicking the underside of her bed until her feet split open and bleed. In October, Anneliese is sitting alone in her bedroom when another voice appears to her, one she has not heard before. It is soft, gentle and loving. The voice announces itself as the Mother of God. It tells Anneliese to be brave and that she must endure all this torment to carry the burden of so much sin that has befallen the world. She need not fear: she will be free soon.

All the while the sessions continue, recorded by Father Renz on his reel-to-reel tape recorder. Some nights he plays the recordings back to Bishop Stangl as together they sit enrapt in the dim light of his office while the voices of Satan's minions echo around the room.

On 29 October the voices deliver an unexpected message: they will leave on all Hallows night, Saturday 31. Gathering again two days later in the small back room, an air of cautious optimism descends as the family take their places around the stricken Anneliese.

'In the name of the Holy Trinity, in the name of the Father, the Son, and the Holy Ghost, I command you to go out, never to return,' repeats Father Renz.

A splash of blessed water is followed by Anneliese's agonising screams but the voices refuse to appear until finally one of them gurgles up.

'Who are you?' asks Renz.

'Are you Fleischmann?' asks Alt.

'Yes, I have to go now,' it rasps.

'Into Hell?' demands Alt.

'Yes!'

Anneliese retches violently and doubles over, shrieking, before a swift growl of 'Hail Mary full of grace' is heard and the room falls completely still.

Renz is the first to speak. 'Fleischmann is gone, now it is the turn of the others.'

Hitler, Cain and then Nero all take their leave, accompanied by horrific screams begging not to be sent back to Hell, until finally it is only Lucifer left.

'I will not go!' the voice growls, but soon it too cries, 'Hail Mary full of grace,' sending an exhausted Anneliese collapsing back on to the sofa.

The sliver of a waning moon hangs outside the window in the dark autumn night, as a long-forgotten silence returns to the

Michel household. It is 10.30 p.m., and the last of the demons has left. There are gasps and apprehensive murmurs as Anneliese begins to stir, coming round as if from a deep sleep.

'Is it over?' she asks meekly.

The congregation weep with joy and break into song; the elated voices rising as a majestic euphoria floods the room. So much so that they don't hear it at first, the shallow gurgle snaking through the gentle choral melodies, turning into another horrifying scream that brings the joyous hymn to an abrupt end. They turn in terror towards Anneliese, now sitting up again on the sofa, a strange smile playing about her face.

'But I am not yet out,' comes a coarse voice.

Despite the failure to complete the exorcism, a rare window of good health the following week enables Anneliese to return to Würzburg to take her theology exams. The next few months are spent travelling back and forth to Klingenberg, as Father Renz continues unsuccessfully to coax a name from the demon who refuses to be exorcised. When Anneliese's friends ask where she's been she offers only that an illness has kept her from her studies. As the year draws to a close there is no let-up from the unnamed voice that plagues her every waking hour and who spits and rages at Father Renz whenever he comes near.

In the new year, the voice reveals itself: I am Lucifer, it says.

One evening in the dorm, Lucifer tells Anneliese to press her face to the floor.

'Do it until you can't breathe anymore,' he says. 'Now strip naked and go to Anna's room and climb under her sheets.'

Anneliese screams until she is released. She puts on her clothes and climbs terrified and shaking into bed, shivering all through the night and begging for a peace that never comes.

Above all else, Anneliese is terrified at the thought of anyone at the university other than Peter and Anna finding out the truth about what has been going on. Despite occasional trips to a number of physicians on the order of Father Alt, Anneliese never mentions the voices or the faces and certainly not the exorcism. What she fears above all else is that she will be judged clinically insane, carted away and stripped of any right to speak for herself, poked and prodded by clueless doctors intent on denying her the only thing that will bring her salvation: her faith. But perhaps there is something deeper that haunts Anneliese, something lingering in the psyche of a nation still struggling to come to terms with its past.

When Adolf Hitler signed the national euthanasia decree in September 1939, it was members of the church such as Catholic bishop August Von Galen – although less concerned when it came to the persecution of Jews – who most vehemently opposed it, while it was those such as Werner Hyde, Professor of Psychiatry and Neurology at Anneliese's own University of Würzburg, who were its most enthusiastic supporters. Between 1939 and 1945, in an operation dubbed Aktion T4, as many as 100,000 German citizens considered physically or psychiatrically deficient – many of whom had already been sterilised by the state in a mass eugenics programme – were murdered by their own government.[5]

In March, Anneliese is attempting to board the train home when her body becomes oddly stiff and she is unable to move. Deciding she can't go home she returns to her dorm and is later attempting prayers in the local church when an invisible force throws her repeatedly on to her knees in an act of strange supplication. Concerned by the recent events, Roswitha is despatched to Würzburg to look after her sister who is now also refusing to eat. One morning Anneliese's friend Ursula opens the door to Anneliese's room and gasps in horror. Roswitha quickly ushers her out, but Ursula can't shake the image from her mind, and Maria has seen it too; Anneliese staring into space without moving, skeletal arms contorted in front of her in an inhuman pose. Her friends grow increasingly concerned, but Roswitha refuses to let them call a doctor, reassuring them it is all under control.

The following month more terrifying screams send Roswitha running to Anna for help, but by now almost every light in the dormitory has been switched on as anxious faces gaze quizzically at each other from across the hall. Anna does her best to control the gossip and promises that a doctor has been sent for, but it is Father Alt who has been called. After a brief stay with Alt that ends with Roswitha being injured in a mysterious fall, a weak and emaciated Anneliese is collected by Peter and her parents, carried to the car and driven home. Despite the deterioration in her condition, Anneliese attempts to reassure them all that everything will be fine, the Mother of God has delivered a message that it will all be over in July.

Once home, Anneliese's behaviour only becomes more erratic as the voices continue their unremitting torment. Some days she is found rubbing her face or banging her head against the wall until it bleeds. She asks her family to tie her up at night and sometimes during the day for fear of what the demons might make her do. But when Father Renz continues the exorcism the demonic voices remain silent, and he seems only to send Anneliese into violent fits of rage as Peter and Josef fight hard to keep her restrained. During one particularly brutal session, just like in the church weeks before, Anneliese falls to her knees, stands, then throws herself to the floor again until the skin splits and her knees bleed. She will repeat the gesture 600 times before collapsing from exhaustion. Anna tries tearfully to comfort her daughter by throwing pillows and blankets under her bloodied legs but she seems determined to miss them every time she hits the floor.

Haunted by the news of Anneliese's vicious genuflections and continuing refusal to eat, knowing the family's reluctance to involve the medical profession, Alt secretly invites a physician friend to one of her exorcisms. With the session underway Dr Richard Roth follows Alt into the Michel family home as the sound of inhuman shrieking is heard coming from the back. A single lamp illuminates the hall as Alt leads Roth up to the second floor where the doctor gasps at the sight of the skeletal young woman standing before him. Her face is swollen and beaten and her eyes are sunken into discoloured flesh. Father Renz stands in front holding out his crucifix as he talks. Dr Roth decides he has seen enough and returns shaking to the kitchen. When Father Alt asks if he will administer help if things get too bad, Dr Roth replies, 'There are no injections against the devil,' before gathering his things and hurrying out of the house.

When Alt returns a few days later, Anneliese tells him with fading light in her eyes that she fears it is still to get worse before it will get better. She reminds him that he mustn't be afraid; all will be well in July, just as the Mother of God has deemed it. Father Alt notices that one of Anneliese's teeth has been chipped. When he leaves he notices a peculiar mouth shaped dent in the wall and a glass panel appears to be missing from one of the doors. It was Anneliese, Josef informs him: she had run through it head first.

Another five exorcisms take place before 30 June when, in a thick summer heat, Renz arrives at the Michel household for what will be the sixty-seventh session since he started in 1975. As she has done in all sixty-six so far, Anneliese waits patiently and eagerly for her deliverance surrounded by Anna, Josef, Barbara, Roswitha and Peter. There is reason to be cheerful, for despite her temperature running at 38.9°C, tomorrow it will be July, the moment, as has been foretold, that she will finally be released. Anneliese is placed on the sofa with barely the strength to lift her own body but as Father Renz begins the ritual, once more she begins to slither and moan, her teeth and withered gums gnashing at the sound of the prayers. On the bridge of her nose, a large open sore weeps from a wound sustained the previous week. As Renz continues, a voice cries out but it is not the growl of the demons or the hiss of rage but the gentle, sweet and exhausted voice of a young woman.

'Absolution.'

Father Renz stops and asks, is she sure?

'Yes.'

Renz looks to Peter who stares long and hard into Anneliese's eyes, before confirming that the words are her own. Finding a momentary reserve of strength, Anneliese drops from the couch and kneels on the floor. Renz makes the sign of the cross and places his hand on her head.

'God, the Father of mercies, through the death and resurrection of his Son, has reconciled the world to himself and sent the Holy Spirit among us for the forgiveness of sins; through the ministry of the Church may God give you pardon and peace, and I absolve you from your sins in the name of the Father, and of the Son, and of the Holy Spirit.'

When it is finished, Anneliese is taken to her bed and left to sleep. A hopeful Anna follows Renz to the door.

'What happens now?' she asks.

Father Renz pats her arm and smiles.

'We pray.'

Later as Anna makes her way to bed a quiet voice comes out from Anneliese's room.

'Mama, I'm afraid.'[6]

Anna sits with her daughter until she falls asleep. At midnight a scream rips through the silence of the night, sending Josef running to Anneliese's room to find her being thrown about the bed. Josef commands the demons to leave his daughter alone and the violence subsides, but it will be well into the early hours of 1 July before Anneliese is finally calmed enough to turn on to her side and fall asleep. A few hours later, Venus, the morning star, having hung so bright and prominent in the sky slowly fades before vanishing altogether into the warm light of the rising sun. At 7 a.m., before heading off to work, Josef makes sure to check in on his daughter and finds her sleeping peacefully.

An hour later, he receives a phone call from Anna to inform him that Anneliese is dead.

An autopsy on her body finds all her inner organs healthy, including the brain, with no damage noted that could have caused any epileptic seizures. Her death is recorded as being caused by starvation, and possibly overexertion. The report also notes that her pupils were 'unusually' dilated, and that she had none of the bedsores or ulcerations of the skin associated with starvation[7] despite weighing only 68lbs at the time of death.[8] She is buried a few days later at the outer edges of the cemetery, next to her sister Martha.

In the aftermath of Anneliese's death, the West German state charged Anneliese's parents Josef and Anna, along with Fathers Arnold Renz and Ernst Alt, with negligent homicide. Two years later, in a heavily publicised case, all four defendants were found guilty of manslaughter due to negligence and sentenced to a term of six months in prison (later suspended) and three years' probation. All four defendants maintained to the end that Anneliese had been the victim of demonic possession.

Much later, when Father Renz's taped recordings of Anneliese's exorcism are made public, an analysis of her pained and anguished responses reveal some of them to be hitting two registers at the same time, as if two people had been speaking simultaneously.

Fathers Ernst Alt and Wilhelm Renz on trial for negligent homicide in spring of 1978, following Anneliese's death.

Josef and Anna Michel also await trial for the negligent
homicide of their daughter, a portrait of Anneliese inset.

*   *   *

Whichever way we look at the terrifying and tragic case of
Anneliese Michel, it is impossible to escape the horror of it. If you
believe in the existence of demonic spirits that can inhabit your
mind, intent on condemning your soul to an eternity of damna-
tion, then such a horror is self-explanatory. If you don't, we still
find a number of equally unsettling ideas lurking.

During the exorcisms, when she would yell and fight with
Father Renz, Anneliese claimed that it was as if somebody had
taken over her mind, leaving her 'self' stranded on the edges of
her psyche while someone else pulled her strings.[9] If, like me, you
find this notion terrifying, then perhaps it's best not to think too
deeply on just what that self is exactly.

We often talk of how our actions define us, that the choices we
make, from our moral standpoints to the clothes we wear to the

partners we 'choose', all combine to form an impression of who we are. Yet if we live in a deterministic universe, as most leading scientists and philosophers think – certainly those working in what might clumsily be referred to as the 'western' tradition – which, if any, of our decisions could we reasonably declare to have been made entirely of our own volition? To paraphrase Arthur Schopenhauer, you may have a thought, and then act on that thought, but *what* thought to have that thought in the first place?

Free will in the purist sense – a will that is completely free from any influence – does not exist. Through a combination of nature and nurture, even before we are born we are programmed to behave in distinct ways. At a very basic level our behaviour is controlled by the biological demands of our bodies. We eat because we're hungry, drink because we're thirsty, rest because we are tired. We could choose not to eat, drink or rest but, for the most part, the consequences of doing so prevent us from making such decisions. Often we are not aware of what impact such basic functions are having on us. A 2011 study led by Jonathan Levav of New York's Columbia Business School revealed one particularly startling example of this. Levav and his team, having analysed 1,112 cases across four Israeli law courts, found that the more mentally fatigued a judge was, the more likely they were to deny a prisoner parole. The prisoners were judged to have a 65 per cent chance of parole if their case was heard at the beginning of a session, but if heard towards the end their chances dropped to almost zero.[76]

The neural networks in our brains that influence our behaviour, how quick we might be to get angry or why we prefer oranges to apples for example, are partly determined by genetic events (many of which take place before we are born) that constantly affect behaviour. Epigenetic imprinting, as mentioned in Chapter One, also takes place before we are born and can even continue during our lifetime. The Nurse-Family Partnership (NFP), established in the US in the 1970s, offers support to vulnerable, low-income, first-time mothers in the form of regular home visits by registered nurses beginning when the mother is pregnant and continuing for up to two years after giving birth. Recent studies on the efficacy of the programme revealed that children raised with the help of NFP exhibited a 67 per cent reduction in behavioural and emotional problems by age six,[10] a 28 per cent reduction in mental health problems at age 12[11] and a 59 per cent reduction in arrests by age 15,[12] showing behaviour to be fundamentally affected by our environment. Crucially, as Professor Raymond St Ledger of Maryland University notes, babies who benefited from NFP may not only be gaining from better parenting skills, but the programme may also alter the epigenetic expression of their genes, biologically compelling them to act differently to how they might have otherwise.[13]

Our will is continually influenced in other more subtle ways too. Often when we feel we are being freely assertive, our actions are in fact reactions to stimuli. Priming is a profound case in point, demonstrating the way in which our behaviour can be manipulated by something as simple as word association. One striking example was revealed in a 2006 study conducted by psychologist Professor Kathleen Vohs of the University of Minnesota who demonstrated that people who carried out tasks whilst being exposed to reminders of money, either through images placed near them on screens or the use of Monopoly money left out in plain sight, were likely to be more self-sufficient and less willing to help others in any later tasks that they were instructed to perform as part of the experiment[14] – and all this before we even take into consideration how moral and religious beliefs are shaped by upbringing and the social groups we predominantly interact with.

We could say that in some of the cases outlined above, through education and raised awareness, we learn to recognise the ways in which our choices are being influenced by things we can't control and in turn learn to make better, more thoughtful choices. As thinkers such as Daniel Dennett have proposed, maybe that's enough. Dennett argues that even if we reject the purist's idea of free will, there are parameters within which we can retain a satisfactory degree of freedom that at least leaves us with 'the varieties of free-will worth wanting'.[15] In this sense, free will is possible if we understand it essentially as a useful fiction, much in the way we hold the notion of a 'game of baseball',[16] as cosmologist Sean Carroll puts it, expanding on Dennett's ideas; it doesn't exist as a fundamental law, you couldn't test for it in a lab, but it can reasonably be said to exist in our practical experience of the world. In other words, although we should accept that we can't have full authority over our decisions – be it the biological impulses we can't control, like who we fall in love with, or the myriad ways in which our environments influence us – we might find we have enough choices to meaningfully affect outcomes, thereby providing a satisfactory feeling of autonomy.

If we say that free will amounts to the number of options available to us within any given situation, how do we incorporate the many limitations on those choices to keep social groups functioning? How should we account for the way in which for each of us – due to the influence of our individualistic pre-determined genetic make-up and the varied subjective experiences of our lives – the choices at our disposal will be different? The simple answer is that we can't. The best we can do is agree collectively on what we deem to be acceptable behaviour, then negotiate the parameters of acceptability, either explicitly through the enforcement of laws or implicitly through tacitly agreed social mores. What happens, then, when those parameters shift?

The terror of becoming the victim of demonic possession is about much more than control. For the devout, the ultimate fear is that something fundamentally 'evil' has taken over their 'soul', threatening to commit 'evil' acts in their name, or the sin of suicide, condemning them to Hell in the process.

Yet, if we are never truly in control of our actions, what might any of us be capable of, given the right set of circumstances?

In July 1961, twenty-three-year-old Bill Menold came across an advert in the *New Haven Register*, a Connecticut-based local paper, requesting 'Persons Needed for a Study of Memory' with the offer of '\$4 for just one hour of your time.'[17] Having recently left the army, Bill figured he could use the money and, since he would be in New Haven that day anyway, decided to put himself forward.[18] A few days later, he arrived at Yale University's Interaction Laboratory where he was introduced to another volunteer, an accountant named Mr Wallace and 'the experimenter', an officious-sounding man dressed in a grey lab coat, who would be supervising the experiment. After it was explained to Bill and Mr Wallace that they were taking part in a study to examine the effects of punishment on learning ability, they drew straws to determine which roles they would take.[19] Mr Wallace was assigned the position of 'learner' and taken into a room, where, watched by Bill, he was strapped into an 'electric chair'. Now assuming the role of 'teacher', Bill was taken to an adjacent room containing an electric shock generator that he was led to believe was hooked up to the 'electric chair'. Under the watchful eye of the experimenter, Bill and Mr Wallace – no longer able to see each other – proceeded to carry out a series of simple word-based memory tests. All Bill then had to do was administer an electric shock whenever 'the learner' got the answer wrong – with one additional instruction: each time this occurred he was to increase the number of volts. On the generator there were 30 switches clearly marked with different levels of power ranging from 15 volts, described as 'Slight Shock' to 450 volts, described as 'Danger: Severe Shock'.

With the experiment underway, Bill dutifully increased the shocks by 15 volts with each wrong answer, even when Mr Wallace could be heard screaming in agony and demanding to be let out from the other side of the wall. At each scream Bill would turn to the experimenter for guidance, each time being told, calmly but forcefully to 'please continue'.[20] 210 volts ... 255 volts ... 345 volts. Up it went, until something occurred that Bill had not been prepared for. Mr Wallace stopped responding. The young former soldier had been instructed earlier to treat a non-response as an incorrect answer but was understandably concerned that something terrible had happened. He looked to the experimenter, who again asked him to continue. He flicked the next switch: 435 volts. There was no response. An anguished Bill, now utterly convinced that he had killed Mr Wallace looked again to the experimenter.

'The experiment requires we continue,' he commanded, flatly.

Against all his better judgement, Bill flicked the highest and final switch on the generator: 450 volts.

Of course, thankfully for Bill, none of it was real. There were no electric shocks transmitted to Mr Wallace, who it turned out wasn't an accountant at all but a stooge named Bob McDonough. Bill had unwittingly taken part in a hugely controversial experiment designed by psychologist Stanley Milgram to test our obedience to authority figures. After the revelations of the Holocaust were exposed in the aftermath of the Second World War, Milgram, like many others, was left completely stunned as to how so many 'ordinary' people could be convinced to perpetrate such acts. The Milgram experiment was conducted in the wake of the trial of Adolf Eichmann who, as a member of the National Socialist German Workers' Party, played a leading role in the organisation of the Holocaust. Eichmann famously stated he should not be considered culpable for his actions since he had merely been following orders. Eichmann's uncomfortable defence inferred that anyone in his situation could very well have made the same choices. Milgram set out to discover if there was any truth to this.

Bill was one of forty male subjects with varying occupations and levels of education who were tested. Prior to the study, Milgram asked fourteen Yale psychology majors to predict how many test subjects could be coerced into administering the highest level of shock, to which they gave the mean answer of 1.2 per cent. The eventual answer was in fact 65 per cent.[21]

For me it is here that we find the true horror: we might well evolve a natural aversion to certain types of behaviour if it serves no benefit to us, but often the only thing standing between us and the perpetration of what we might consider 'evil' acts is the tenacity of our fictitious social conventions and whether we are lucky enough, either through a genetic pre-disposition or through developing the requisite sense, to 'wilfully' adhere to them. Which in turn leaves us with the even more uncomfortable truth that far from 'evil' being an aberration of human behaviour, it is entirely normative.

The search for the truth (with a capital T) of things has invigorated thinkers throughout the history of humankind, and has become an especially fraught issue in an era of uncertainty characterised by fears over the impact of 'fake news' and the increasing reliance on dispassionate algorithms to aggregate information. What rarely gets acknowledged is that the truth is not necessarily important to the function and survive of humanity. In fact, we could reasonably say that, in terms of how we model societies and come together to collectively operate, it might be irrelevant, and in some ways even detrimental.

In 2008, Kathleen Vohs, this time in collaboration with psychologist Jonathan Schooler of the University of California, carried out a fascinating study to test how belief in free will affects moral responsibility. Vohs and Schooler gave two sets of participants a different passage to read from *The Astonishing Hypothesis*, a 1994 book about the study of consciousness written by Nobel laureate and co-discoverer of DNA, Francis Crick. One passage asserted that 'although we appear to have free will, in fact, our choices have already been predetermined for us', while the other gave no mention of the concept. After completing a quick survey about their respective thoughts on the idea of free will participants were then asked to take a quick maths test with one caveat: whenever a question appeared they were asked to press the spacebar to prevent the answer appearing on the screen. Incredibly, those who read the passage dismissing free will cheated more often, with the level of cheating being higher the more sceptical the participant was about having it.[22] Perhaps, then, with this in mind (provided you think cheating is an undesirable behaviour), there is reason to maintain the idea of free will regardless of whether it is true or not.

Ultimately, we may find that the extent to which we cling to notions of free will and ownership of the self has far more to do with what we consider the purpose of life to be, as opposed to any real truth as to who or what we are – something that may itself be driven by pre-programmed genetic data and unconscious responses. Do we choose to see ourselves as all valid occupiers of a minutely small shared space in a vast universe that should do what we can to ensure as many of us as possible can experience a life that is worth living? Or do we choose to act selfishly to survive and thrive at any cost? Or are we merely, in the words of *True Detective's* Rusty Cohle:

[just] things that labour under the illusion of having a self; an accretion of sensory experience and feelings, programmed with total assurance that we are each somebody, when in fact everybody is nobody.[23]

Chapter Five

TO MORN NAMES

'If I'm gonna tell a real story, I'm gonna start with my name.'

Kendrick Lamar – in conversation
with Amos Barshad for Vulture.com

It is just after 2 p.m. on 11 December 2015 when a stranger walks into The Clarence pub in the village of Greenfield at the edge of Saddleworth Moor in Britain's Peak District. On brighter days the nearby moors can seem a place of stark majesty coloured by vibrant tufts of pink and purple heather and swathes of fawny grass; a place where from any number of its rocky ledges, you feel you need only hold out your hand to reach through to the heavens. But on days like these, in the dreich and dreariness, the moors seem charged with a far more ominous beauty; the green and greys of their gritstone crags are turned black, and all colour seems washed from the land. The shadowlands at the edge of an apocalyptic John Martin painting perhaps, shortly before the ground is ripped asunder and the fiery bowels of the earth are revealed from below.

The man is middle-aged, around 6 feet tall and wearing a cedar brown mac. He has white and greying hair at the sides, and only a small tuft of it on top. After approaching the bar, he asks for nothing but directions to the 'top of the mountain', and is pointed towards Chew reservoir by the pub landlord. It's the highest place he can think of, but one, he warns the man, that he will not be able to return from after dark.[1] Undeterred, the stranger thanks the landlord and as a light drizzle begins to fall, sets off into the gloom.

The following morning, on a path between the Dovestone and Chew reservoirs, a cyclist spots a body lying parallel to the road that is oddly unresponsive to the unforgiving rain lashing down and the bitter coldness of the air. It is the stranger from The Clarence. When police and mountain rescue arrive they find no form of ID and only some cash, train tickets and a container emptied of its thyroxine sodium tablets with which to determine his identity.

In the months that follow, media outlets across the globe pick up the news of the body's discovery. It's hard not to be intrigued by the mystery of why the man, who is eventually discovered to have committed suicide, chose to end his life in such a way. But more than anything, we are gripped by the mystery of the man's identity. We seem compelled, regardless of whether anonymity had been his desire, to want to name him.

Although it is fairly likely names were used verbally for many years before, the first to be recorded by Homo sapiens appear sometime around 3500–3000 BCE in Sumeria, Mesopotamia, scrawled on to what were essentially ancient receipts made from clay. The Kushim Tablet, thought to describe the transaction of 29,086 measures of barley, also seems to bear the name of the person who had regulated the transaction.[2] Written in a corner, from the combination of two symbols that are believed to translate phonetically as *ku* and *shim*, the name Kushim may well be the first ever name to be recorded in the history of humanity.

As writing and language evolve so too does our capacity to comprehend ideas and, by extension, the world around us. In this sense, the Kushim Tablet represents a key moment in the evolution of communities; as Yuval Noah Harari notes in *Sapiens: A Brief History of Humankind*, it's a reflection of how increasingly complex societies needed more sophisticated ways of keeping track of their engagements.[3] Perhaps the recording of the first name marked another transition of sorts, into a world whereby we all began to think personally about who we were and our place in that world, and how as individuals we could shape it. Before the written name we could leave handprints or unique symbols painted on to the rocks, such as those found in the karst caves of Sulawesi in Indonesia, but their ownership has long since been lost to time. Without recorded evidence to attest to who we individually were, whole swathes of society could be forgotten, ignored and left out of the conversation but now – exemplified by Kushim's bureaucratic cornerstone – here was the chance for anyone to be able to exist in print; you would know we existed because it says so right there. It equipped us with the tool with which, even in the most forgotten and marginalised of corners, like a New York graffiti artist of the 1970s, you could scream your refusal to be ignored in fire and thunder, emblazoned on the side of subway carriages as they rolled out of the Bronx.

In January 2017, after an exhaustive search lasting over a year, the body found on Saddleworth Moor was finally identified as being that of David Lytton who had been living in Lahore, Pakistan for the previous ten years before returning to the UK when he decided to take his own life. David's story, or at least what little we know of it, has parallels with another that began seventy-five years earlier, halfway across the world. Like all such stories, it, too, begins with the discovery of a body . . .

He was lying on a ledge of rocks down by the water's edge when they found him. Judging by the state of the corpse and the newspaper dated 20 May 1945 tucked neatly under his head, he'd been dead just over two weeks. The calm, cobalt waters of Sydney's Taylors Bay – a little duller than usual that afternoon under the overcast skies – lapped gently against the rocks below as the officers inspected the scene. To the left of the body they found a small glass and a half-emptied bottle of lemonade next to an opened sachet now void of its contents. On his chest, still nestled in the grip of his right hand, a small hardcover book, no more than 5 inches in length. Pages flapped back and forth in the light breeze as one of the officers bent down to pick it up. He blew the sand from the cover and held it out to read: *The Rubáiyát of Omar*

Khayyám, printed in gold across the front. A quick glance inside revealed a faint cross, marked in pencil, next to the lines:

> Ah, make the most of what we yet may spend,
> before we too into the dust descend;
> dust into dust, and under dust to lie
> sans wine, sans song, sans singer and – sans end![4]

The man was later identified as thirty-year-old Joseph Haim Saul Marshall, who had lived in Sydney for the past six years after arriving from Singapore in 1939, although Joseph would some-times prefer to be called George, and the name Marshall had in fact been changed from Mashal – an all too common attempt, perhaps, to disguise the family's true Jewish and Baghdadi herit-age, for fear of how others might receive them.

The inquest into Joseph's death revealed the empty sachet found next to his body to have contained barbituric acid, and death by suicide was confirmed. It was also revealed that the night before Joseph was thought to have died, he met with Gwenneth Dorothy Graham, a young Sydney-based hairdresser. Graham, who had become close friends with Joseph over the last four years or so, attended the inquest as a principal witness in the case. Less than two weeks later, Dorothy Graham's body was discovered bent over and partially submerged in the bath tub of her Roslyn Road flat in Kings Cross, Sydney; her wrists were seemingly cut by the razor blade found at the bottom of the bath, yet her autopsy later revealed that her death had in fact been caused by drowning.

Just across from Taylors Bay, barely 3 kilometres from where Joseph Marshall's body was discovered, lies Chowder Bay, a popu-lar scenic spot for twilight walks by the sea or swift dips in the sheltered waters of its grand sea pool. One especially popular loca-tion there, owing largely to the Army barracks located nearby, was the Clifton Gardens Hotel. Built in a striking Federation style, it was perched just a few yards inland from the bay, peeking out from a surrounding cover of woodlands. The perfect place to spend an evening with friends in the soft glow of the winter sun; the perfect place too, perhaps, to surreptitiously watch the movement of warships as they pull out of Sydney Harbour, past Watson's bay and beyond into the treacherous waters of the South Pacific.

There was something special about evenings at the Clifton during wartime, often materialising out of the moment; an embodiment of the spirit of the age for those only too familiar with how precious such moments might ultimately prove to be. One night in early August, around the time of the inquest into Joseph Marshall's death, a group of friends from the barracks chanced their luck at the back door despite it being past the usual six o'clock closing time. Moments later, ensconced in the bar and raising toasts to the hotel staff for letting them in, one of the group, thirty-nine-year-old Army Lieutenant Alfred Boxall, is introduced to a young trainee nurse of the Royal North Shore Hospital. The pair strike up an instant rapport, so much so that at only their second meeting, with Boxall due to ship out the next day, the nurse is moved to offer him a parting gift: a copy of the *Rubáiyát of Omar Khayyám*. Inside the front cover is written:

> Indeed, indeed, Repentance oft before
> I swore – but was I sober when I swore?
> And then and then came spring, and Rose-in-hand
> My thread-bare Penitence a-pieces tore.[5]

The number of the verse, '70' is marked just below and the inscription is signed 'Jestyn'. The following day, Boxall leaves for the Northern Territories to join up with the rest of the 4th Water Transport Company. The pair will never see each other again.

THREE YEARS LATER

'Look at the way that man's slumped,' says Helen, as they make their way across the sand.

On warm evenings like this, with the sound of waves lapping

softly at the shore and the light turning pink and gold under the darkening sky, Helen and her husband John Lyons could often be found taking a stroll along Somerton Beach. Today is Tuesday 30 November 1948, the last day of spring, and as Helen and John amble north towards the quiet Adelaide suburb of Glenelg it has just gone seven when Helen first spots the smartly dressed man lying on the sand just below the Somerton Children's Home.

John looks to where his wife is pointing, at the figure lying down with his legs crossed and stretched out towards the ocean. He certainly seems strangely propped, as if he hadn't quite the strength to pull himself fully up against the wall. Helen is greatly relieved to see the man raise his arm as they pass.

'Someone's had a bit too much to drink, by the looks of it. Maybe we should report him to the police,' jokes John.

Helen smiles, then turns her head for one more look at the prostrate man – her smile becoming a little less sure as she turns back to John, threading her arm through his and pulling him a little closer as they continue along their way.

Moments later, a young couple pull up outside the children's home on a motorbike. Olive and her boyfriend Gordon have come for the sunset too and pick a prime spot on a bench just next to the small set of steps leading down to the beach. They have only been there five minutes when Olive notices a pair of legs in striped brown trousers sticking out from the base of the sea wall. She taps Gordon and points.

'Leave it out, you should mind your own business.'

'What if he's dead?'

'You mean sleeping more like.'

The pair laugh it off but for the next thirty minutes it certainly seems odd that the man hasn't moved once, especially with so many nuisance mosquitoes buzzing about. But each time Olive tries to get a better look Gordon pulls her back, telling her it's rude to pry. As twilight descends and all around them the streetlights are coming on, Olive notices a man in a blue suit walking past before stopping just above where the man is lying. She watches him as he looks down at the obscured figure on the sand for what seems like a good few minutes before turning away and disappearing down one of the streets off the seafront. Not long after, Gordon and Olive are back on their bike and driving off into the warm, hazy night.

The following day, John Lyon is back at the beach for an early morning swim. After emerging from the water, he notices two men with horses looking at something close to the sea wall. As John draws closer the object of their interest slowly begins to reveal itself. Although he can't be sure, it looks for all the world to be the same man from the night before, still lying strangely slumped with his head hanging limp to the right. The two other men, local jockeys Neil Day and Horrie Patching, had just been passing they said, when they found him like that. As John draws closer still, in the starkness of the early morning light he is able to see him clearly now for the first time: his broad shoulders and coarse reddish hair that recedes from the front, greying slightly at the sides. He is dressed in a white shirt with a red and blue tie under a brown wool knitted pullover, with a grey and brown double-breasted jacket and brown leather shoes. John sees too, immediately and without question, that the man is dead.

Police Constable John Moss of nearby Brighton police station arrives to find John, Neil and Horrie, along with a steadily growing crowd of onlookers, waiting by the corpse. Moss inspects the body, finding it cold, stiff and damp from the morning dew, then opens the eyelids to briefly examine the grey irises and dilated pupils. He makes the routine and ultimately unsuccessful check for a pulse and discovers a half-smoked cigarette between the man's right cheek and jacket lapel but no sign of blistering, suggesting it had perhaps fallen from the mouth after it had already gone out.

The constable judges the man to have been somewhere in his forties or fifties. He notes the loose hanging arms by his side and the lack of obvious signs of violence or damage to the body, nor does the surrounding sand appear to have been much disturbed. He notes also, with some surprise, how clean the man's shoes appear for someone who might have been walking along the seafront. Searching the pockets for ID, he finds instead an unused second-class rail ticket from Adelaide to Henley Beach, a 7d tramway bus ticket numbered 88708, a thin aluminium comb, an opened packet of Juicy Fruit chewing gum, a packet of Army Club cigarettes and a box of Bryant & May matches.

A short time later, with the pale morning sun lifting ever brighter and higher into the sky, a warm breeze sweeps loose grains across the beach as Lyons watches the body being placed into the ambulance and finally driven away.

Dr John Bennett is on hand to meet the vehicle as it pulls into the forecourt of the Royal Adelaide Hospital. Going on the extent of cyanosis and degree of rigor mortis, Bennett judges the man to have died no more than eight hours previously, putting the time of death loosely at some point around 02:00 that morning. Dr Bennett formally declares the man deceased, suspecting a possible seizure as the cause, although he is unable to ascertain exactly how he died at this point. From here the body is driven directly to the city morgue at West Terrace cemetery in the south-west corner of Adelaide's central parklands.

After getting it on to the gurney, PC Moss helps to wheel the body inside where moments later coroner John Dwyer removes the clothes and ties a blank cardboard label round the big toe. Dwyer places a sheet over the body and wheels it up to the refrigeration unit, opens the door and eases it on to one of the racks. Moss bags up the items found with the body along with each piece of clothing, noting with some curiosity how most of the labels appear to have been snipped out, leaving only frayed remains. With Moss's work complete the task to identify the man is transferred to the Adelaide Metropolitan Police where Detective Sergeant Lionel Leane is instructed to oversee the investigation.

Committed as they are to putting a name to unknown bodies, even with little suspicion of any foul play, such cases can often prove to be lengthy distractions from more pressing work, so there is some relief when later that evening, Leane's department receives a call from Sgt. Fenwick of Glenelg police station with a strong lead on the man's ID. Fenwick suspects the body to be that of fifty-five-year-old Edward Cecil Johnson, who had recently gone missing from his home in Payneham, a north-eastern suburb of Adelaide. Fenwick tells them to look out for a fractured elbow and partially missing little finger.

The following morning, 2 December, Constable Sutherland of the Metropolitan Police, joins Dwyer to oversee the unknown man's autopsy and watches patiently as the sheet is pulled back, only to reveal five fingers clearly intact on each hand. Edward Johnson is not their man. As Dwyer meticulously carries out the two-hour autopsy procedure, something even more unexpected is about to come to light.

Dwyer finds the body to be that of a man in good physical condition, who had taken reasonably good care of himself. His finger- and toenails are recently clipped and clean, and his face is clean-shaven, neither of which tallies with the police's first suspicion that this man was a drunk or vagrant of some description, although there are a significant number of teeth missing from both the upper and lower jaw, eighteen in total. Dwyer puts him at roughly forty-five years old and measures him at 5ft 11in height. He has a significant physicality with the broad and muscular body of a man possessed of considerable strength. Dwyer pauses for a moment at his eyes. Looking a little closer he notes an odd unevenness in his pupils, as if they had been unnaturally reacting to something just prior to his death. Moving round the back, Dwyer finds a deep lividity behind the ears and neck where the blood has settled, consistent with the position the body had been in after the man had died. He also finds a small amount of sand in the hair but nothing in the nostrils or mouth, suggesting, along with the cleanliness of his shoes, that he had not been long on the beach before he passed away.

Like Dr Bennett, Dwyer too assumes a condition of the heart to be the most likely cause of death and duly finds a congestion of blood in all the major organs, a tell-tale sign of heart failure. So it's with some surprise that when he examines the heart itself, he finds it not only in a healthy condition, but tough and firm like the heart of a younger man. He is even more surprised when he opens the stomach to find blood inside, which points to a very different cause of death indeed.

Dwyer can't yet be sure but going on the evidence so far, he is left with the suspicion that, although it may well have been heart failure that killed the man, the man's death had not occurred naturally; he had been poisoned, either by his own hand, or by someone else's. With no obvious signs of anything lethal having been ingested, Dwyer wonders for a moment if a hypodermic needle had been used. He checks in between the toes and the knuckles for a puncture wound but finds nothing save for a light scar on the left arm and a few abrasions across the hand. Later that afternoon, Constable Sutherland delivers tissue samples to the State Government Department of Chemistry, in the north of the city, along with samples of blood and urine. Each is received by Dr Robert Cowan, the deputy government chemical analyst, and will be tested for cyanides, alkaloids, barbiturates and carbolic acids although it will be a few days before the results can be known.

The following morning, Detective Leane, in his white panama and dark seersucker suit grabs a copy of the *Advertiser* from a newsstand. Leane's attention is momentarily caught by a front-page article announcing the arrest of two spies, captured in the British Zone of Vienna, before he flicks past to page two and finds what he is looking for: DEAD MAN STILL UNIDENTIFIED, reads the title. Satisfied that that will do the trick, he returns the paper to the newsstand before heading off to work.

A hot day is steadily brewing as Leane makes his way to the Detective Office on Angas Street. The South Australian task force consisted of fifteen or so personnel of men and women spread out across four small rooms, and space was at a premium. It wasn't uncommon to see any one of Constables Sutherland and Storch or Detective Canney squeezed on to the windowsills or perched on the end of tables as they compiled their reports and checked their paperwork. That morning as they gather round, Leane takes the team through Dwyer's report, advising them to start considering the case as a suicide or a possible homicide and to step up their search for the man's identity. Later, after receiving photos of the body and fingerprints from the morgue, the team put together case packs, to be mailed with copies of the prints and photographs to all major police HQs in the nation.

Original autopsy photo of the unknown man found
on Somerton Beach in December 1948.

*   *   *

In late-1940s Australia, identifying a dead body could be a particularly arduous task. The end of war had triggered a tidal wave of mass migration as many people, unwilling or unable to return home, looked to re-establish their lives elsewhere. For Australia, the sheer scale of the hostilities, not to mention the attacks on Darwin and Sydney Harbour, had left many in government – perhaps recognising the manner in which the nation had itself been established – terrified that such a young and under-populated country was dangerously susceptible to invasion. Between 1947 and 1952 alone a 'populate or perish' policy resulted in 180,000 people arriving to take up homes and jobs. The policy was heavily racially controlled with Minister for Immigration Arthur Calwell terrified that the 'yellow races' might one day take over. Calwell had hoped also that most of the new arrivals would come from the British Isles – however, with British shipping crippled by war, the government was forced to open its doors to eastern and southern Europeans, who often arrived on makeshift papers, with no friends or family to receive them, and were set to work on the most manual and transitory jobs.

Thanks to the newly revised article in the *Advertiser*, more than twenty police have contacted the Detective Office by the end of the day – mostly with info from distraught relatives worried for the safety of their lost sons, brothers and fathers. But one call stands out.

It came from a Brian Joseph Dittmar.

Nineteen months back, while working the sugar boats in Port Adelaide, he'd got acquainted with a man called Jack Thomas McLean, though, as he said, with the way things were on the docks those days, he wouldn't put much stock by that name. Dittmar knew McLean as a man who could handle himself and suspected that he may have got himself in a few scrapes throughout the years. The following day, Dittmar stands watch as the sheet is pulled back from the dead man's face. Dittmar instantly confirms the body as that of Jack McLean before curiously correcting his previous statement saying now that it had in fact been four years since he had last seen him, not one and a half. Nonetheless, armed with a possible ID, Leane's team contact the New South Wales Central Investigative Bureau in Sydney to see if they have any record of a Thomas McLean. Dittmar had suggested contacting them, believing McLean might already be in their files due to a previous arrest. The team are overjoyed when a positive hit comes back – only, as Dittmar had suspected, his name isn't Jack McLean, but William Edward Price. What's more, despite Dittmar's positive ID, Price/McLean is confirmed to have had brown eyes instead of grey and measured only 5ft 6in in height. The team are back to square one.

Over the next few weeks a steady stream of friends and family of the missing call into the Adelaide Detective Office offering possible identities with many travelling up to the West Terrace Cemetery to view the body. A mother from St Kilda is looking for her thirty-four-year-old son, missing for some time, another searches for hers who disappeared six weeks previously. Both will inspect the body but leave the morgue with desperate hope renewed that somewhere out there still, their boy is alive. The owner of a local hotel suggests it might be a guest that had left recently without paying. When the police trace his family they discover they haven't seen him in months either, but his description doesn't fit and he is soon scratched from the list.

A woman from Salisbury hasn't seen her husband in twenty-two months, a chain smoker in the habit of cutting the labels out of his clothes, in a way similar to those found on the deceased. One man, a former inmate at Alice Springs Jail thinks it could be a fellow former inmate who'd arrived on a boat from Bulgaria back in 1945. Many make appointments to visit the body but don't show up, others make positive IDs only to later retract their statements while most fail to recognise the body at all. One by one the leads are chased up, but all of them come to nothing.

With hope of a swift resolution to the case receding, it is decided to have the body embalmed. On 10 December at the morgue, local funeral director Laurie Elliot wheels his brand-new Turner portiboy next to the autopsy table, before filling its large cylindrical glass with a formalin embalming fluid. Together with the assistance of Constable Sutherland, he removes the corpse from the refrigeration unit and places it on to the table. After massaging the body to warm it up a little, with great care he makes two arterial incisions with a scalpel and places a cannula into each of the marks, one connected via rubber tubing back to the machine and the other connected to separate tubing that is left to dangle above the drain at the foot of the table. Satisfied the cannulas are locked in place, Laurie flicks a switch on the porti-boy, which sends it whirring loudly into action. The two men watch as blackened blood, pulled slowly from the right of the dead man, begins to snake its way through the tubing, while from the machine, a clear liquid is steadily creeping towards the inserted cannula in the left side of the body. As the blood begins to drip out on to the floor and down the drain, the formalin finally eases into the body.

Within three weeks most leading newspapers in the country have published pictures of the dead man, while in Adelaide, all boarding houses and hotels have been scoured for any useful information, to no avail. The following day, the case files are dispatched to every English-speaking country in the world as Leane's team look to widen the net, and on 22 December, Cowan, the deputy government analyst, delivers his chemical report to the detectives' office. He has found no obvious evidence of poisoning, which is deeply troubling for Leane. Ordinarily, any of the more commonly used poisons in suicide cases, at least those which Cowan tested for, would have left a clear trace in the body. That there is nothing suggests that if a poison had been used, it would have been something far more rare and difficult to get hold of than anything anyone looking to commit suicide would utilise. Cowan hastens to add that it may merely prove that there had been no poison involved, that the man's demise was one of simple heart failure after all. But Leane isn't convinced. How on earth does a man, as powerfully built as he was with that strong heart, just collapse? Even more strange: if it had been a simple heart attack, he didn't appear to have struggled or writhed. And why doesn't anybody know who he is?

As the nation prepares to celebrate the holiday season, the

police are no closer to uncovering the man's identity, but at the turn of 1949, a promising lead emerges. On Sunday 2 January, a smartly dressed woman walks into a police station in Morgan, a small town located on the bank of the River Murray about 160 kilometres north-east of Adelaide. She approaches the front desk clutching a copy of that day's *Sunday Mail* with its picture of the unidentified man printed on the front page, along with a small black-and-white photograph. The woman introduces herself as Elizabeth Thompson and, holding out the front cover of the *Mail*, points to the picture of the unknown man whom she identifies as her friend Robert Walsh, also known as Nugget. Her photograph shows the two of them together years before. Back in Adelaide, Detective Harvey receives a message from an anonymous caller who, having too seen the *Mail*'s picture that morning, identifies the man as someone he had once worked with, also called Nugget.

A few days later, on her way to Adelaide's West Terrace Cemetery to identify the body, Elizabeth calls on Stanley Salotti in Port Adelaide. Salotti had at one time been Walsh's employer when Walsh was lodging at Elizabeth's house. After showing Salotti the paper and an old picture of him and Walsh together, he is also convinced that the dead man is their mutual acquaintance and agrees to accompany Elizabeth to the morgue.

After both formally identifying the body as Robert Walsh, aka Nugget, the pair are taken back to Angas Street to be interviewed by Constable Harry Storch. Elizabeth, who is a widow, explains that she had met Walsh, who would have been sixty-four that year, eight or nine years ago when he first arrived in Adelaide looking for lodgings. He had claimed to have come originally from Wales where his one remaining relative still lived, an estranged sister he had long since fallen out with. Clutching the photo of Walsh a little tighter, Thompson explains that he had left her home just over a year ago, before Christmas 1947, to visit Brisbane, hoping that she might later come out to visit him, but she had never gone. It was the last time she saw him alive.

Salotti, who describes Walsh as quiet and well-liked, had last seen him at the Victoria Park Racecourse eighteen months previously, adding that he suspected Walsh to be something of a gambling man. The following day Jack Hannam, a storeman working in Port Adelaide, turned up at the City Detectives' Office identifying the unknown man as someone he had met at the Morphettville Racecourse back in May 1947. Although Hannam too said the man's nickname was Nugget, curiously he had first introduced himself as Bob Morgan, not Robert Walsh. In early February the following year Jack had bumped into him again by chance at Adelaide railway station. The man was in need of accommodation and Hannam had helped him move into the boarding house he was staying at, a place called Turners. Morgan/Walsh stayed there for the next couple of months in which time he and Hannam became good friends; they would often talk and share the odd drink together. At some point Morgan had let slip that his name was in fact Robert Walsh, and sometimes even called himself Nugget McCarthy. In hindsight, it was a little peculiar, Jack admitted, but at the time he'd thought it funny.

As Storch listened, patiently taking notes, Jack went on to describe Nugget as roughly late forties and 5 foot 8 inches in height with a tattoo on his right forearm.

'I'm sorry,' says Storch, 'did you say a tattoo?'

'Yes,' says Jack, 'it was a faint outline of Australia I think.'

That afternoon, Storch accompanies Jack to the morgue who identifies the body as the man he knew as Bob Morgan. However, when Storch makes sure to look again at the dead man's forearm he finds no evidence of the tattoo.

The next day, Constable Boyce from Minlaton station contacts the Detective Office to inform them of a call he had just received from another man again identifying the deceased as Robert Walsh, adding that Walsh had wanted all his property to go to Elizabeth in the event that anything should happen to him.[6] Then another message, this time from a different caller, confirming the exact same thing. The department decide eventually not to pursue this line of enquiry, perhaps because it was starting to sound suspiciously like a scam.

Back on 2 January – shortly after Elizabeth Thompson had first made herself known – an entirely separate lead was about to come to light. Again in response to seeing the picture of the deceased in the *Sunday Mail*, a man had pitched up at the Adelaide detectives' office with a different name for the police to pursue: Ray Clark. This man went on to describe Clark as being late thirties, 5ft 10in with reddish hair and complexion as well as several missing teeth. The man knew Clark to have been something of a boxer in his youth and he was still in good shape, all in perfect keeping with the profile of the dead man. However, it wasn't until he was asked how he had known this Ray Clark that the detectives really sat up and took notice.

'We worked together for the Commonwealth Department of Parks and Interior,' he says, 'down at Woomera.'

'Woomera?' repeats a junior officer with some confusion.

Detective Leane knows exactly what Woomera is.

On 18 July 1945, unbeknownst to most of the planet, a bomb was detonated at 05:48 local time in the middle of the Jornada del Muerto desert in New Mexico. The device, named Trinity, marked the first successful deployment of the atomic bomb. Less than three weeks later the Atomic Age announced itself in two mushroom clouds of death and destruction when Little Boy and the Fat Man were detonated above the Japanese towns of Hiroshima and Nagasaki. The bombs would go a significant way to ushering an end to the Second World War but they would also mark the beginning of a seemingly endless arms race that to this day continues to haunt every military aspect of foreign diplomacy. After the war, or more specifically, after the detonation of the bombs at Hiroshima and Nagasaki, it was clear to all those governments who considered themselves major world players that the game had shifted. Although the United Kingdom could provide the expertise to compete in the development of nuclear weapons, what they didn't have was the space to test them out.

The word Woomera, taken from the indigenous Dharug language, translates to English loosely as a 'wooden spear-throwing device'. The perfect name, you might say, for a nuclear-grade rocket-testing facility. Developed as a joint venture between the governments of Australia and Great Britain, the Woomera site, located over 500 kilometres to the north-east of Adelaide in a wide expanse of South Australian outback, covered an area of roughly 120,000 square kilometres.

What went on at Woomera was top secret, and Ray Clark had helped to build it. The suggestion that this Ray Clark, a potential murder victim with uncertain origins, had worked on such a top-secret facility is deeply concerning for Leane.

Later that afternoon, PC Horsnell escorts Ray Clark's former colleague to the morgue where he makes a positive identification of the dead body. The following day the *Advertiser* names Clark as a possible candidate for the unknown man. Later that evening, another man who claims to have worked with Clark is also taken to the morgue, where he states that the body is not him. However, a few days later a letter arrives from one of the lead surveyors on the construction of Woomera who confirms that the likeness and description of the unknown man does indeed resemble the Ray Clark he knew. He adds curiously that Clark used a different name on his Royal Australian Air Force driving licence but he isn't able to remember what it was. Despite their best efforts Leane's team are unable to determine Clark's whereabouts but, crucially, nor can they find enough information to identify him as the unknown man.

After six weeks of fruitless investigations, the Adelaide police, now boosted by the addition of the smart and amiable Detective Len Brown, reconvene to go back over the evidence. There must be something they've missed, some clue that they haven't pursued yet, thinks Leane as they pick through the dead man's belongings. Then he sees it: the train ticket! He bolts to the phone and immediately has Adelaide train station on the line.

'The luggage,' he says down the receiver, 'check the luggage department for any unclaimed suitcases or bags that were checked in before December the first. In fact, that goes for every left luggage department,' he says to his startled team.

Soon they are on the line to every boarding house and local transport depot they can think of, urging them to check for any items that might have belonged to the deceased. A similar appeal is run in the *Advertiser* the next day.

Finally, on 14 January, a vital breakthrough.

'It was checked in sometime on November 30th between 11 and 12 p.m.,' explains Senior Porter Harold North as he leads Detective Leane into the back of the Adelaide station cloakroom. Sadly for Leane, Harold has no recollection of who he took the bag from, but it's the only one checked in before December that hasn't been picked up, he says. Harold negotiates his way through the mountain of luggage and coats crammed into the small back room until finally he gets to it, ticket number G52703. He pulls the bag from the shelf and hands it to Leane.

'Here you go, mate.'

Leane takes the medium-sized brown leather case from Harold's hand and places it on the ground. Inspecting the side, he notes a destination sticker has recently been removed, but otherwise finds no other markings. Flicking up the clasps he pauses for a moment before lifting the lid. Inside he finds a stack of neatly folded clothes along with several implements whose purpose he is not yet able to discern. As he slowly pulls out a shirt and pair of brown trousers, almost identical to the ones found on the unknown man from the beach, Leane knows whose suitcase this is. He digs frantically for any sign of documentation, but there is nothing.

Back at the station the team make a proper assessment of the contents. A small card of brown cotton and some buttons appear to match with thread and buttons found on the trousers of the deceased. They also find a red-chequered dressing gown, some slippers, brown leather shoes, a tie, shaving gear, a jacket and handkerchief – that also matches with one found on the man. Curiously, again they find all the labels have been removed from the clothes with three of the items bearing the name Keane, although Leane suspects there is nothing to be gleaned from this. As for the implements, they find a small electrician's screwdriver, a stencilling brush, a pair of scissors and a table knife that has been cut into a smaller and sharper instrument and covered in tape to keep it so. Leane learns subsequently the items are commonly used for stencilling and after speaking with a tailor he discovers that the jacket in the suitcase was most likely made in America. Unfortunately, any hope that this presents a new avenue of enquiry was dashed a few days earlier by a letter sent from the US Dept. of Justice informing the team that the prints they had sent had failed to show up on the FBI's database. In fact, all international police departments contacted by the team come back to them with the same news: there is no record of the man. Despite the initial excitement at locating the suitcase, with no documentation being found inside, they have little more to go on. By April the man is still nameless.

From left to right, Detectives Dave Bartlett, Lionel Leane and Len Brown examine the contents of the suitcase found in Adelaide Station.

At some point it is recommended to Leane that he turn to the University of Adelaide for help. Professor John Cleland, a well-respected and experienced authority on the science of pathology, jumps at the opportunity to offer his assistance in any way he can. The following day, Cleland takes receipt of the case notes as well as the suitcase and its items found at the train station and immediately gets to work. Reading the details of the autopsy, it is clear to the seventy-year-old Cleland that this man had not died of natural causes, confirming Detective Leane's suspicions. He finds blades of barley grass in both the lower part of the trousers left in the suitcase and in one of the socks worn by the deceased suggesting they had possibly been worn together at some point. All in all, Cleland is able to confirm that the suitcase and enclosed items belonged to their man but there is little to add to what they already know.

Going back to the clothes, he runs infrared light over the trimmed labels but finds nothing of interest. Then he looks again at the trousers that the man had been wearing when he was found – made by Wilson according to the little tag on one of the pockets, which he flips inside out to reveal the maker's mark chalked inside: 560-T5-REG-23. The police had made enquiries about this early in the case, leading them to a manufacturer based out of 275 Brunswick Street in Melbourne which produced over 3,000 pairs of similar trousers each week; in other words, it would be nigh on impossible to trace the name of the buyer. Cleland is despondent and close to giving in when, working his fingers around the inside of the waistband he feels a little bump in the fabric next to the opening of a tiny fob pocket. Putting his finger inside it, he finds a small, tightly rolled piece of paper. Careful not to rip it, he unfurls the piece which has clearly been torn from somewhere and is stunned to find two words printed on the inside of it in thick, black, stylised font, reading cryptically: *Tamám Shud*.

Back at the detectives' office the team are stumped as to what it could mean, and Cleland has no idea either. Weeks go by as they try in vain to uncover the meaning of the words until one afternoon Frank Kennedy, a journalist at the *Advertiser*, gets wind of the enigmatic discovery and has an instant jolt of recognition. He races to the phone and calls Detective Len Brown to let him know where he has seen the phrase before: in the *Rubáiyát of Omar Khayyám*.[7] Brown grabs the slip of paper and heads straight out to a nearby bookstore. He runs his fingers across the spines in the poetry section until finally he comes across a Collins Press 1st Edition of the *Rubáiyát*. He pulls it from the shelf and rifles through the pages, turning over the final one to discover, right there staring back at him in bold type, the words: *Tamám Shud*. Holding the page up to the light, he pulls out the torn piece of paper and holds it over the words on the page: it's a perfect match.

Later, after consulting with a librarian, Brown and the rest of the team learn that the phrase is Persian, its English translation meaning 'To End' or 'Finish'. They go into overdrive, contacting all bookshops and libraries in the hope of finding the original item from which the slip had been torn but the search comes to yet another dead end.

Back at the morgue, despite the continuing of the embalming process, the dead man's body is beginning to disintegrate, and in the absence of a positive identification the police are left with little option but to finally lay him to rest. Local taxidermist Paul Lawson is brought in to make a cast of the upper torso and head should anyone later turn up wanting to ID the body, before it is dressed and prepared for burial. On the morning of 14 June, the nameless man is transported by hearse from the funeral parlour of F.T. Elliot & Sons in Hindmarsh and delivered to the West Terrace Cemetery. It is hard to escape the strange sombreness of the occasion, laying to rest a body for which there is no identity; this unnamed man, with no apparent friends or family to claim him as their own. Those who had spent over six months trying to decipher his riddle are united in a peculiar sadness as his body is lowered into the ground.

The case touched the public's hearts to such an extent that a local bookmaker covered the cost to grant the man a proper funeral, and a few days later a small headstone is placed at the top of his grave, a gift from local stonemason Mr A. Collins. It reads, 'Here lies the unknown man who was found at Somerton Beach, 1st Dec 1948'. A few days later an inquest is held into the man's death, concluding that he had most likely died from unnatural causes, which appears to draw a final line of sorts under the investigation. The man's bust is placed on display at the South Australian Museum for anyone caring to examine it and although the detectives continue their hopeful search for the vital *Rubáiyát*, it's hard not to suspect they have reached the end of the road.

That is until something extraordinary comes to light.

Late one Friday evening in July, Ronald Francis is reading the newspaper at his home on Jetty Road in Glenelg when he comes across a story about a local police search for a book with a partially torn-off back page. Remembering a road trip he and his wife had taken with her brother and his wife the previous year, Roland gets up and heads out to his Hillman Minx parked up on the street just by his house. He opens the door and reaches over to the glove compartment, pulling out the book from inside that his brother-in-law had placed there when they had returned from their trip. *Rubáiyát of Omar Khayyám*, it says on the front. Roland flicks immediately to the back page and is astonished to find a large chunk of it is missing, ripped from the middle. What's more, there appears to be something written inside the back that looks suspiciously like a phone number. As it will transpire, Roland's brother-in-law had found it under the seat and had placed it in the glove box thinking erroneously that it was Roland's.

The next morning, Roland arrives at the Detective Office and is introduced to a beaming Detective Leane. He hands the book to Leane, who wastes no time in comparing the strip to the back page, finding it an exact match. After confirming Roland's story and subsequently clearing him of any involvement in the man's death, the team immediately get to work analysing the book. Placing the inside of the back cover under ultra-violet light they are amazed to find not one but two phone numbers indented on to the card. Underneath those numbers, they find something very peculiar indeed: five rows of letters written out in an unrecognisable sequence:

WRGOABABD
MLIAOI
WTBIMPANETP
MLIABOAIAQC
ITTMTSAMSTQAB.

The second line seems to have been crossed out and there is an 'x' written over the 'O' in the fourth. It looks like a foreign language, suggests one of the officers. No it doesn't, says another, it looks like a code.

The numbers, at least, are more easily deciphered. One is discovered to belong to a bank, but the second is found to be residential and tracked to a property in Moseley Street in Glenelg, which incredibly runs directly off Jetty Road – right next to where Roland Francis kept his car. A short time later, Detective Errol Canney, who had been tasked with tracing the phone number, makes his way up the porch steps of the requisite home in Moseley Street. It's a pleasant tree-lined street just one back from the beachfront and barely fifteen minutes' walk from where the unknown man's body had been found the previous year on that bright December morning of 1948.

Canney can barely contain his nervous excitement as he knocks on the door. Hearing movement from inside he catches sight of someone approaching and moments later is greeted by a young, confident woman with wavy brown, shoulder-length hair. She shields her eyes from the light to get a better fix on Canney as he introduces himself before he suggests politely that perhaps they had better go inside to talk.

The woman, who introduces herself as Jessica Thomson, is completely dumfounded as to why her number might have been written in the back of the found copy of the *Rubáiyát* but is happy to answer Canney's questions. She goes on to explain that she has lived in Glenelg for the past few years working as a nurse in the city. She had moved here after completing her training in Sydney and lived with her husband Prestige, who was presently out of town, as well as their three-year-old son Robin. After a lull in the conversation, Canney asks one final time if she can't think of anything that might be of significance to the case and then something occurs to her. There was a soldier a few years back, she says, whom she'd met a couple of times during the war while out with friends – back when she was a trainee nurse. She had given him a copy of the *Rubáiyát* shortly before he had been due to ship out again. In fact, the man had later tried to contact her after the war had finished but she had written back to him letting him know that she was married and that it would be best that they no longer speak. The man's name, she says, was Alfred Boxall and she also gives an address where the police might find him.

Canney reads out the strange sequence of letters found at the back of the book and asks if Jessica has any idea what it might mean but she is as stumped as anyone. Canney thanks Jessica for her time and suggests they arrange a date for her to come down to the station and make a formal statement as well as to take a look at the cast of the man. Finally, as he turns to go, Canney asks if Jessica ever went by any other names?

'Yes,' she replied. 'People often used to call me Jestyn.'

Back at Angas Street, Detective Leane asks all personnel to find out what they can about Alfred Boxall. With Boxall's link to the *Rubáiyát* and Jessica's rejection of him, Leane is beginning to think they might finally have their man and that perhaps it had all been a case of suicide after all. On the afternoon of 26 July 1949, seven months since the body of the unknown man was found, Detectives Leane and Canney accompany Jessica to the South Australia Museum where taxidermist Paul Lawson is on hand to take them to the bust. The men watch with bated breath as Jessica approaches it. For a moment Leane discerns a glimmer of recognition on her face before she quickly averts her eyes to the floor where they stay for the remainder of the conversation. She seems momentarily unsteady on her feet, almost as if she might faint, but when Leane asks if she is OK, she insists she is. He asks her to confirm whether she has seen the man before.

There is the briefest of pauses before she answers.

'No, I have not,' she says.

Three days later, after tracking Boxall's last known address to a property in the beachside suburb of Maroubra in Sydney, the man is found alive and well working maintenance at a bus depot in nearby Randwick. When Boxall is later interviewed at his home by the Sydney CIB, he confirms Jessica's story about that night at the Clifton Gardens Hotel when she had given him a copy of the *Rubáiyát*, and even shows them the original book to prove it, pointing out the inscription in the front signed by 'Jestyn' before returning it back to his bookshelf. He apologises for their wasted journey.

There is no luck with the possible code, either, not even when it is offered to the country's finest naval intelligence officers to crack. With nothing left to lose, Detective Leane releases it to the press in a move that, over the next seventy years, will see a vast army of amateur sleuths try their luck at trying to break it.

To this day nobody has been able to offer a satisfactory answer as to what it means.

Many things will come to light further down the line that, had the detectives known them then, may have proved significant. One piece of information being that Alf Boxall's wartime engineers unit hadn't merely been a glorified home guard but was also involved in intelligence gathering; one other being that Jessica Thomson, as she is alleged to have told her daughter shortly before dying in 2007, had indeed known the man – and so too had others who she allegedly described as being of an authority above the police.[8]

Time has done little to dampen interest in the unknown man found dead on Somerton Beach in December 1948, with speculation as to what he was doing that evening in a quiet Adelaide suburb as rife today as it ever was.

Was he the mysterious Ray Clark? A secret agent and cohort of Jessica Thomson's perhaps, who could no longer be trusted or – worse – having served his purpose, was no longer of use?

Was he a passing acquaintance of Thomson's, destroyed by an unrequited love?

Or was he one of many people who had been forced to leave their war-scarred homes and families behind on the other side of the world, finding any job they could in the hope of building a better future for their loved ones, whose heart had unexpectedly given out as he took a moment to enjoy the sunset and to think upon the day when they might finally be reunited.

We may never know.

Although it's the failure to successfully identify the 'Somerton Man' that has given his existence more visibility than most, it has certainly not been on his terms. Whether or not he cared himself for posterity, his fate is one that will surely haunt many of us; the sadness of a life destined to be forgotten, an affirmation of a degree of meaningless too profound to comprehend even if, in reality, it is a fate that may well befall us all.

The notion of individuality may seem peculiar to an omnipotent godhead observing our insignificant speck of rock from outside our universe, seeing the rapidity with which we come and go, watching as the busying, minute shapes scurry about the globe while hundreds of years tick by, seeming to them like nanoseconds. Watching as points of mass emerge and structures rise and fall, noticing with amusement perhaps how with such predictable regularity, lights begin to flicker and turn on as the great shadow of night curls around the planet.

From this perspective, provided we were considered significant enough to even warrant observation, we would appear to them how many of us might regard a colony of ants, or a slide of bacteria – singular components of an irrelevant species that jostles, evolves, lives and dies, completely interchangeable and indistinguishable from the next, appearing merely to be fulfilling the objectives of some sort of hive mind. How shocking it would be to move closer and discover a very different world indeed – a world of fierce uniqueness and breadth of individuality, and all the many ways we might distinguish ourselves from each other. It is this world that begins with our name.

In the Arthur Miller play *The Crucible*, a fictionalised account of the Salem witch trials and an allegory of the communist paranoia that gripped the US in the 1950s, lead character John Proctor finds himself forced to confess to witchcraft to avoid execution. However, such a confession comes at a cost: not only will it condemn other prisoners to their deaths, but with his name written in ink and pinned to the local church door, he and his family will forever be marked by his confessed sins. In the play's climactic scene, Proctor changes his mind and rips up the confession. In answer to why he had done so he cries: 'Because it is my name! Because I cannot have another in my life . . . I have given you my soul, leave me my name!'[9]

What, then, is in a name? Certainly, as Shakespeare would have us believe, it is 'not hand, nor foot, nor arm, nor face, nor any other part'[10] belonging to us. We rarely choose them for ourselves, sometimes we don't even like them, and yet for most of us, for better or worse, it is our name that most signifies our existence. It is our name that will remain on the administrative records, certificates, censuses, gravestones and social-media accounts long after we have gone. For all that we attempt to project ourselves into collective spaces, be it through written, audio or visual means, it is the simple magic of our names that serves as the primary trigger from which we are conjured up and held in the minds of others; how in our absence we might remain something solid and real. A name then has power. It is where we begin and end.

It is quite odd then to think how few of us take the route of the eponymous Lady Bird in Greta Gerwig's brilliant 2017 film, and choose our own name for ourselves. For many, a name you don't like might be an annoyance, but it can at least be a source of pride, a connection with one's family or tribe. We will often take for granted that we have a name at all, but what a luxury it is when you consider the millions of German Jews with names of 'non-Jewish' origin forced by law on 1 January 1939 to adopt the name Israel or Sara to make it clear to authorities who was Jewish or not. Or the hundreds of thousands of women, men and children abducted from their homes in Africa, anonymised and stripped of their identities, often only 'granted' a name in their newly forced places of residence to make it easier for administrative purposes, or as a mark of a master's ownership.

Given the horrific experience of victims of the Holocaust or slavery, a given name can then be a complicated and wholly unwelcome signifier that you exist, and one that can bury the truth of who you are underneath. When Muhammad Ali became the heavyweight-boxing champion of the world in February 1964, he did so under a different name, Cassius Clay. When he decided to change it, many people in the predominantly white U.S. media refused to recognise it: but Ali would not be refused. He told them, 'Cassius Clay is a slave name. I didn't choose it and I don't want it. I am Muhammad Ali, a free name – it means beloved of God, and I insist people use it when people speak to me.'[11]

Perhaps this concept of individuality is just an additional layer of sophistication in what is nothing but part of a DNA-driven strategy to heighten the illusion of self that keeps us fighting to live. We might argue that to do away with such ideas of individual self is where true liberty lies – to be removed from our delusions of separateness and our desire to be noticed. Until that day comes it is hard to argue with Gerwig's Lady Bird; hard to fail to understand the torment of Margaret Atwood's handmaid, Offred, or indeed to fail to understand the shedding of names, such as Alice Faye Williams for the luminescence of Afini Shakur instead.

David Lytton, whose body was found on Saddleworth Moor in 2015, had in fact been born Lautenberg. At some point later in life he had decided to change his name to Lytton which, as long as the records exist to show it, will stand as a more truthful mark of who he considered himself to be. Consider, too, our propensity for social media to so often operate not as a tool with which to explore each other, but a means with which to validate ourselves; not only a way of saying who we are but, in the way of old-school graffiti, a way of saying *we were here*. That we did exist. If all this – life, the universe and everything – is meaningless, perhaps at the very least we can say that we were here, material and extant in our own right.

What is in a name might be nothing but the beginning of a truth that your entire existence is founded on.

Chapter Six

ALL THAT WE SEE

'Now the thing about seeming is that seeming is never quite
as it seems . . . appearance is always strange.'

Timothy Morton – *Dark Ecology*

When Christopher Columbus' ships first neared the shores of the
islands known today as the Bahamas, it is said that the islanders
didn't see them coming. Not until they saw the unfamiliar fluctuations in the water caused by the wash from the galleons did they
realise that something was awry. This same story is told in a variety
of ways; replace Columbus with any number of European explorers 'discovering' supposedly 'uncharted' territory and you will get
the same effect: the implication that the ships were so alien to the
local communities that they were effectively rendered invisible.

These apocryphal tales are thought to stem from diary entries
recorded by botanist Joseph Banks in 1770 during his time spent
accompanying Captain James Cook aboard HMS *Endeavour*.[1] On
making its way into what is now called Botany Bay, the *Endeavour*
passed a number of canoes piloted by local fishermen but when 'the
ship passed within a quarter of a mile of them . . . they scarce lifted
their eyes from their employment; [Banks] was almost inclined to
think that attentive to their business and deafened by the noise of
the surf they neither saw or heard [the ship] go past.'[2]

Later, with the seemingly unmissable 100ft-long vessel
anchored less than half a mile opposite a small village, the fishermen gave it barely a moment's notice as they paddled back to the
shore and pulled their canoes on to the beach before returning to

their homes.[3] Although there could be any number of reasons for this peculiar behaviour, Banks's own suggestion, that the people were simply too distracted by the standard regimen of their daily lives to notice the ship as it moved into the bay, is particularly insightful.

In 1998, psychologists Arien Mack and Irvin Rock published a paper for the Massachusetts Institute of Technology, entitled *Inattentional Blindness*.[4] Building on the earlier work of cognitive psychologists Ulric Neisser and Robert Becklen, the paper outlined the results of a series of simple experiments that highlighted a fundamental deficiency in our sense of perception. The study concluded that due to our brain's natural tendency to band multitudes of objects and stimuli into single groups, we often fail to notice the most obvious of stimuli, even if they occur directly in front of us. One well-known example of this was demonstrated in an experiment known as The Invisible Gorilla[5] in which participants were shown a film of people passing a basketball amongst themselves and instructed to count the number of times the ball was exchanged. Afterwards, as participants congratulated themselves on guessing the correct amount of passes, almost 50 per cent were surprised to learn that they had missed something quite irregular: the person in a gorilla suit who walked straight through the shot, stopping in the middle and turning to the camera to beat their chest before walking out again.

Although inattentional blindness wouldn't explain how something could remain hidden in plain sight, as opposed to it not being 'seen' momentarily because we are more intently focused on something else, it remains a startling example of the limits of our perception. It is hard not to wonder then, just what else we might be missing?

Certainly, it is fascinating to think that there might exist technologies or beings formed of materials so beyond our comprehension that we can't see them, let alone understand them, or that within our lifetime we could become so conditioned that we might *always* be blind to them.

In Ancient Greece, the Pythia – the high priestesses of the Temple of Apollo, who served as his Oracles of Delphi – were thought to originally have been young children, ideally farmers' daughters who were chosen for their perceived purity and innocence.[6] It is a common theme in the history of divination found in many cultures. In ancient Rome, children often performed the drawing of lots, a process used to determine the will of the gods by the reading of small tablets usually made of wood that were thrown into water.[7] Classicist Prof. Sarah Iles Johnston of Ohio University attributes this to the strongly held belief that children were simply 'able to see gods, demons, and ghosts that other people could not',[8] a skill that they would invariably lose once they had grown up.

Interestingly we find hints of this theme with regards to a number of especially compelling UFO sightings. In 1977, fourteen pupils from a school in Broad Haven, a small village on the south-west coast of Wales, reported seeing a silver cigar-shaped craft land in a field beside their playground. Parents and teachers, quick to dismiss the event, were later left scratching their heads after the children were asked by their headmaster to draw a series of pictures describing what they saw. Despite being separated to perform the task, their drawings were found to be strikingly similar.[9]

Just over fifteen years later, on the other side of the world, a remarkably similar event unfolded in a small rural village in Zimbabwe. It remains one of the more extraordinary accounts of an apparent close encounter of the third kind ever documented.

Many have wondered like the great Enrico Fermi, if there really are other sophisticated life forms out there, then where are they? Others might say that just because we don't see them, it doesn't mean they aren't there . . .

It had just gone 21:00 on the evening of 14 September 1994, when Cynthia heard the explosion. Startled from her paperwork, she turned to the window and hurriedly scanned the horizon for any sign of an attack. Though it had been over fourteen years since Zimbabwean independence, the intervening years hadn't been easy, mired in the social and political upheaval one might expect of a postcolonial nation grappling with the complications of the past. The affluent and leafy suburb of Mount Pleasant, where Cynthia lived, was an exclusive district of north Harare and home to some of the city's wealthiest residents, including a number of dignitaries and government officials. That the former Ethiopian dictator Mengistu Mariam lived nearby was as good a reason as any to suspect, as Cynthia did, that what had just rattled her windowpanes was a bomb.

Unable to see anything from her desk, Cynthia made her way out to the garden where she was joined by her friend and granddaughter who had also heard the bang. As they scanned the dusky sky for remnants of the explosion, they were surprised to see no thick plumes of smoke or flashing emergency lights. Instead of the sirens that they had expected to hear, there was only the gentle sound of water trickling through the filter of the swimming pool to break the silence. All things considered, it was unusually quiet, with even the neighbourhood dogs seeming unnaturally stilled. Ever eager to get to the bottom of things, the curious Cynthia soon had the three of them jumping into her car and setting off in search of the source of the explosion. As they slowly trawled the neighbourhood for any sign of damage, back home Cynthia's telephone was ringing off the hook.

Cynthia Hind was born in South Africa in the 1920s and spent a number of years in North England with her husband and two children before moving the family to the Mashonaland region of Southeast Africa to help run her father's furniture business. Cynthia's true passion, however, was writing, and what fascinated her more than anything else was the paranormal. Although primarily a writer of short stories for radio and women's magazines, she developed an interest in the UFO phenomenon in 1966 after securing an interview with 'alien abductee' Elizabeth Klarer. In 1956, Klarer alleged that she had been conducting an affair with an astrophysicist named Akon who had travelled to Earth from the distant planet Meton. Cynthia was dubious of Klarer's story but also fascinated as to why she would make up such an extraordinary claim if it wasn't true. When the resulting article was eventually published in a 1969 edition of *FATE*, a popular American magazine specialising in the possibility of the paranormal, her life would never be the same again. Within weeks Cynthia found herself inundated with letters from countless others desperate to share their experiences from around the continent. Representatives of a newly established American organisation known as the Mutual UFO Network (MUFON) were also quick to get in touch.

The MUFON organisation, originating from an earlier group known as the Aerial Phenomena Research Organization, was established to bring a measured, scientific approach to the investigation of UFOs. They had written to Cynthia, excited at the prospect of developing a relationship with a fellow researcher operating from the African continent, but Cynthia was reluctant. Her interest had stemmed from the personal story behind the phenomenon rather than the phenomenon itself, and being at the start of her career, she feared the inevitable ridicule and stigma of associating herself with such a group. Despite finding most of the stories she received too ridiculous to be true, Cynthia reasoned that simply presenting personal accounts was not an admission of belief, but a useful contribution to the understanding of a curiosity that deserved closer inspection, whether the origins were unearthly or not. After accepting MUFON's invitation in 1974, Cynthia was appointed an official field researcher, spending the next few years investigating all manner of alleged UFO sightings from across the continent.

In July 1978 Cynthia travelled to Dayton, Ohio to attend her first MUFON conference and was utterly spellbound by the speakers in attendance; giant names in Ufology such as J. Allen Hynek and Major Donald Keyhoe, a man often considered a leader in the field.[10] She felt at home among the other members of MUFON whom she was pleased to discover were not at all like the deluded crackpots that she had first imagined, many being learned individuals with distinguished academic records in physics, psychiatry, geology and medicine. In 1981, Cynthia returned to the conference to present her own paper on African encounters where she rubbed shoulders with the likes of retired nuclear-physicist-turned-Ufologist Stanton Friedman – considered the first civilian to have documented the site of the infamous Roswell Incident, an alleged cover-up of an alien spacecraft that had supposedly crash-landed in 1947 in Roswell, New Mexico. By the time she published her first book, *UFOs – African Encounters* in 1982, Cynthia had become something of an authority on the subject and was regularly invited on TV and radio to talk about her research.

It was this reputation that explained the incessant phone calls that hadn't stopped since Cynthia left the house that September night in 1994. On returning, she would pick up the first of many that night as various friends and acquaintances called, eager to share their stories of that evening's peculiar events. It hadn't been a bomb – at least, not one exploding on the ground – but rather something unusual that had taken place high above the land. Strange lights they kept saying, streaking across the sky in a parade of colour and sparkle, like a giant Roman candle shooting out across the heavens. Cynthia worked tirelessly to scribble down each report as it came in but could barely keep up, deciding eventually to call the editor of the *Herald* with whom she had a good relationship to find out what information they had received. As Cynthia expected, they too had been inundated by calls from as far away as Johannesburg attesting to the strange lights, but her enthusiasm was soon dampened after learning that their origins had already been determined. As the editor explained, it was simply a meteorite shower. Extraordinary and beautiful in its own right no doubt, but not what Cynthia had been hoping for. Yet, as the calls continued late into the night, Cynthia couldn't escape the feeling that perhaps not all was as it seemed.

One person Cynthia spoke to that evening was Vivienne Pascoe, a teacher living in Bulawayo, over five hours drive west of Harare. Vivienne recounted how at precisely 20:54 she had caught sight of something in the clouds after stepping outside her cottage for some fresh air. Looking northwards she watched for over a minute as 'flashing, shimmering, smeary lights'[11] moved low across the sky, heading south towards the nearby Matopo Hills. Then there was the report from a Mr Alexander, a specialist in aircraft fire prevention who, along with a friend, had spotted what they assumed to be an aeroplane in distress with flames shooting off the wing. Describing a 'cluster of small white lights extending across the fuselage from one wing to another',[12] he watched as the apparent craft, similar in size to a 747 jumbo jet, moved silently from north to south at a low altitude barely 20 metres above the tree-tops. As it moved it kept a level flight path, which Cynthia thought strange for a meteor shower, but even more so since the object appeared to be metallic in nature. Many sightings came in from the shores of Lake Kariba, a popular tourist destination in the north-west of Zimbabwe. Alexander Law who was staying at the lakeside Cutty Sark Hotel had first seen it as a white light growing on the horizon, before realising it was in fact moving with what he counted to be fourteen other lights flashing around it. Looking closer he was able to make out a dark centre in the primary object as well as a long orange tail that streamed behind it.[13] Similar accounts flooded in from the region with many reporting that the objects had been observed changing direction. Cynthia worked hard to make a record of the sightings, but with most media outlets content to accept the meteorite explanation, the event seemed destined to become little more than a forgotten celestial quirk. That was, until something completely unexpected came to light.

Children pour into the playground in a blur of khaki shorts, sky blue dresses and bright red jumpers, spilling out into the acres of scrub with wild abandon before finally coalescing into more orderly groups; they whizz around chasing balls, or take to the see-saw and climbing frames while others are content to settle in under the shade of the big eucalyptus tree. It's a beautiful late-winter day without a cloud in the sky. Alyson, a physiotherapist who is today volunteering at the tuck shop, can't help but smile as she watches the children shriek and giggle about in the bright morning sun, looking like flowers in their wide and floppy sun hats. She senses a little more crackle than usual in the air that morning, probably owing to the fact that the teachers are still gathered inside for an early term staff meeting, giving the pupils free rein of the field. It has been left to Alyson, whose ten-year-old daughter Fifi attends the school, to single-handedly supervise the 250-odd children.

Built in 1991, Ariel School was constructed on the site of an old farm, roughly twenty miles east of Harare in the town of Ruwa, a small rural community that also serves as a municipal hub for the many surrounding homesteads. As a fee-paying facility, its pupils, who attend grades 1 to 7, come from the wealthier parts of Zimbabwean society and are comprised of a broad mix of ethnicities; from the children of Shona, Ndebele and Karanga, among other tribes, to first- and second-generation European immigrants. The playground is divided into an area for swings and climbing frames used mostly by first to fourth graders and a two-acre stretch of dirt and grass. A thick scrubland and line of tall gum trees form a natural border at the end of the dirt flat beyond which lies a dry creek and vast swathes of savannah merging into a series of low rolling hills that slope gently at the horizon. Children from these parts know better than to disappear beyond such natural boundaries; after all there is no telling what creatures might be lurking in the tall grass waiting either to pounce or to defend themselves with deadly venom at the slightest hint of a threat.

As eleven-year-old Salma makes her way towards Emma at the back of the playground, she becomes aware of a loud buzzing noise that seems to be emanating from a row of wooden utility poles and power cables that run under the trees at the eastern edge of the playground, stretching off into the plains beyond. When Salma gets closer, the buzzing seems to intensify until a flash of light flares up from somewhere in the distance.

'What was that?' asks Salma, as the pair turn to see where the light had come from.

'Look!' says Emma pointing to the far end of the playground.

Salma and Emma watch bemused as a small group of children gather by the trees at the edge of the playing field, as if they had just been called over by someone. They keep watching as more children join them, running across from all ends of the playground.

'Come on!' says Emma excitedly, grabbing Salma's hand.

Back at the tuck shop, Alyson has just noticed how quiet it's become when twelve-year-old Luke comes tearing up to the hut.

'Miss! Come quickly!'

Alyson listens patiently as Luke struggles to get his words out; something about a tiny man in a black shiny suit, with large eyes and a silver lace tied around his forehead. Alyson, suspecting it might be a trick to lure her away from the sweets, has little intention of heading off to investigate but as she tries to make sense of the boy's peculiar story she becomes aware of the faint sound of crying. When she looks up there are more children heading towards her. Some are wide eyed, while others are inconsolable with tears, but each arrives with the exact same story: that some kind of object has just landed in the trees at the back of the playground and two little beings in silver and black suits with strange eyes have got out of it. Suddenly concerned by the obvious distress of the children Alyson looks around for her own daughter Fifi, and finally spots her running towards the sweet shop.

'Why are they all crying?' Alyson asks.

'Because of the glowing white thing that landed,' she says.

Alyson stares at her daughter, detecting no trace of mischief in her eyes.

Headmaster Colin Mackie is just starting to wrap up the meeting when an urgent banging comes from the staffroom door. He opens it to find a pupil in an agitated state. A ship has landed in the playground he says. Mr Mackie chuckles at the boy and tells him the meeting will be over shortly before closing the door. Ten minutes later, the teachers emerge, chatting amiably as they walk into the light of the playground before one by one each of them falls completely silent. There before them, instead of children laughing and playing as they had expected they see instead twenty or so children huddled together with tears streaming down their faces as other classmates try to console them. Many others are standing around in small groups deep in conversation, while a few others wander about in a strange daze. Alyson is comforting some of the children when Mr Mackie approaches her.

'What an earth's been going on?' he asks.

Before Alyson can explain, the children drown her out, speaking rapidly over each other as they try desperately to articulate exactly what they've seen. Some say they saw it land, others that it was already there when they arrived. They speak of how it glinted in the trees and its oddly circular shape, but most of all they just want to talk about the two beings that came out of it and their peculiarly large eyes that seemed to wrap around their whole face. The teachers look to each other in disbelief.

Despite his scepticism, Mr Mackie is eager to get to the bottom of it all and asks anyone claiming to have seen something to follow him into the school hall. With over sixty children gathered inside, Mr Mackie and two other teachers ask them all to spread out with paper and pens and draw exactly what they saw. For the next thirty minutes the children sit in concentrated silence, sketching and colouring, while the teachers talk amongst themselves. Relieved to have finally calmed the children down, little attention is given to the array of saucer-like shapes and stick figures appearing on pieces of paper throughout the hall. One after the other the children hand in their work as the teachers ask them, was it not a helicopter you saw? Are you sure it wasn't just a farmhand from the homestead next door? You've been watching too much TV, they say. But mostly they tell them it was just their imagination and that there's no such thing as aliens from outer space. At the sound of the bell, the teachers gather up the last of the drawings and suggest the children try and forget about whatever it was they think they saw.

But eleven-year-old Salma knows exactly what she has seen. Like many of the kids her family don't even own a TV, and although some of her classmates talked about aliens and UFOs she had never heard the terms before today. By the time she makes it home from school she feels she has done nothing but speak about the event all afternoon yet not one of the grown-ups has heard a word she's been saying. So when her mother asks her what's up, she is reluctant to talk.

'You won't believe me if I tell you,' she says, as she pushes her food around the plate. 'None of my teachers do.'

But her mother perseveres and finally Salma relents, telling her about the flash of light and about how when she and Emma had got nearer to it, they had the feeling that time had squished, as if it were no longer a part of her thoughts. Also how, when they had reached the crowd, they pushed through to the front and saw a large silverish object on the left of the trees. She couldn't tell what it was but it seemed mechanical, like it might move at any moment, only it didn't look like any material she had seen before.

What she couldn't stop looking at, though, was the creature that stood in the long grass barely five yards away from where they were gathered. It looked human-like but was no taller than a child, and its whole body was covered in a shiny black suit like scuba divers wear, she said. And its face. She couldn't take her eyes off its face: a blank smooth space, like the surface of a porcelain jug. Although it seemed to have no eyes, nose or mouth, as she looked at it she had the very distinct feeling that it was looking directly at her, as if it was trying to understand her.

'I felt that it knew me,' she says.

What's more, it kept jumping; back and forth from one place to another, only, as she explains, she never saw it actually move, almost as though whenever she blinked it had moved somewhere else.

'Were you afraid?' asks her mother.

Salma looks up suddenly from her plate.

'You believe me?'

'I don't know what it is you saw, but yes I believe you.'

Salma's mouth burst into a wide grin.

'No, I wasn't afraid.'

That evening, despite being advised to forget about the day's events, similar conversations take place throughout the homes of the sixty-odd children who claim to have seen the extraordinary incident, who too had felt the being studying them. Those unlike Salma, who are afraid, endure a sleepless night, staring out their bedroom windows, terrified at the thought of the small black-suited creatures returning to steal them from their beds. Those too afraid to even tell their parents are left to suffer their night-mares alone in the dark. Many others also stay up all night, their young minds whirring as they try helplessly to piece together what they have seen. Perhaps the teachers had been right, they think, maybe it really was just their imaginations playing tricks. That evening, back home in his living room, Mr Mackie sifts through the drawings properly for the first time, becoming more and more troubled as one after the other he finds the same set of images depicted by each of the children: pictures of a craft on the ground and humanoid figures with wide bulbous eyes stretching high around the face.

British journalist Tim Leach moved from London in the 60s to study journalism at the University of Rhodesia (renamed the University of Zimbabwe in 1980). By 1994, with almost twenty

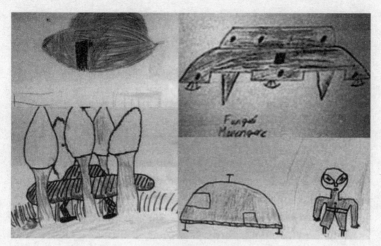

Four drawings made by pupils of Ariel School
depicting the 'craft' they claim to have seen.

years' experience as a reporter and cameraman, he has risen to
become the BBC's Bureau in Chief of southern Africa having
covered some of the most devastating events imaginable from
war in Angola to genocide in Rwanda. Tim is alerted to news of
the strange incident at Ariel School on the afternoon it occurs,
and quickly he informs his friend Cynthia Hind. Tim suggests
they go down to the school at the first opportunity on Monday to
scope it out. Never one to sit on her hands, through the help of a
veterinarian friend who lives in Ruwa, Cynthia is on the phone
within minutes to Alyson's daughter Fifi, listening sympatheti-
cally as Fifi takes her through what she has seen that morning. Fifi
carefully fills in as many details as she can remember, like how a
strong wind had swept across the playground just as the bright
light had dropped into the trees. She also explains again how
some of her classmates had reported seeing peculiar little men in
black suits but that she herself hadn't seen them. Eleven-year-old
Barry and twelve-year-old Fungai, however, who Cynthia would
later speak with that night, both attest to having seen the 'beings'.
Both boys had clearly seen their large black eyes shaped like rugby

balls and had also experienced a weird slowing down of time when they neared the 'ship', as they called it. Later that evening, when Cynthia finally gets off the phone it is hard for her to resist the thought that she is possibly sitting on one of the most extraordinary close encounters of the third kind which the world has ever known.

The following Monday, Tim and Cynthia, accompanied by Gunter Hoffer – a friend of Cynthia's and fellow UFO researcher – drive east out of Harare into the pale grass and farmlands of the surrounding countryside before finally pulling up at Ariel School shortly before nine. After being greeted by Mr Mackie they are promptly led into the staffroom where a few of the teachers have assembled to take them through the events of the previous week. None of the teachers want to believe for a second that a UFO had really landed in the school playground, but neither could they answer the question of how sixty young school kids could even begin to coordinate a hoax like this, if that's what it is.

Tim films Cynthia as she examines the drawings made by the children. She is instantly struck by the level of detail but also the subtle differences in each one, suggesting to her this was not something they concocted together. A few minutes later, six children from seventh grade, the oldest group in the school, file into the small white room to speak with her. Mr Mackie instructs them to take a seat along the back wall.

Cynthia waits for them to settle before asking if they had definitely all seen something, to which they all reply yes, nodding enthusiastically. The first to give his account is Nathaniel.

'Did it have a shape?' asks Cynthia.[14]

Nathaniel thinks for a moment then describes a dome shape with his hands. 'It had a long top and a platform coming round the sides,' he says, as he moves his hands around, drawing a saucer-like shape in the air.

'I didn't see the spaceship but I saw the little guy. He was all in black and looked like he had long hair,' says twelve-year-old Luke, who sits on Nathaniel's left.

'Could you see his face?'

'No,' he says softly.

'Why was he among the trees?' asks Cynthia.

'It was just like . . . like a shadow,' says one of the other boys jumping in.

'What's your name?' asks Cynthia.

'Trevor.'

'And you also saw this, this creature?'

'Yes we were all there.'

'Did you see it land?'

'I just saw flashes on the side of my eye, and that's really all I saw,' he says quietly.

'You didn't see anything on the ground?'

'No.'

Daniel, who has been close to bursting with excitement as he waits for his chance to speak, is next.

'I'm Daniel and I saw this silver thing in the trees with this one thing sitting on the side and another running up and down the top, it almost looked like a real person except it was a bit more round,' he says, squeezing his waist.

'At first I thought it was a boy from the compound just playing,' says Emily, the next in line and who like most of the children had identified the black-clad creatures as men. 'They had longish hair and it was all black and they had big black eyes. They kind of turned around and stared then went back to a kind of ship, there was one big one with quite a few little ones scattered around.'

'When you say he had big eyes,' says Cynthia, 'show me with your hands.'

Emily brings her hands up to her face and, pinching her fingers and thumbs together, holds them over her eyes. 'They were oval, like that,' she says.

'Were you afraid?'

'Yes,' she says, smiling anxiously.

'What did you think it was?'

'Well everybody was saying they were UFOs and everything.'

'Were you perhaps influenced by what the other children had said?'

Emily thinks for a moment then dips her head to the side before looking back at Cynthia with confidence. 'Sort of, but I did definitely see what I saw.'

Finally, Cynthia turns to Charity, who stood to the side of the others. 'What did you see?'

'I saw something silver on the ground amongst the trees and a person in black, that's all I saw.'

'What did the silver thing look like?'

'It looked like a saucer but the shape wasn't really round.'

'Have you heard about UFOs before this?'

'No.'

'Were you afraid?'

'Yes,' she says quietly, as she turns her eyes to the ground.

Tim, who has been filming the entire exchange, tries to keep the camera steady while all the hairs rise up on the back of his neck. As a veteran journalist of some of the worst and most complex human conflicts imaginable, until now he thought he had seen it all. He knew what deception looked like too, but as he watches the children's faces through the disinterested lens he sees only honesty and sincerity. Whatever had happened, he thinks, they really had seen something.

After meeting with the children, Cynthia decides they should venture out to the playground and examine the 'landing area' for any radioactive traces. Mr Mackie has twelve-year-old Guy and Fungai, who Cynthia had spoken to on the Friday evening, walk them over to the 'site'. With the group making their way into the playground, tiny faces cram into the classroom windows behind as the children fight for a glimpse of the TV crew. Stepping from the sheltered area into the wider dirt flat, Guy recounts his experience of the event. He had first noticed a small group of children pointing at something in the tall grass and shrubs at the edge of the playing area. Naturally, he thought the children were messing around or that someone had been hurt. Being one of the taller kids he was able to push to the front easily, which, he says as the team finally near the edge, was when he saw it. Guy points out the spot just beyond in the shade of some gum trees, where he saw the large, silvery, round object and another smaller object just to the right of it. Some of the children had started walking towards the larger one, he explains, when the 'being' climbed out of it.

Cynthia listens intently as Guy takes his time between questions, clearly still wrestling with what exactly it was that he had seen. At some point Guy noticed that two of the younger girls had started to cry, and had watched as they grew increasingly frightened before running away to the back of the playground. Then he noticed others, who were also crying, seemed rooted to the spot with fear. The word Tokoloshe spread through the group, murmured on the lips of the various tear-streaked and trembling children. It wouldn't be until later that Guy found out what it meant.

In Zulu mythology, the Tokoloshe is a short, malicious water demon with long hair and glowing eyes that can be summoned to inflict grave harm on its victims. One local story has it that many years ago a young woman, wearing nine bracelets on her arm, was bathing in a river a few hundred miles east of Harare, when she was attacked by a Tokoloshe who tore off her arm and threw it into the water. Although many doubt the existence of such a creature, in 1924 a prospector named Captain Valentine, searching the same stretch of river, is said to have discovered the remains of a human arm while digging around the riverbank. When he pulled it from the silt he was amazed to find there were nine metal bangles wrapped around it.[15]

When Guy finishes his account, Fungai leads Cynthia and the others to the exact spot where the 'craft' had landed. Here he explains how after the event some of the students, examining the area with one of their teachers, found what looked like six burn marks on the grass and hundreds of dead ants scattered about. Gunter pulls out the Geiger counter and directs the probe towards the ground but finds no evidence of radiation.

Over the next few weeks, news of the peculiar event at the little rural school in Zimbabwe spreads across the globe with reporters from Holland, the UK's BBC and South African TV flocking to the region to meet with the children. At first the kids welcome the attention, but they soon grow weary of having to repeat themselves over and over again, mostly because they know perfectly well that they are being made fun of, but also because every reporter and interviewer, with the exception of Cynthia, tries to talk them out of what they had seen. There is one other person, however, from the most unexpected of quarters, who does not dismiss their reports so easily, even if it comes at a considerable cost to his professional reputation.

In the early 1990s Dr John Mack, a well-respected child psychologist and Professor of Psychology at Harvard Medical School had become interested in reports from people who claimed to have been contacted by aliens; a fascination that would eventually lead to a decade-long study on the subject. Mack's initial interest stemmed not from whether the subjects had been abducted or not, but rather the sheer scale of the phenomenon, which suggested to him that in one way or another there was some truth to what the people were saying.

His first assumption was that the 'witnesses' were suffering from some kind of psychological disorder. However, many of his subjects exhibited no pathologies whatsoever. What Mack found most interesting was how often the subjects appeared to have had their whole perspective of the world changed after their encounters. Although often ridiculed for his new obsession, Mack was encouraged by his good friend and pioneering philosopher of science Thomas Kuhn to pursue his investigations regardless. Kuhn had himself been at the centre of some controversy years before with the 1962 publication of his ground-breaking treatise *The Structure of Scientific Revolutions*. Kuhn's book challenged the prevailing notion of the time that scientific progress was based on the steady accumulation of accepted facts and theories, suggesting instead that such periods of conceptual continuity were frequently interrupted by revolutions of thought. Such revolutions, he argued, often presented new perspectives in which to explore ideas. Kuhn famously termed this idea, the 'paradigm shift'.

In May 1994, Dr John Mack, in his capacity as a professor of psychiatry at the Harvard Medical School, published his first set of findings in his book *Abduction: Human Encounters with Aliens*. Shortly after publication the Dean of Harvard Medical School, troubled by Mack's subject matter, appointed a committee to investigate his work for potentially bringing the institution into disrepute. Mack was staggered by the decision, but taking solace in his good friend Thomas Kuhn's work, reasoned that although accounts of alien encounters were incompatible with our current scientific knowledge, we might yet discover them to be real in a way we don't presently understand.[16] Undeterred, Mack vowed to carry on his research, confident that he had neither violated the university's code of ethics nor slipped below their high standards of academic rigour.

With the investigation into his work still ongoing, Dr Mack decided to expand his research by looking into cases outside of the US and had just arranged a trip to South Africa when news of the Ariel School incident first broke. Deciding it was too good an opportunity to miss, Mack adjusted his plans and, accompanied by research assistant Dominique Callimanopulos, made a visit to the school. Over the course of two days, the pair brought their considerable academic experience to bear on the case. What they would discover was nothing short of extraordinary.

The children are at first reluctant to go through it all again, but the amiable and charismatic Mack, whose technique of pulling up a small classroom chair to sit beside them on their level and question them with a gentle enthusiasm soon puts them at ease. It is as if they recognise one of their own, someone they can trust, who is genuinely interested in what they have to say. Time and again, Mack, like Cynthia, is astonished at how much detail the children remember as they recount their stories to him. As the teachers would later attest, rarely would the children's accounts deviate from the ones they had first given on that strange morning in September.

Mack was particularly interested in the reports of those who had found the event traumatic, for whom the trauma had very evidently stayed with them. Asking one child what scared them most about the incident she replies it was 'the noise'.

'What noise?' ask Dr Mack, gently.[17]

'The noise that we heard in the air,' says the young girl.

As she spoke, John can almost see the memory spreading across her face, the fear of it growing from somewhere within her.

'What was it like, a roar or a buzz?' he asks.

'It was like someone was blowing a flute,' she replies enigmatically.

To another young girl he asks, 'Where were the eyes?'

Consistent with what many others had done before, the girl responds by making that same shape with her hands, holding them up to her face.

'And what was the feeling when you looked in the eyes?'

'It was scary.'

'Scary why?'

'The eyes looked evil.'

'What was evil about them?'

'It was just staring at me, as if it wanted to come and take me.'

'Did you want to go with it?'

The girl shook her head and tears start to well up.

It was certainly nothing like talking to psychiatric patients who would often seem desperate for him to believe them or be obviously distorting reality in some way. The minds of these children, he believed, were completely sound. In their answers he can hear a reticence in their voices, showing concern at how what they are saying might be received, and a constant doubt of their own recollections. Dr Mack is convinced that at the very least the children genuinely believe what they are describing had truly happened to them.

Ten-year-old Lisa had been one of the first pupils to spot the object and had run across to it with some friends.

'I felt scared,' she says.

'What was scary about it?' asks John, perched low on the small chair beside her.

'I felt scared because I'd never seen such a person like that before.'

John asked Lisa to draw her memory of the event on a blackboard. He watches as she outlines the craft; a bulbous saucer shape with two landing feet and antennae on the top, next to which she draws a stick figure with wrap-around eyes on the head. What she said next was most astonishing.

'What I thought, was maybe the world is going to end, maybe they were telling us the world is going to end.'

Just as he had found in the accounts of many other 'experiencers', Lisa appears to have taken some kind of message from the encounter.

'Why do you think they might want us to be scared?'

'Because, maybe we don't look after the planet and the air properly.'

'Is this an idea that you have had before? That we don't look after the planet properly, and the air? Or did this idea come to you when you had this experience?'

'When I had this experience.'

'How?'

'I just felt all horrible inside. It was like in the world all the trees will just go down and there will be no air and people will be dying.'

'How did he get those thoughts across to you?'

'He never said anything, just through the face and the eyes.'

'Would you like to see him again?'

'Yes.'

'Do you think you might see him again?'

'I don't know.'

'And if you saw him again what would you do?'

'I'd ask him what are you doing on Earth and what do you want from us?' She pauses before adding emphatically, 'I believe in it because I *did* see it.'

She isn't the only one to have apparently received messages from the being. Emma, who had been with her friend Salma at the time, also reports something very similar.

As the creature had stared at her, she recounts, her heart was beating faster and faster until a thought started to emerge in her mind.

'I think they want people to know that we're actually making harm on this world and we mustn't get too tech-knowledged,' remarks the ten-year-old girl.

These 'messages' aren't unique to the children of Ariel School; it was something Dr Mack had come across time and time again in his interviewing of 'experiencers'. With a striking regularity, many of Mack's case studies reported being warned about humanity's destruction of the environment leading Mack to suspect that, in one way or another, this was central to the 'abduction' experience.[18]

Dr Mack concludes his interviews and returns to the US shortly after to continue his research. After fourteen months the Harvard investigation into his academic credibility is eventually brought to an end, resulting in a complete exoneration and reaffirmation from the university dean that Mack has the 'freedom to study what he wishes and to state his opinions without impediment.'[19] As for the pupils of Ariel School, the media interest soon dies down and the children return to focusing on their studies.

Although the story would ultimately drift from the public consciousness, not one of the children will ever forget what happened on that peculiar day in September. Now adults, with jobs and children of their own, with some emigrating to distant corners of the world while others remained to make their homes in Zimbabwe, not one of those sixty-odd pupils has revealed the story to have been a hoax with many continuing to speak about it to this day; some still suffer from the trauma.

All have watched, with mounting horror, as year on year, those warnings of environmental concern have appeared increasingly prescient with each passing day.

What then are we to make of the Ariel School mystery? In the absence of any irrefutable, empirical evidence, we are left with only anecdotal eyewitness accounts from which to discern truth from falsehoods. Most would not unreasonably conclude that due to the sheer improbability of such an event, the children were at best mistaken in their interpretation of what had occurred, or at worst they deliberately lied about it. What intrigues me about this particular story, far more than whether it occurred or not, is the romantic inference that the children were able to see something that the adults could not; that failure to 'see' the spaceship was only a matter of perception.

Perceptual narrowing is the way in which our brains will ignore certain information in our environment in order to better focus on other types of information. Writing in *Scientific American* in 2016, neurologist Susana Martinez-Conde explored a number of studies that show how human infants younger than six months can see things that adults cannot. One study conducted in 2002 revealed that babies under six months were better at telling different monkeys' faces apart than adults were. Another study, conducted by a team of psychologists led by Jiale Yang of Chou University in Japan, shows that up until the age of five months, human infants have a much broader sensitivity to the effect of light on an object, being able to detect subtle variations in images and colour that are invisible to adults.[20] When we age, as our sense awareness narrows we become blind to these realities and 'objective differences become subjective similitudes'.[21]

The flip side to this narrowing of perception is that it is likely a beneficial evolutionary tool that helps us to better survive our environments. I wouldn't go so far as to say it would account for our inability to 'see' alien technology, yet if it did, such a notion would be entirely consistent with a basic fact of our everyday reality: that due to the limitations of our singular perspective much of the world is continually hidden from us. Or as Susana Martinez-Conde so eloquently put it, there may well be 'such a place as reality,' out *there*, 'but it's not a place that any of us have ever been.'[22]

The emergence of colour is a perfect case in point. That babies are able to distinguish shades of colour we don't see as adults is down to the way we perceive an object not as it is, but how our brains interpret it for us. More profoundly, it has nothing to do with 'colour' at all. Colour does not exist in and of itself. A green ball isn't green unless something observes it to be so. When light hits the ball, depending on its molecular structure, certain wavelengths will be absorbed and others reflected. Through the mechanics of the eye, our brains interpret those reflected wavelengths as colours. The colour of the ball as it appears to us at any given time is dependent on how much, and what type of light it is exposed to, as well as how much our brains compensate for the difference. Once we understand it as green, we maintain that it is so, even if under low light it might in fact appear grey. So what then of the ball itself?

Philosopher Immanuel Kant made the distinction between *phenomenon* as being something as it is described and comprehended by our senses, and *noumenon* as being the object as it exists independently of our senses. We may observe a 'ball', which, if it were to hit us on the head, we would say is extant as something that we can physically interact with; but defining what it *is* exactly is a little more complicated. Anti-realist philosopher Hillary Lawson pointed out while debating 'The Strangeness of Things' for the Institute of Art and Ideas that phenomenon, in this case the idea of a 'ball', is merely a useful metaphor; its true, real substance – its noumenal property – is not something we have ever been able to identify.[23] Democritus, living in the 5th century BCE, would say that the 'ball' was fundamentally made of atoms. Since then we have discovered that atoms are only the tip of an even more curious world of previously unknown sub-atomic particles and quantum-level forces, with nothing to suggest we have reached the final, base property that defines all noumena.

Probing a little further we find ourselves confronted with an even more complicated truth about 'reality'. We already know of species on Earth that physically see and interpret the world in different ways to ourselves. What's to say, then, that there isn't a sentient species somewhere in the universe that understands and exists only in electro-magnetic waves or impressions of ultra-violet light, or in a manner that we have yet to even conceive? If we and this other species apprehend the 'moon' in different ways, what exactly is it that *we* are observing, and does something even have to be animate to be considered something that can observe? Which is not to say that there isn't something there with proper-ties that appear to us in the form of the 'moon' but it would certainly be problematic to claim our version was the absolute, objectively correct one. Imagine a being with perception in the manner of Alan Moore's Dr Manhattan who, being able to observe sub-atomic particles, would therefore no longer be capable of distinguishing a mug from the coffee table it is resting on (or a spaceship as it landed in the playground of a rural school in Zimbabwe).

Perhaps this is all fine; what we see is our perspective of reality and we don't know any different. Our brains and bodies do a pretty good job of keeping us alive and functioning in our shared practical experience of reality. In the extreme – if we were to walk into oncoming traffic or be in need of open-heart surgery – it serves us no good if we aren't able to consistently identify the object of a car or a heart; both clearly share a solidity and existence of sorts that to ignore would have fatal consequences. I often think, what would it even matter if, like Neo from *The Matrix*, we discovered we were in fact living in a computer simulation? Little, if any, of our physical experience of life would change as a consequence. There is only one crucial problem. If this is the only perspective we know, it tends to follow that it is the only perspective we care about. Setting aside how this clouds our understanding of space, time, the universe and everything, it first and foremost clouds our understanding of the very place we live in.

As our biological make-up will limit our perspective and hide the true nature of reality, so too does our subjective understanding of things distort the way in which we see the world around us. The apocryphal tales of European explorers and invisible galleons mentioned at the beginning of the chapter are meant to reflect the native people's inability to 'see' the ships, but there is something else invisible in the stories: the native people. These tales are told from the perspective of the valiant explorers 'discovering' and 'mapping' uncharted territory that is in fact already inhabited by other people. The assumed failure to 'see' the ships is a partial reflection of the perceived intellectual inferiority of the local people that have been 'discovered'. We may not know for sure what Joseph Banks thought about the people living in what is now known as Botany Bay, but we can be sure that little importance was granted to their culture and perspective by the people who would subsequently colonise the land they lived on.

How unsettling it is to think of how much we are losing when we fail to accommodate other perspectives; to think of how many of our interactions are susceptible to all-too-common prejudices towards each other based on our individual biases of sexuality, race, gender and class that have no basis in objective fact. Are ideas of masculinity and femininity biological manifestations for example, or constrictive social constructions blinding us to a more honest understanding of the human being?

We see similar ideas explored to devastating effect in *Black Mirror* episode 'Men Against Fire', where American 'super-soldier' Stripe, played by Malachi Kirby, fights to eliminate a race of feral humanoid creatures, known as 'roaches' that appear to be terrorising the human race. Stripe, like the rest of his team, has been fitted with a neural implant to enhance his combative capabilities. However, after one particularly tough mission, Stripe's implant is corrupted revealing to him the truth behind the enemy 'roaches'.

As the implant malfunctions Stripe no longer sees his victims as monstrous mutants that scream an indecipherable language. Instead he sees them as they really are: ordinary human beings. The implant had been fooling him all along so he could better his execution of the job.

For a more terrifying real-world example, consider the National Socialist German Workers' Party's virulent racist campaign to affiliate the Jewish and Traveller communities with rats and cockroaches. It wasn't based on any objective truth or empirical evidence. It was to construct a reality whereby killing them would be less complicated if people considered them less than human, and it was horrifically effective.

This is a profound reflection of the practical reality in which we live. It is a place where a phrase as seemingly innocuous as 'to run like a girl' can alter entire perceptions of expectation, a place where people can be driven to suicide because their community has arbitrarily pathologised their sexuality.

As inconvenient as it can sometimes be, we could argue regardless that perceptual narrowing is a useful survival tool, but might our failure to escape our perceptual limitations ultimately prove our undoing?

According to philosophers such as Timothy Morton – and other advocates of the theory that we are presently living in an epoch known as the Anthropocene – our very survival may hinge on learning to do away with our human-centric perspectives, especially ones that have deluded us into thinking ourselves somehow above and separate from nature.[24] The term Anthropocene refers to a proposed era that dates back from the present day to roughly 12,500 years ago to the period when Homo sapiens transitioned from hunter-gatherers to agrarian societies. Such a time, they believe, marks the beginning of the era when human societies began to have an inextricable impact on the planet, an impact that has left it, and everything on it, in a state of peril. Morton and similar thinkers, are looking for a way to avert the impending ecological crisis of our time, chiefly but not limited to climate change, encouraging us to find a better 'logic of coexistence' with the natural world.[25] One of Morton's central tenets as laid out in his most recent work *Dark Ecology* is the idea that all things, from inanimate rock to jungle vines to ourselves, have an existence and place in the universe, whose perspectives, as it were, are all equally valid, and that too often we see them merely as either the decoration of our space or as things to be exploited.[26]

If you aren't quite ready to accommodate the perspectives of a rock then perhaps you might consider how we are learning with increasing horror – explored to amusing but devastating effect by Simon Amstell's 2017 mockumentary *Carnage* – that those animals we have been rearing en masse, and regularly in squalid conditions, only to murder them for their meat, may not be the dumb, unthinking, edible machines we have been taught to think they are. Who knew that instead, these living creatures, extant in the exact same universe as ourselves, are intelligent sentient beings capable of cultivating relationships, who have memory, family bonds, and who also feel pain and mourn for their lost loved ones just like we do.

In a 2017 study led by evolutionary biologist Susanne Shultz at the University of Manchester analysing the social skills of ninety different types of cetacean – whales, dolphins and porpoises – Dr Shultz and her team discovered that not only do many of the species use tools with a complexity not previously realised, but they can also strategise in ways not previously imagined. They discovered that some dolphins have been observed assisting humans to fish, helping to round them up in nets completely unprompted, realising that by doing so they will be given fish in return. It was also discovered that the most advanced species of cetacean pass down their understanding of techniques for hunting and tool use to successive generations.[27] They have also been observed conversing in more sophisticated ways than once thought, with regional dialects and names for individuals: perhaps they even have a name for us.

There is no reason to think, of course, that having alerted somebody to a different perspective, they will then care about it. How

blinkered it would be to assume someone's failure to accommodate other perspectives is merely an unconscious bias. It may very
well be considered beneficial to ignore another perspective or
remain committed to your own interpretation of phenomena. To
bemoan the human instinct of assuming a superior status above
nature and other animals is to ignore the idea that this very behaviour is in itself a *natural* process of the *natural* world. Some
people, as much as it pains me to think about it, might enjoy killing non-human animals. It would certainly be naïve to think that
alerting a friend to the fact that a pig may be more intelligent than
they might have thought would be enough to prevent them from
eating one in future. We know very well how intelligent human
beings are, yet it does little to prevent us from slaughtering each
other.

In any case, why should we all see the world in the same way?
It may seem desirable to align our perspectives into one common
point of view, that striving to see the world as one is the ultimate
human goal, but one thing we can almost guarantee is that it would
be a world in which much would remain hidden to us. The tension
and conflict of our differing perspectives, for better or worse, is the
human experience. As inconvenient as it may seem, the survival of
our species, the manner in which we and our societies evolve – we
hope into something 'better' (whatever that means) – may very
well depend on the fact that we don't all see the world in the same
way, that we don't all converge into one homogenous understanding of how things should and shouldn't be. That isn't to say that
we can't find ways to align our points of view more closely, to work
at improving our collective experience of life, but it's worth
remembering that much of our shared understanding is realised
not through objectivity but through the exchange of our uniquely
individual perspectives.

Far more useful then, even at the risk of allowing for viewpoints
we don't agree with, is for us not to focus on eradicating different
truths, but that we learn to embrace our multifaceted perspectives
as an inherent trait of our species; that we learn never to turn from

the strange and unfamiliar. We cannot be expected to know, understand and see everything instantaneously, but perhaps it is only through recognising different perspectives that we are able to fully 'see' what would otherwise remain hidden to us. In this process of becoming more aware of, and comfortable with, the existence of different points of view, we might begin to better understand our world, and each other.

Chapter Seven

IF THESE WALLS
COULD SCREAM

'Our flesh doesn't sweat and pimple here for the domestic
mysteries, the attic horror of What Might Have Happened so
much as for our knowledge of what likely did happen.'

Thomas Pynchon – *Gravity's Rainbow*

The world of horror is littered with unnerving locations, places
that both draw from and have in turn seeped into the public
imagination. There are the places of what we commonly call the
'natural' world, seemingly imbued with a timeless spirit that
transcends the human imagination: the mystical island mountain
Uluru, also known as Ayers Rock, found deep in the Australian
outback; the mythical rocky outcrops and abandoned mines of
Cheshire's Alderley Edge in England, as evocatively portrayed in
the work of Alan Garner. Then there are the places of the 'natural'
world that we often find portrayed metaphorically as extensions
of our own psyches; the darkling forest or black shimmering lake,
those Jungian, Freudian locales of the subconscious that hint at
something lurking either deeper within or just below the surface,
something unseen pulling at us, daring us to confront an unsettled past or innermost fear.

The psychological effect of these places tends to be generated
by our own projections; they become, in the post-modernist sense,
not 'places' but 'spaces', whose ability to unnerve us is dependent
on our individual perspective – fears encapsulated within, our
own to decipher and overcome. There may well be a noumenal,

objective place underneath but as far we know, these features of nature don't name themselves[1] and if they did, whether they could truly be said to be ominous, eerie or weird would be expressed in a language that we do not currently speak.

Far more chilling, therefore, are those places that require us to cross a threshold to enter, arriving in a world that is resolutely not our own to interpret: the human constructions. Locations, not only for the housing of our darkest unconscious, but those of others too . . .

In his Gothic masterpiece *The Fall of the House of Usher*, maestro of the macabre Edgar Allen Poe presents to us a stately building alive with 'eye-like windows',[2] as foreboding as any of its gloomy inhabitants; its manifestation, being also a metaphor for the Usher family line, is so inextricably linked with the 'souls' of the eponymous Madeleine and Roderick Usher that upon their death it is immediately split in two by a great fissure 'extending from the roof of the building, in a zigzag direction, to the base,'[3] before it crumbles to pieces.

Moving from the realms of the weird towards something a little closer to horror, if we travel along Route 39 towards Ashton, turn left on to Route 5, pass the small village of Hillsdale, and up into the high lands beyond, we might, if we are unfortunate enough, find ourselves chancing upon the gates of Hill House. This most unnerving of places marks the main location for Shirley Jackson's chilling classic *The Haunting of Hill House*, often considered one of the finest haunted-house stories ever written.[4] In Jackson's novel, Hill House, scene of a number of troubling deaths throughout its eighty-year existence, becomes the focus for a paranormal investigation led by psychical researcher Dr John Montague. Montague is aided by a group of assistants, selected because of their past paranormal experiences in the hope that they will be especially receptive to anything supernatural. It is primarily through the perspective of Eleanor, one of the assistants, that we become acquainted with a number of increasingly disturbing events that take place. However, as the novel reaches its tragic conclusion we are left to wonder whether anything at all had occurred or if we had merely been witnessing the unravelling of Eleanor's mind. Montague insists, 'the evil is the house itself,'[5] and whether it had been by design or simply the idea of the house's ghoulish history pressing in, something of the building had got inside her head.

A similar theme emerges in many true-life cases of alleged domestic supernatural disturbances, such as those that took place at 30 East Drive in Pontefract, or at number 284 Green Street in Enfield.[6] In these stories we find the recurring notion that any new resident of the property is an invader, occupying a space that isn't theirs to occupy. At times it might seem that, in some way or another, the property itself has developed a spirit all of its own.

For me, although Robert Clatworthy and Joseph Hurley's iconic Bates Mansion[7] as depicted in Alfred Hitchcock's *Psycho* comes a close second, the true house of horror comes complete with its own abattoir, bespoke skin-clad interiors and a fridge stocked with meat; you may recognise it as the family home of Leatherface, disturbingly depicted in Tobe Hooper's mesmerisingly deranged *The Texas Chainsaw Massacre.* Leaving aside the more cerebral interpretations of Hooper's classic (which some have gone as far as to suggest as a metaphor for the cannibalistic tendencies of capitalism), as a visceral experience alone, watching *TTCM* for the first time was to be exposed to a level of horror previously beyond the comprehension of my teenage mind.

What these fictional buildings have in common is a location so inextricably linked to their original occupants, or unsavoury events occurring within, as to be almost inseparable from them. There is the sense that even when empty they have somehow incubated the things that have happened inside. They are places of events so unfathomably monstrous that no level of will can expunge them from the space. Incidentally *Psycho* and *TTCM* were partly based on the life of murderer Ed Gein whose proclivity for manufacturing ornaments and furniture from human bone and skin continues to shock the world more than sixty years later.

After Gein's conviction, it was decided that his house should be torn down. So incapable were the local community of separating the location from the events that had taken place inside, there was no other option but to remove it entirely.

Above all other locations, the hotel emerges as the creepiest of dwellings, both in fact and fiction. Little wonder when you consider the daily comings and goings of hundreds of guests; the many events and bodies criss-crossing through time, a chaotic, psychical intersection, clashing and held together in one singular place.

Some may be familiar with H. H. Holmes and his 'Murder Castle' formerly located on the corner of South Wallace and 63rd near Jackson Park in Chicago. Holmes had begun construction of his two-storey multipurpose building in 1887, home to a variety of commercial properties and private apartments. Five years later, he added a third floor, with the apparent intention of constructing a hotel to take advantage of the many tourists due to visit the city's World's Columbian Exhibition (renamed latterly as the World's Fair). That Holmes was a ruthless serial killer is in little doubt; as to whether he really killed over 200 people, squirrelling their bodies away in secret passages and channels that he had built into his infamous 'hotel' is anyone's guess. Holmes' 'Murder Castle' was mercifully burned down by the man himself in an insurance scam shortly before his capture in 1894 and subsequent execution two years later.

Fans of Stephen King have the Stanley Hotel of Estes Park, Colorado, to thank for inspiring his most iconic location. Situated overlooking Lake Estes in the shadow of the Rockies, it was there in 1974 that King spent a fraught night terrorised by nightmarish visions of his three-year-old son being chased through the hotel's corridors by something dreadful and unseen. As you may have guessed, these night terrors would inspire King to write *The Shining* with the Overlook Hotel replacing those disquieting halls of the Stanley. There will be few who peer down the corridors of King's Overlook who don't feel something of those nightmares that he had experienced back in '74, and who, having done so, will fail to sense something of the strange and eerie in almost any hotel they have stayed in since.

There is one place that, for reasons we will soon explore, holds a special place in the pantheon of hotels with a strange and sinister past. In 2013, this place became host to one of the most disturbing and tragic deaths of recent times; a mystery that remains to this day, unexplained.

Sarah scanned Elisa's Facebook and Twitter pages again. Knowing her sister's avid use of social media, it seemed unusual that she hadn't posted anything in the last twenty-four hours. Meanwhile, David tried Elisa's number one more time as an anxious Yinna watched on. David held the phone to his ear and gazed out of the window as an afternoon sun threatened to break through the clouds, concern rippling across his face when the call once again clicked through to voicemail. Ordinarily it wouldn't be so uncommon that a twenty-one-year-old woman on a solo trip to Los Angeles might forget to call home once in a while, but this was Elisa, and they had an agreement. She could take the trip on one condition: that she called in with her parents every day to let them know she was safe. Besides, Elisa was happy to do it. She knew how difficult the last few years had been on them.

Sarah scrolled through Elisa's pages again. Her last tweet was from 27 January 2013, five days ago, that read 'SPEAKEASY': but that was back in San Diego. Then there were the photos from the zoo, also in San Diego and finally the live recording of a Conan O'Brien show in LA that she had attended two nights back. She seemed to be having a great time. Sarah told her parents not to worry, that it was probably nothing, but suggested they try calling the hotel just in case. What did she say was the place she was staying at again, 'The Stay on Main'? David pulled up the number and called it immediately, relieved to finally have a voice to speak with on the other end of the phone. Sarah and Yinna watched expectantly as David spoke to the front desk. Their relief at the prospect of getting some information soon turned to worry at the look on the father's face as he hung up. Elisa had been due to check out that morning, he explained, only she had never appeared and wasn't in her room. With a new guest set to use it, the hotel would keep her things in the basement until she returned. He shouldn't be too concerned, they'd said, there could be any number of reasons why his daughter wasn't there. David fought to remain optimistic but couldn't shake the gnawing in the pit of his stomach.

Something was wrong.

Friday evenings were one of the busiest at Paul's on Hastings Street, North Burnaby, the Chinese restaurant owned and run by David and Yinna. It was a small but popular place in the quiet Vancouver suburb, recognisable by its large yellow light box at the front. The family had arrived from Hong Kong in 2003 and since then, they and their restaurant had become a much-loved asset to the local community, serving some of the best-value Chinese food that side of Vancouver. On that night of Friday 1 February, however, David and Yinna were finding it increasingly difficult to focus and as the customers continued to arrive their distraction was becoming noticeable. Unable to hold off any longer, the pair decided to make the call. A short time later, David stood in the kitchen waiting to be put through to the Royal Canadian Mounted Police in order to make an official report that his youngest daughter, Elisa Lam, was missing. Though there was some relief to finally have the police involved, it was tempered by the assertion that nothing much could be done until the following morning. That night the Lam family failed to get any sleep as they waited, desperate for any contact from their daughter.

Having made the call on a weekend, it wasn't until Monday that the Los Angeles Police's Missing Persons Unit was alerted to Elisa's disappearance, and not until the following day that a call was put through to Detectives Wallace Tennelle and Greg Stearns of the LAPD's Robberies and Homicides to formally begin the investigation.

The timing could not have been worse. The department would

never want to be seen to prioritise one case over another but it had been understandably distracted. Two days previously, in Orange County, a young woman and her fiancé had been shot in their car after a night out. Such a killing was rare enough, but that the woman, twenty-eight-year-old Monica Quan, happened to be the daughter of former LAPD captain Randal Quan had hit the department hard. When a manifesto claiming responsibility for the crimes appeared online the following day, purportedly written by former LAPD officer Christopher Dorner, all hell broke loose.

Nonetheless, the Lams couldn't have had a better person for the job than Detective Tenelle, a man who knew only too well what they were going through. In 2007 on a mild May evening, Wallace had just wandered out to his garage when a young girl, trembling and with tears in her eyes, approached the house. Wallace recognised her as his neighbour and a friend of his youngest son Bryant. He recognised too the blood-stained cap clutched in her hands, which belonged to Bryant. Wallace learned soon after that his eighteen-year-old son had been shot in the head at point-blank range only blocks away from their home. He died later that night.[8]

Tennelle, a diligent and methodical worker, listens patiently in his Los Angeles office to the Missing Persons officer on the other end of the line in Vancouver, making a note of the important details: age 21, Chinese Canadian, 5ft 4in with long black hair and brown eyes and weighing approximately 115lb, name Elisa Lam. Last known location: Stay on Main hostel on South Main Street, part of the Cecil Hotel building. Tennelle knows it well. It's located on Seventh and Main, Downtown, formerly a major business and financial-district once referred to as the Wall Street of the West, now home to the city's Skid Row neighbourhood, one of the largest stable populations of homeless in the United States. Although there are many who would be quick to portray it as a no-go area for that very reason, that isn't an immediate concern to Tennelle. Yes, there is crime there, much like any other bustling city of the world, but petty theft and drug dealing is one thing: the possible murder of a Canadian tourist, if that is what he is dealing with, is quite another.

In fact, due to a recent relaxing of development laws, the area had been experiencing a quiet upturn in fortunes and had become an increasingly popular location for tourists keen to take advantage of the area's comparatively low rates. As for the Cecil Hotel itself, that remained something of a local oddity, a stubborn but long since faded paean to a distant more glorious past. Hard to imagine it now but the Cecil (pronounced see-sil), built at a cost of $1 million, was once considered one of the more glamorous establishments of the area. Opened in 1925 to great fanfare in all its Beaux-Arts grandeur, the Cecil, comprising 700 rooms across fourteen floors, was opulently decorated throughout with marble and pretty mosaic patterns, its lobby a grand Art Deco fantasy of the finest stained glass and brass.

No more than five years after opening, however, a global depression, triggered by the Wall Street Crash had taken hold. Within ten years, many of the city's banks and businesses would go under, taking with them the vibrant nightlife and movie theatres of Downtown's Broadway district. As the region's wealthier residents flocked to the suburbs in the 40s and 50s, Downtown's bubble had well and truly burst. Over the next fifty years, although you might still find fragments of its former majesty peeking out from under its yellowed and peeling wallpaper, the Cecil eventually became home to a number of transient and low-income residents as its once-pristine façade steadily faded along with its prices. In 2007, however, three floors of the Cecil were given over to a team of designers hoping to captialise on Downtown's recent gentrification. In 2008 the Stay on Main opened its doors for the first time, covering floors four to six of the original building, promising a boutique hotel experience for the cost-conscious traveller. Despite some early teething problems, the Stay on Main had established itself as one of the better low-cost hostels in Los Angeles and it was easy to see why it might have appealed to Elisa. But there was one other thing about the Cecil, something that you wouldn't find on any of the building's hotel listings.

The Cecil Hotel shortly after construction.

Something rather unsavoury.

The first to die was forty-six-year-old W. K. Norton. His body was found in his room in November 1931 after ingesting poison capsules. Next came twenty-five-year-old Benjamin Dodich, found by a maid one morning in September 1932, dead from a self-inflicted gunshot wound to the head, the remnants of which remained stained on the walls for months. Former Army Medical

Corps Sgt. Louis Borden, fifty-three, was found in July 1934. Borden had checked in one evening and proceeded to write suicide notes to various family members before slitting his throat with a razor.

The first of the jumpers was Grace Magro. In March 1937, she dropped from the ninth floor of the hotel, only for her fall to be broken by telephone wires strung across Main Street below. She would later die at a nearby hospital. In January of the following year, marine fireman Roy Thompson had been staying at the hotel for several weeks when maids discovered he hadn't been in his room for days. He was found dead on the skylight of a neighbouring building having presumably leapt from the top floor. Robert Smith and Helen Gurnee jumped from the seventh floor in 1947 and 1954 respectively. Julia Frances Moore did the same from the eighth in 1962. Later that year, police investigated what they assumed to be the double suicide of twenty-seven-year-old Pauline Otton and sixty-five-year-old George Gianinni but later concluded that it was Otton who had leapt from the building and collided into Gianinni on the street below, killing him instantly. In December 1975 a still-unidentified woman is believed to have leapt to her death from a twelfth-floor window

Then there were the other suicides through poison (W. K. Norton's being the first): Navy Officer Erwin Neblett in 1939, and Dorothy Sceiger the year after, both found dead in their rooms by staff. And although there is no putting a grade on such a litany of tragedy, perhaps the most shocking death to occur at the Cecil was that of a newborn baby in 1944. Nineteen-year-old Dorothy Purcell had recently moved in with Cecil resident thirty-eight-year-old Ben Levine when she found herself going into labour. Unaware that she had even been pregnant and not wanting to disturb Levine, she stumbled to the bathroom and almost immediately gave birth to a baby boy. In a state of post-natal shock, Dorothy believed the child to be dead and threw it out of the window.

In the summer of 1964, retired telephone operator and full-time resident of the Cecil, Goldie Osgood, was found raped, stabbed and beaten to death in her room. Her murder remains unsolved to this day. All in all, fourteen deaths by 'unnatural' causes.

That wasn't all.

According to former hotel resident Raoul Enriquez, in late July and August of 1985 when rates had dropped as low as $14 a night, he had lived next to a man on the fourteenth floor who had introduced himself as Richard, saying he was from Ciudad Juarez in Mexico. The man would turn out to be twenty-five-year-old Richard Ramirez who between April 1984 and August 1985 brutally murdered at least sixteen people, raping and mutilating many of his victims before his eventual capture and arrest in 1985. His horrific crimes, often perpetrated after walking into people's homes at random, would land him the nickname The Night Stalker. In 1991, it is thought that Jack Unterweger stayed at the Cecil Hotel over the period of time in which he terrorised, raped and murdered at least three women. Unterweger had previously been convicted for murder in Austria after strangling an eighteen-year-old woman to death in 1974. Whilst in prison, he began to write about his experiences, reflecting on the nature of his crime. His work would earn plaudits from the country's literary elite, with his novel *Purgatory* even becoming a bestseller. By the time of his release in 1990 he was already a national celebrity and widely heralded as a model of rehabilitation. A year later Unterweger was commissioned to write a radio piece about prostitution. It was during a research trip for this piece that he murdered the three women.[9]

Many have suggested that Unterweger elected to stay at the Cecil entirely because of its association with Richard Ramirez, the hotel effectively drawing him in with the screams of its past – a sinister siren call broadcast on only the rarest of frequencies. There are some too who claim it was no accident that Ramirez himself had found his way to the Cecil, nor why so much death and depravity had been concentrated in this forgotten corner of LA. They say there was always something unsettled about the place, something dark and unfathomable that lingered within its many dimly lit corridors. To some it seemed sometimes as though the building itself were alive.

In the early afternoon of 5 February, shortly after getting off the phone with Missing Persons, Detectives Tennelle and Stearns, along with a small team of officers, made the short journey from their offices to the Stay on Main in the Cecil building. As they approached, Tennelle observed the vast building as it came into view, looming hulking and high over the street; it had recently been re-painted in alabaster, the colour of new beginnings; a colour of skin. On the side a large burgundy sign read, 'Cecil Hotel, Low Daily, Weekly Rates'. Tennelle and Stearns pulled up outside and stepped into the cool winter air as thick, dark clouds hung low in the sky above.

Once inside Tennelle and Stearns took a moment to admire the recently refurbished grand foyer, no less spectacular than the day it had opened. You could almost imagine the boisterous guests of eighty years ago sweeping through in sharp suits and party dresses, on their way out to see a show. An image soon punctured by the sign on the wall warning that no visitors were allowed upstairs, and for guests to show keys upon request for their own protection. A few residents shuffled in and out as Tennelle and Stearns snooped around before a member of staff directed them to the Stay on Main reception located next door – as it transpired the main entrance was only used by Stay on Main guests after 11 p.m. A single receptionist manned a bright white and orange desk as Tennelle approached requesting to speak to the manager. A moment later, general manager Amy Price greeted the detectives. After getting confirmation that Elisa had been travelling alone, Tennelle asked Price if she could remember seeing the young woman entering or leaving the hotel with anyone else during her stay? Price confirmed that Elisa had last been seen by a member of staff entering the building, alone, on the afternoon of 31 January.

Price took the men through Elisa's booking history, explaining that she had initially made reservations to stay for three nights, starting on the evening of Monday 28 January, with the intention of checking out on 31 January, but had decided to extend her stay for one more night. Then she mentioned something intriguing; Elisa had originally booked into room 506b, a six-bed shared dorm, but had later been moved to a private room after some of Elisa's roommates had made complaints about her odd behaviour. The detectives made a note and requested all CCTV footage covering the duration of Elisa's stay to be handed over. Next, the detectives examined the belongings that had been removed from her room. They found a backpack full of clothes as well as a large handbag, an overnight bag full of cosmetics and Elisa's laptop computer, but conspicuously, no mobile phone. Such a collection of items was troubling to Tennelle and Stearns. These weren't ordinarily the type of things you left behind out of choice.

There was one other item amongst Elisa's possessions that the detectives hadn't expected: a small bag of pill bottles. Tennelle didn't recognise all the names but knew enough to understand it was psychiatric medication. Tennelle had an officer bag it all up before they made their way to the fifth floor, led by maintenance worker Santiago Lopez.

Tennelle and Stearns stepped into the quiet of an empty corridor that stretched out in front of them, its walls an oppressive shade of dark brown. Muffled sounds emanated from behind closed doors as the detectives made their way down the hall and deeper into the heart of the building, finally stopping outside room number 511, where Elisa had last stayed.

Inside, it was small and cramped, taken up mostly by a single queen-sized double bed, the orange and white sheets of which clashed garishly with the sky blue walls and umber carpet. A small flat screen bolted to the back wall played soundless scenes of the day's news as Tennelle inspected the tiny en-suite, its shower and lavatory separated only by a flimsy shower curtain. Tennelle listened for a moment as the sound of clanging pipes drifted up from the depths of the building.

Stepping back into the dimly lit corridor, Tennelle noticed the communal bathroom and shower area at the far end of the floor. Lopez confirmed each floor was set up in a similar fashion, with a fire exit at each end allowing access on to the floor from any one of the building's other levels. It became clear to the detectives just how big a task they had on their hands: though the Stay on Main operated independently to the Cecil, any of the main building's temporary or permanent residents technically had access to the Stay on Main's rooms, meaning a full 700 rooms of potential suspects related to Elisa's disappearance.

By early afternoon, with more officers requested to join the search, a command post was set up in the lobby of the main building. Officers were grouped in pairs and instructed to go from room to room, searching for any sign that a body might be hidden inside. Lopez was requested to assist in the opening of doors, along with chief engineer Pedro Tovar, who had worked the hotel for over thirty years. A team of sniffer dogs, who had been given some samples of Elisa's clothing, were also brought in to help.

Back in Vancouver, Elisa's family waited with increasing desperation for any more news. Having learned that afternoon that there was still no sign of Elisa, they decide to fly down to Los Angeles together.

The last floor to be checked was the fifteenth, though as Lopez explained to Tennelle, technically it was actually the fourteenth since the hotel, for superstitious reasons, had no thirteenth floor. Although it was possible to climb to the fifteenth in the lift, it was off limits to guests and residents alike and the doors would not open without a maintenance key. After a sweep with the dogs, nothing of note was found and attention soon turned to the roof. There were four ways to gain access: by one of the three fire escapes that ran the full height of the building, or through the fifteenth floor access door. The fire escapes could be accessed from any floor of the hotel, but Tovar suspected it would be difficult for anyone to get up them without being noticed. As for the access door, not only was it located on the top floor, but it was also kept locked at all times and was linked to the fire alarm system, as Tovar demonstrated when he opened it up for Tennelle and his team.

The detectives let the dog team head out first before following them on to the roof. Tovar pointed out the four large water cisterns raised on a 4 foot-high platform next to the roof entrance. Each of the tanks stood roughly 10 foot high by 6 foot wide and could hold up to 1,000 gallons of water, pumped up from below street level. A small and empty maintenance hut overlooked the tanks.

Tennelle gazed out at the Downtown Los Angeles skyline, rendered even more flat and dull than usual by the low-hanging cloud. Remembering again the pills found in Elisa's room, he wandered across to the edge of the roof and peered over the side, taking in the fourteen-storey drop, then looked back across the empty roof. There was nothing here.

'OK, let's wrap it up,' he said.

The following day, Elisa's parents Yinna and David and sister Sarah flew to LA to assist the police with their enquiries. Needing to widen the search, and with the press beginning to sniff out the story, the LAPD held a press conference. As a host of journalists and photographers assembled outside 100 West First Street, Lieutenant Walter Teague took to the microphone and announced that Elisa Lam, a Canadian citizen who had last been seen at the Cecil Hotel on 31 January was officially missing. As the press shouted out questions, Sarah, Yinna and David, who was barely able to bring his eyes up from the floor, stood in sombre silence behind. A photo of a smiling Elisa in puce-coloured glasses and pink and blue chequered hoodie was displayed prominently on a Community Alert poster to Teague's right, which was soon to be plastered throughout the Downtown area.

For the rest of the day, Tennelle and Stearns took the opportunity to interview the family in the hope of getting a better understanding of Elisa's character. First they wanted to know about the pills they found. In total, among the sinus and pain-relief tablets, the officers had found 70 Lamictal tablets, 20 Seroquel tablets, 124 Effexor XR capsules as well as 57 Bupropion tablets.

As the detectives had suspected, Sarah confirmed that Elisa suffered from depression having been diagnosed with bipolar disorder in her final year of high school, and had taken medication for it ever since. The medication was not insignificant. Lamictal is a brand name of Lamotrigine, an anticonvulsant that prevents the rapid fire of neurons that can lead to epileptic seizures, but is also used to treat bipolar depression by preventing the onset of mania. Seroquel, a brand of Quetiapine, helps manage the balance of dopamine and serotonin levels in the brain. Although both medications are fairly common in the treatment of bipolar, they are not without potentially harmful side effects. Lamotrigine can lead to blurring of vision, loss of balance and memory loss, and Quetiapine can often cause a hellish combination of insomnia and fatigue, although Elisa's prescribed dosage was at the lower end of the scale for this drug. Venlafaxine, the chemical compound of Effexor, is commonly prescribed for sufferers of depression, which like Quetiapine is used to help potentially dangerous chemical imbalances in the brain that can lead to suicidal thoughts. Bupropion was one of the most frequently prescribed anti-depressants in the States.

It was a difficult subject to broach but one that had to be addressed. The detectives enquired if Elisa had ever expressed any suicidal tendencies, but Sarah was adamant she hadn't. It's not uncommon for sufferers of depression to have long periods of lucidity and apparent happiness only to be offset by one event or other that could trigger a dangerous and sometimes irretrievable downward spiral. The detectives wondered whether anything specific might have happened in Elisa's life recently that could have caused such an event? The family weren't entirely sure, but the more they told the detectives, the more tangible their sense of the woman they were searching for became.

Elisa was twelve years old when she arrived in Vancouver with her family in 2003. It hadn't been an easy adjustment for a

young girl to make, coming to a new culture and facing stereo-
typical prejudices. But Elisa was smart, warm and approachable
and despite being a little self-conscious she was outgoing and
always eager to meet new people. At school she was a high
achiever, but as she neared the end of high school, things began
to change. Elisa's parents sensed her listlessness but talking
about it was complicated and nothing they did seemed to help.
A doctor was consulted, prescriptions were written out, and by
the time Elisa was applying for college she was taking medication for depression.

Elisa earned a place to study history at the University of British
Columbia, but by the summer of her third year in 2012 she had
yet to complete a single year of her studies. David and Yinna were
all too aware that she was failing her course, but perhaps they
didn't know how much she appreciated what it took for them to
afford her that opportunity, only for her to be throwing it all away,
and how much that crippled her. Neither did they know about the
anonymous blog and tumblr pages she kept online, headed with
the Chuck Palahniuk quote, 'you're always haunted by the idea
you're wasting your life,' and how isolated her feelings would
often leave her. But Sarah knew, as she now explained to Tennelle.
Elisa wasn't suicidal; like most people she just wanted time to
figure out who she was supposed to be, before the world and all
its potential spiralled away from her.

In August 2012 Elisa was told that she wouldn't be kicked out
of college after all, but was advised to take the year off and return
the following summer to begin again. Slowly she found a renewed
sense of purpose and determined to make the most of her unofficial year out. In October she made enquiries about volunteering
on a farm through the WWOOF organisation, and found the
perfect location in Santa Cruz. She had always wanted to visit LA
and made the plan to stop off there on the way. In November Elisa
suffered a sudden drop in her mood and unbeknownst to her
family, she had written anonymously about suicidal thoughts on
tumblr. However, things had sufficiently lifted by the end of the

month for her to undertake a seemingly much-enjoyed solo trip to Toronto and Ottawa.

Tennelle asked the family about relationships, learning that Elisa had a relatively long-term boyfriend until recently. Although they had broken up shortly before the New Year, she hadn't seemed too upset by it. But perhaps Elisa hadn't shared with anyone how the emotion of the break-up had suddenly caught up with her in the weeks prior to leaving for America. Another area of concern for the detectives was the possibility that Elisa may have come off her drugs, but as Elisa's parents attested, she had always been good at taking her medication and did not seem to suffer any obvious side effects. What's more, the drugs appeared to be working. Prior to the trip, the family had enjoyed a pleasant holiday season together with Elisa appearing in good spirits right up to the time she had left. Having booked the flights in early January, Elisa was looking forward to getting out there, and from what they could tell from her daily calls back home, she had been positively buoyant.

Elisa began what she called her West Coast Tour on 22 January and spent a week in San Diego before she arrived in Los Angeles by train on 28 January. The family didn't know if she had planned to meet up with anyone, but she had definitely been alone when she checked into the Stay on Main. They knew little about her subsequent movements other than the fact she had attended that recording of the Conan O'Brien show on the night of Wednesday 30 January – presumably alone. Every day she had called to speak with David and Yinna, and had sounded happy. Tennelle asked if Elisa had mentioned anything about having to move rooms at the Stay on Main, but it was the first they had heard about it. The detectives thanked the family for their time and reassured them they would do everything they could to find their daughter.

The press conference led to a flood of phone calls and speculative reports of Elisa's whereabouts, but nothing of use turned up until the following day, when Katie Orphan, the manager of The Last

Bookstore, located just a few minutes' walk from the Stay on Main got in contact with the police. Orphan had seen Elisa in the store on the afternoon of 31 January, the day she had last been seen by hotel staff. Orphan even remembered speaking with the young woman, who had dropped in to buy presents for her family around about noon, which put her whereabouts at least in the vicinity of the hotel prior to returning there later that afternoon. Most significantly, Orphan remembered that Elisa was not only alone, but that she was outgoing, friendly and completely lucid.

Then, after days trawling through over 800 hours of CCTV footage taken from inside the hotel and surrounding ATMs, the tech team finally made a breakthrough, picking Elisa up on security footage recorded from inside the lobby of the Stay on Main on the afternoon of the 31st. The first piece of footage showed Elisa engaged in a short and seemingly innocuous conversation with two men who appeared to hand her a small box before they left the hotel with Elisa heading off alone in the other direction towards the lift and presumably back to her room. Hoping they finally had a suspect, Tenelle and Stearns, having been called in to watch the footage, were disappointed to learn soon after that neither of the men were picked up again entering or exiting the building. But that wasn't the footage the team wanted them to see. The footage the team really needed them to watch was something altogether different.

They loaded up the next clip and hit play.

This footage had been recorded in one of the hotel's lifts later that evening. Tennelle and Stearns moved in closer to the screen as a silent colour shot flickered up on the monitor of an empty lift. The car then begins to move up through the levels until stopping at the fourteenth floor, or what would have been the thirteenth if it wasn't for the superstitious contractors. A short time later the lift doors open to reveal an empty corridor from which a young woman, matching Elisa's description, enters the lift from the left-hand side. The woman, wearing a burgundy hooded sweater, black shorts and sandals turns immediately to the control panel, bends in close to the buttons and bizarrely presses the entire middle row, lighting up floors 10, 7, 4, Mezzanine level, the Basement and one further button below. Having pressed the buttons, the woman steps back into the corner of the lift and stares out vacantly past the open door with her hands dangling by her side. But the doors don't close. Then something even more unexpected happens. The woman takes a step towards the open door, slides herself forward on one leg before sticking her head out and hurriedly looking both ways down the corridor, before stepping back into the car and retreating further into the near corner, as if she is hiding from somebody.

A moment later the woman steps again into the open doorway and this time takes a small jump into the empty corridor as if trying to catch someone out. Again, there is nobody waiting outside the lift. All the while, the doors remain open, refusing to shut. As Tennelle and Stearns struggle to comprehend what it is they are looking at, the footage gets increasingly strange. Now standing outside the lift, the woman brings her arms above her head before walking back into the lift, her movements suddenly languid and off-balance. She turns back to the control panel and once again presses the same middle row of buttons, going back over each a number of times before stepping again into the empty corridor beyond. As she waits for a moment she turns to the right and for a brief second it appears she is speaking to someone; but still there is nobody there.

Tennelle and Stearns watch transfixed as the woman makes a peculiar dance of hand gestures. At one point, after she holds her hands out to the unseen 'presence', she begins to move them speculatively in front of her as if she were fumbling her way across a dark room, before suddenly grabbing at her fingers, twisting them as if wringing out a damp cloth. After a few more seconds the woman finally spins to the left and walks away from the lift. Tennelle keeps his eyes locked on the corridor beyond the unmoving lift door, waiting for a glimpse of whomever she had been speaking to, but nobody comes. As the time-code continues running, the doors close softly and the deserted lift begins to move, slowly making its way through each of the different floors that the woman had selected.

The footage was taken a matter of hours after an 'outgoing, friendly and lucid' Elisa had been spoken to by bookshop manager Katy Orphan. But that isn't all. With no subsequent footage found of Elisa leaving the building, Tennelle and Stearns can only assume, whether she is alive or dead, that she is still somewhere inside the hotel.

On the morning of 19 February, Sabrina Baugh, who was staying at the Cecil Hotel with her husband Michael, had some trouble getting their shower to work. Unable to get more than a dribble from the showerhead, she turned it off and tried the sink instead, hoping to at least get her teeth cleaned. With just enough water to work with she held the toothbrush under the tap then applied the toothpaste and brought the brush to her mouth only to immediately spit the water out in disgust. It was putrid. By the time she made it down to reception to complain, maintenance worker Santiago Lopez was already investigating the third such complaint of that morning. Over in the bathroom of room 720, he lifted the single faucet lever and watched with revulsion as discoloured water trickled into the white ceramic basin below.

A few minutes later, after taking the lift to the fifteenth floor, Santiago made his way towards the roof. Having disabled the alarm and unlocked the access door, he pushed it open and stepped out into the cool air. With the sounds of the morning traffic rising up from the streets below, Santiago climbed up the steps leading to the cistern platform and squeezed through to the main tank at the back. Taking a small wooden ladder tucked in behind, he leaned it against the tank and started to climb.

The cisterns were completely covered by heavy metal lids, each with an 18-inch by 18-inch access hatch cut into them. Ordinarily these hatches were left shut, but as Lopez neared the top of the ladder he was surprised to find this one was open.

And there was something floating inside the tank.

He pulled himself over the hatch to get a closer look and recoiled in horror.

At 13:10 Detective Tennelle received a call from Lt. Cheryl MacWillie to let him know that a body had been found on the roof of the Cecil Hotel, the same roof they had searched just over ten days previously. He arrived half an hour later and was led up to the fifteenth floor by LAPD Patrol Officer Sanchez who had been first on the scene. Stepping out on to the roof under a light drizzle Tennelle made his way up to the platform and to the top of the main water tank. Moments later he was staring down through the hatch at the naked floating body of a young female of Chinese descent; her long black hair, stretched out behind her head, waving gently in the dark water below. A marbling of livor mortis covered the abdomen, and much of the body had turned a pale green in colour. Despite significant decomposition and skin slippage, Tennelle recognised the face immediately as Elisa Lam's.

For the next two hours news helicopters circled overhead as LA Fire Department #9 worked to extricate the body from the cistern. Unable to lift it out of the small access hatch, the fire crew were forced to drain the tank before cutting a large hole out of the side of it. The body was finally pulled free shortly before four o'clock in the afternoon. With a light rain continuing to fall, the body was carefully laid out under a forensic tent and inspected momentarily by Tennelle and Stearns before it was placed in a black bag and taken to the Department of Coroner. With the body removed, fire crew also discovered inside the tank Elisa's room key and her watch as well as a pair of black shorts, a green shirt, underwear, a red American Apparel hoodie and a pair of black polka dot sandals. They were the exact same clothes the woman was wearing in the lift footage from 31 January. Elisa's devastated family were informed of the discovery only moments before images of their daughter's body being taken from the water tank were played out live and nationwide on the news.

For Tennelle and Stearns, although never wanting to presume anything, given the circumstances it seemed likely that Elisa had been murdered and placed inside the water tank. An assessment of the scene was quickly initiated with Tennelle ordering a dusting of the area for prints and anything that could contain DNA. Attention soon turned to theorising how Elisa could have found her way on to the roof in the first place. It was unlikely that she had been carried up via one of the three fire escapes since all required scaling a vertical ladder up the side of the building before squeezing through a small square hole at the top. Such a feat would require an inordinate amount of strength. However, the only other option was through the roof access door, but as maintenance chief Pedro Tovar again insisted, the door was locked and alarmed at all times. Perhaps Elisa had been murdered elsewhere and brought on to the roof by a member of staff, or at least someone who was able to get hold of the requisite access keys? Or perhaps instead, Elisa had accompanied somebody willingly to the roof either through the door or up the fire escape? Or could she in fact have been followed on to the roof by the perpetrator, or perpetrators even? Such immediate assessments are hard to resist but for the diligent and methodical Tennelle, who was more than aware of any number of possibilities, such hypotheticals were pointless. All that mattered were the facts and right then they had very little to go on. He also knew only too well that with Elisa's body likely to have been lying in the tank for over two weeks, and with no CCTV footage covering the roof, any vital evidence to the crime would have long since been washed or blown away.

Elisa's body arrived at the Hertzberg-Davis Forensic Science Center shortly after 2 p.m. The building, perched just above Route 10 on the eastern fringes of Los Angeles, stands out monolithic and pristine against a surrounding backdrop of soft rolling hills topped with desert shrubs and colourful suburban villas. However, few motorists who passed the centre daily on their regular commutes recognised the squat five-storey building as one of the leading forensic science centres in the world. That afternoon, in one of its newly constructed labs, Elisa's body was carefully laid out on a service table by medical examiner Dr Yulai Wang and his associate, Dr Jason Tovar. Around 17:30 Senior Criminalist Mark Schuchardt diligently took snippets of fingernail, hair and pubic hair from the body as well as a number of swabs before bagging it all up along with Elisa's clothes for further analysis. The tests would help to determine whether Elisa had suffered any kind of physical or sexual assault before her death.

Two days later, Wang and Tovar conducted the autopsy in anticipation of finally discovering a cause of death, as detectives Tennelle and Stearns looked on. Incredibly, after three hours of procedure, the examiners were unable to determine it, finding no evidence of trauma whatsoever. No bones were broken and there were no abrasions or bruises in evidence on the skin; nothing was found to be obstructing the body's airways. Inside the stomach they discovered the remains of tablets and capsules suggesting that Elisa had been taking at least some of her medication shortly before her death. When Dr Wang investigated the chest and abdominal cavity region he found the lungs to be filled with water, suggesting that Elisa had been alive when she entered the cistern. With no clear cause of death, Dr Tovar had no choice but to mark it down as 'undetermined'. Frustrated by the findings of the autopsy, Tennelle and Stearns, not to mention Elisa's devastated family who had travelled down to retrieve their daughter's body, are left waiting on the toxicology report.

Both Santiago Lopez and Pedro Tovar were spoken to by the detectives but promptly discredited as suspects, and with no DNA or fingerprint evidence to suggest the involvement of unknown persons the detectives remained stumped as to how Elisa could possibly have got inside the tank. When the toxicology results finally came back they revealed no evidence of intoxication save for the smallest trace of alcohol, along with traces of Venlafaxine and Lamotrigine. Having analysed the results of Mark Schuchardt's swabs and clippings they also determined that Elisa had not been the victim of a sexual assault. After a further month of investigations, the detectives were left with only one explanation: that Elisa, who the police knew to have a history of mental health complications, had climbed into the tank herself. On 19 June Dr Wang and Dr Tovar, in agreement with Detectives Tennelle and Stearns, and ultimately Los Angeles coroner Lt. Fred Corral, ruled Elisa's death to be caused by accidental drowning, with her bipolar disorder considered a significant contributing factor.

In a final peculiar coincidence to the case, a few days after Elisa's body was discovered, Los Angeles County health officials are alerted to a serious outbreak of tuberculosis among the homeless population of Skid Row just minutes from the Cecil Hotel. Health workers eventually called on federal assistance from the Centers for Disease Control and Prevention in order to stem the outbreak. The causative agent of TB is a bacteria known as *mycobacterium tuberculosis* with the most common strain found in America being the type 4 Latin American–Mediterranean strand, or LAM for short. One popular and frequently used technique to detect the presence of antigens in the body (a substance that causes the immune system to produce antibodies) is known as an enzyme-linked immunosorbent assay, or ELISA for short.

The test kit, specific to the type 4 strain of TB found in Downtown LA around the time of Elisa Lam's death, is known as the LAM-ELISA.

Inevitably, due to the mysterious nature of Elisa Lam's death, it has been pored over endlessly by Internet sleuths keen to offer all manner of theories as to how she died. Such attention was due in no small part to the questionable decision to release the peculiar footage taken from inside the Cecil's lift. Within hours the clip was a creepy online sensation, going viral across the globe. In China alone, after being shared on the video-hosting site Youku, it was watched 3 million times, racking up 40,000 comments in a week. Never had an ongoing investigation sparked the public imagination in quite this way, and it wasn't long before the hotel's troubled past was unearthed.

Reports emerged of strange activity said to have been occurring there for years. One woman claimed that her father who had lived at the hotel in the 1960s had woken in the night with the sensation of being choked.[10] Former staff claimed guests staying on the fifteenth floor, in the room in which Goldie Osgood was murdered in 1964, often complained of similar experiences. One couple had apparently checked into a room on the eleventh floor only to find it in a state of complete disarray with a woman in a white dress already staying in it.[11] After complaining to the front desk they were led back to the room only to find it in perfect order, ready for their arrival, and the woman nowhere to be seen. In 2014 a young resident of Riverside County apparently photographed a ghostly apparition that appeared outside a window on the fourth floor.[12]

Numerous vloggers and paranormal investigators have also visited the Cecil in recent years, hoping to capture evidence of its apparent inner darkness. Some have pointed out that the fourteenth floor, where Elisa had stepped into the lift and was seen apparently conversing with someone, was the floor on which Richard Ramirez had once stayed. The inference being that maybe something of Ramirez still haunted the hotel's many narrow corridors and had contributed to the young woman's death (presumably those making such claims were unaware that Ramirez died five months after Lam's body was found).

Whether or not a full account of the investigation into the Lam case is made public, it will remain intricately linked to the building in which it occurred. What is particularly interesting, though, in the absence of this, is how easily we seem drawn not to those present in the hotel at the time, but to those who are no longer there; we seem unable to shake the sense that somehow something of all that had happened previously within its walls was responsible for the horrifying event. Similarly, what spooked and inspired Stephen King so much during that terrifying night at the Stanley Hotel, had nothing to do with what was present during his stay; it was because he and his wife Tabby were the only guests.[13] With the place due to close for the winter, the building was almost completely deserted. That evening, when King had wandered the empty corridors and lifeless dining rooms, ringing with the silence of people's pasts, something in the emptiness had bled into his mind.

In classical mythology everything from rivers and valleys to the forests and mountains could be home to unnamed spirits that would have to be placated with shrines and offerings in order to bring good fortune. The Ancient Romans termed these spirits *genii loci*, or spirits of place. Today the term, unmoored from its theistic connotations has come to signify something more abstract, described by writer John Reppion as the 'echoes of people, of events, of ideas which have become imprinted upon a location for better or worse ... the disquieting atmosphere of a former battlefield, the comfort and familiarity of a childhood home.'[14] Nowhere are these spirits more noticeable than in ruined and abandoned urban archaeology.

In Nikolaus Geyrhalter's hypnotic 2016 documentary, *Homo Sapiens*, the filmmaker presents us with a series of long, locked-off shots of nothing but abandoned buildings and empty human-scarred landscapes, accompanied only by atmospheric sound; flies buzzing round a long-disconnected vending machine, standing solitary in a wilderness of ferns; the interior of a crumbling snow-covered theatre, the ice-melt from the rafters dripping steadily into muddy puddles below; a deserted hospital ward with beds placed at odd angles and the wind, entering through an open window, blowing sheets of plastic about the floor. It is utterly captivating. Ruins of antiquity are not without their charm but there is something especially evocative about this more recently abandoned detritus of human existence, mesmerising in its sense of being both familiar and modern yet distant and strange. I have always been fascinated by such places.

At first there is something profoundly unsettling about old and decaying structures, and how the un-human elements of the natural world claim them with such utter disinterest. What unsettles is their temporality; they present as manifestations of passing time holding us between life and death, confronting us with the inevitability of our own obsolescence.[15] There is the distinct impression of looking at ancient artefacts from a once great but lost alien civilisation only to realise with Ozymandian horror that that civilisation is us. To observe these places is to be left with the uncanny sense of being haunted by our future mortality through echoes of the past.

Tim Edensor, a reader in Cultural Geography at Manchester Metropolitan University who has written extensively on the evocative power of ruins, points out that the 18th-century fashion for depicting ruins in art and the construction of follies – grand ornamental buildings with no purpose other than to stir the spirit – was 'allied to a sense of melancholia which saw ruins as ... symbolic of the inevitability of life passing.'[16] These ventures were also heavily emblematic of the sublime in their attempts to conjure a sense of 'magical forces that remain unseen'.[17]

But for Edensor, and myself, however, it is something a little closer that grips. Whilst researching this book I visited some of the most entrancing abandoned places I have seen in the British Isles. From the eerily deserted airbase at RAF Rendlesham and the magnificent desolation of Orford Ness, to the interstitial scrublands of Middlesbrough's industrial past where I walked along the train line from the site of Heinrich Richter's plane crash, past the towering structures of the vacant Dorman Long steelworks, to the Grangetown signal box where Carl Edon was so tragically murdered. In each of these places I was spellbound by the magnetic presence of absence.

Like every deserted office, disused theatre or empty hotel lobby, all these places tell a story, confronting us with 'weird vestiges of the past, unfathomable artefacts, cryptic signs, [and] unfamiliar textures'[18] that we can't help but try and piece together. And once we see beyond the obsolescence, something else begins to emerge: ghosts.

This is true for any site of past human activity but the ones that are constructed by humans are especially evocative because they are so often of a language that we understand. As Edensor notes, these places are full of 'signs of the past' that can be 'intuitively grasped', even if their 'significance ... [is] ... ultimately evasive and elusive'.[19] As we intuit its previous use, like a projector our minds will conjure the past back into the space – we sense the ghostly movements of 'absent presences'[20] across a factory floor or walking down a hotel corridor, feel the soft feet and flow of long-vanished revellers as we step across a disused ballroom, because they are the lines we all trace.

Whether you believe in autonomous ghosts and spirits or not, it is difficult not to at least think of the spectral echoes of those whose pasts we retrace as we move through the spaces we share. As such, paradoxically, it isn't necessarily the presence of the spirits of place that haunt us, but their absence, and as long as we have the clues with which to construct them, ghosts will always be ready, just waiting to emerge.

Chapter Eight

INTO THE BADLANDS

'. . . (people) with minds sensitive to hereditary impulse will always tremble at the thought of the hidden and fathomless worlds of strange life which may pulsate in the gulfs beyond the stars, or press hideously upon our own globe in unholy dimensions which only the dead and the moonstruck can glimpse.'

H. P. Lovecraft – 'Supernatural Horror in Literature'

Many of us are terrified of the thought that we are ultimately alone. Not in the metaphorical sense, but rather, literally, that we and our fellow creatures of Earth might exist as the sole sentient beings in the universe, with no reason or ultimate purpose for ever having existed in the first place. Perhaps it is to counter this fear that we share tales of other creatures and other worlds, to serve not only as metaphors to better understand and order ourselves but so that, in some ways, we might feel less alone. From ancient tales of omnipotent and eternal deities to hidden folkloric fairy worlds, to the wildest speculations of intergalactic and inter-dimensional travel, we seem always to be conceiving new ways to incorporate the possible existence of life beyond the world we know. Even the subconscious spaces of our dreams have been considered potential locations for beings as real as any we might find in the conscious realm. (Or at least try telling an eleven-year-old who just watched *A Nightmare on Elm Street* for the first time that such beings aren't possible.)[1]

For others, it is precisely the possibility of what we might find in these places that scares them the most. Who could blame them, considering how many of these tales end in disaster. From the terror of Ridley Scott's *Alien* where all but one of an entire space-flight crew are wiped out by a previously unknown organism, to the damningly self-reflexive satire of *Gulliver's Travels* (travels which leave the eponymous Gulliver so appalled by humanity he becomes a recluse), such stories seem designed to prevent us from exploring the unknown. They are handed down as hard-earned truths, a warning to anyone foolish enough to venture beyond the comfort of their known environment; if it doesn't kill you, at the very least you run the risk of discovering something about your-self you don't want to know. As a species not only have we proven deaf to such warnings, we seem almost pathologically predis-posed to ignore them. Far easier was it for the British nation to celebrate the achievements of Captain James Cook, for example, than to dwell on the fact he was murdered at the hands of the distant 'savages' he had 'discovered';[2] even less so to interrogate the possible truth of what Mark Twain described as his 'justifiable homicide'.[3] When we look at such tales from the point of view of those on the receiving end of efforts to colonise 'distant' and 'exotic' lands, the business of exploration starts to look very messy indeed. Either way, we carry on regardless.

We might argue that this yearning to illuminate the darkest unknown corners is driven by survival instincts (we search to understand what, 'out there', could be a threat to us), or through the simple impulse to find new and better places to exist. Perhaps it is a Freudian, unconscious desire to name and conquer that ultimately drives us. Or more simply it's the selfish pursuit of personal gain. Yet when we look at the incredible achievements of our species' most eminent adventurers, such as Abu Bakr II, ruler of a huge West African empire considered by some to have been the largest and wealthiest ever, who in 1311 is alleged to have given it all up in search of what lay on the other side of the Atlantic,[4] or the indomitable Jeanne Baret, who in 1775 – after disguising herself as a man – became the first woman to circum-navigate the globe, it is possible to discern a different driving force. Look past the cynical political motivations of the Apollo 11 moon landing, and you see it there in the engine fire of a Saturn V rocket; it propels NASA's *Voyager 1* space probe beyond the heliosphere towards interstellar space, blows the sails of Charles Darwin's HMS *Beagle*, and fixes together the nuts and bolts of the Hubble telescope that enable us to peer ever deeper into the furthest reaches of the universe: the irrepressible force of human curiosity.

It's this adventurous spirit that fuels the search for other kinds of truth, set apart from the pursuit of the hard sciences. We find it in the ever-seductive lure of the occult and the Gnostic philosophies; the powerful idea that beyond the realities we can comprehend lie other, more majestic, places waiting to be discovered if only we had the requisite knowledge and tools to get there.[5] For these alternative truth-seekers and transcendent philosophers, what satisfaction is to be found in the 'mundane' worlds of fields and sub-atomic matter, when there are far deeper, hidden geometries to explore, buried within the fog that clouds human perception?

Doubtless, there is a strange comfort in contemplating things beyond our everyday practical experiences; furthermore, it is through the potential of the unknown and the unseen that many of our wildest ideas are given birth; thoughts on consciousness, eschatology and the very nature of reality. But might we have forgotten something in all this? For what if those tales we tell of other worlds and other creatures weren't just stories and we aren't, in fact, alone? What if it isn't only our species who are doing the exploring?

Gwen gazes longingly at the vast blue sky as Terry turns their battered old pick-up off the Ar88 Fort Duchesne. It's the summer of 1994 and the Shermans are travelling through a northern stretch of the Uintah Basin in the north-east corner of what is commonly known as the American state of Utah. This part of the basin, which stretches out for hundreds of miles to the south, forms a clash of desert and rich pastures fed by the Uintah River and nearby Bottle Creek Reservoir; it is a stark landscape marked by rare pockets of oases in otherwise desolate swathes of rock and dust. Some might call it the Badlands, but to others it's plain old cowboy country, and everything that Gwen and Terry are looking for.

The truck kicks up dust as they make their way deeper into the plains, hemmed in on their right by a 200 foot-high mesa ridge of red dust and sandstone – one of those otherworldly structures you might think had more in common with Mars than planet Earth – while to their left a pale scrubland speckled with milky green sagebrush and spindly Russian olives stretches out to the horizon. All is framed by the widest, bluest sky you could possibly imagine. Such places have a magical quality, a hidden history that lies compressed and fossilised underground and painted on to the rocks at the back of darkened caves. It rings with a silence, but it is not the silence of emptiness. It is the silence of absence; the silence that remains when so many things have been and gone. Of course, the state hasn't always been called Utah; nor indeed has it always been a state. The vast ranges to the north haven't always been named the Uinta Mountains, and this desert basin hasn't always been desert . . .

Roughly 20,000 years ago a community of bipedal, bare-skinned creatures first ventured forth towards present-day North America, walking from lands of ice and snow to the northwest across a land bridge newly emerged from the depths of once impassable waters. Confronted by walls of ice and inhospitable terrain, the intrepid pioneers were forced to remain on that bridge for thousands of years, before a thawing of the surrounding glaciers and perma-frost brought new routes for them to explore. In their isolation they had been changing deep within their blood. When they finally move on to greener pastures to the south, they emerge new and distinct from the people they had been before. These people, whose names have long since been lost, are thought to be the first human inhabitants of what we now call Utah, arriving there some 13,000 years ago.

Forming small communities these people drift with the seasons, eating cattails and sedge and crafting nets for the creatures that swim and fly. They hunt with spear points made from bone and stone, delicately fluted on both sides. Just like the world of those who came before them, theirs is tuned to the cycles of the golden orb of day and the white disc of night. Eventually they make it as far as the stretch of land Gwen and Terry are driving through, perhaps sheltering under the ridge to their right or tracking animals in the scrubland to the left. Three and a half million curves of the golden orb later, however, the surrounding waters rise and flood the basin, forcing these ancient people from the land where they will be lost to the mists of time. A thousand years later, a shift has taken place and a new people arrive from the southwest with bows and arrows to complement the spear. Although some are nomadic, others prefer a more stationary life, growing and harvesting crops. They wear shoes made from deer hide, make pottery and weave baskets, and paint detailed pictorials of creatures both strange and familiar on to the rocks of their homes. Just 700 years later, a great drought forces them, too, from the land.

It's not long before yet another group of biped creatures arrive, this time bringing a name: Nūche, which translates in English as 'the people'. The Nūche eventually stretch out across 225,000 square miles of the surrounding deserts and prairies, building tipis and wickiups from piñon and juniper branches. To the Nūche, the land is a place of great power, a place revealed in dreams and made manifest by their creator Sinawav, encompassing the upper earth of mountains, a middle earth of foothills, the lower earth of the canyons and the underworld, where the light-giving orb in the sky they call *tavaci* rests at night. It is a land peppered with *puwá-v*: power points where tribal medicine men channel sacred forces. It is also a world populated by the *Mokwič*: the dead. The Nūche never venture into the places of the *Mokwič*, who are said to roam the abandoned homes of those who had come before, manifested in the many spiders and cobwebs that are found in such places.

The Nūche occupy the land for many cycles of the *tavaci*, living out a mostly peaceful existence in harmony with the elements of their world, taking only what they need and fighting only to defend the territory that is crucial to their survival. Unbeknownst to the Nūche, however, there is another world that occupies the exact same space as theirs, and it is beginning to press in on them.

Some Nūche have already heard of this other world, populated by people similar in some ways but different in others. As they discover, it is a place made not by Sinawav but by God Almighty, where time is different and the Nūche are instead called Yuta. In this other world it is the year 1620, the same number of years since a man called Christ was sent to Earth to die for everybody's sins. Early exchanges with the other world's people bring occasional riches, such as the majestic and powerful horses that will later serve to strengthen their communities. There are new ideas that help them make better sense of their own world, discovering, for example, that the golden orb in the sky is not moving into darkness each night, but rather it is they who are travelling around it. Sometimes those from the other world will make raids into Nūche communities and steal their people away to be reared as slaves.

More and more this new world presses in on that of the Nūche, until it has superseded it altogether, and they have little option but to leave their world behind. By this new world's year of 1864, the land occupied by the Nūche, now referred to as Ute by the others, has been declared 'owned' by the United States of America. An agreement is reached to establish a small area of territory for the Nūche, along with other tribes such as the Uncompahgre, Yampa and White River to call theirs. For fifteen years, they are rounded up and escorted into this designated area known as the Uintah and Ouray reservation. No longer free to move with the seasons, the tribe's people struggle to adapt to their zone, an area that is largely dry and poor for hunting. When asphaltum is discovered within this territory it transpires that the 1864 agreement is not quite as resolute as it had first seemed and 7,000 acres are quickly reclaimed by the US government for the mining industry. By 1905 the reservation has diminished to a quarter of its initial size.

Terry brings the truck to a halt having finally reached their destination, a 480-acre stretch of ranch land lying deep within the Uintah and Ouray reservation. Up ahead lies the Myers Ranch house, peeking out from under a row of grand cottonwoods. Although it is true that the ranch occupies land once promised as part of the original reservation, some claim the Nūche were only too happy to be rid of it. It is said that something peculiar stalks these pastures, something not recorded in any of the history books, and the Nūche are terrified of it.

A deep yellow sun hangs in the sky as the Shermans step from the cool of their truck into the dry summer heat before making their way towards the house. Terry runs a hand through his hair before replacing his cap, trying his best not to look too excited as the estate agent approaches.

The building, perched at the base of the mesa ridge and backed by a wide irrigation canal, is a modest-sized bungalow in need of some care and attention. Inside, wallpaper – not changed since the 70s – peels from the walls and ceiling whilst bags of rubbish are strewn throughout. As the Shermans make their way through the rooms, it's difficult for them not to think of the previous owner, living out there all on her own. There's something off about the place that Gwen can't quite put her finger on, but then she realises: every internal door appears to have a deadbolt lock drilled on to it, inside and out, and all the windows, too. Gwen is nudging one of the locks shut when Terry calls to her from outside. She steps out the door to find him holding a heavy chain in his hands that has been bolted securely to the front of the house.

'Must have been some dog,' says Terry.

'I guess so,' Gwen replies, before losing her thoughts in the breathtaking view.

From here, she can see the full acreage of grassy paddocks and scrublands to the south and west, cut through by Dry Gulch Creek and bordered to the north by the irrigation canal and sandstone ridge that run in tandem to the far western border. As she takes it all in, it feels as if they have lived there their whole lives.

Later, after taking a walk through the fields, Gwen and Terry stumble upon the old homestead, a dilapidated stucco cabin built in the early 1900s but now warped and rotted after years under the baking desert sun. How uncanny it looks, almost as if it were still inhabited, with its rusted drainpipe chimney still intact and sticking out through the roof; its brown floral-patterned floor inside just visible under a thick carpet of dead leaves. Spiders and cobwebs cling to every corner. Walking back to the house, Terry notices something peculiar hidden underneath the thick, dry grass: a circular indentation roughly a metre wide and at least a foot deep in the ground. Even stranger is that the soil underneath seems compacted, as if whatever had made the marking hadn't dug the soil out of the ground but had compressed it into the earth.

It's a grey, overcast day when the Shermans return later in the autumn, the proud new owners of the ranch, arriving with all their worldly goods on two heavily laden trucks. With the help of Terry's father Attison, Gwen and Terry's eleven-year-old son T and nine-year-old daughter K lead the way, picking out the pieces from the top of the truck and handing them down to the grown-ups. Terry is just returning for another load when he notices his son staring at something across the pasture picking its way through the field and heading straight towards them.

'What is that, coyote?' asks Gwen having clocked it too.

'Too big,' says Terry, not taking his eyes from the animal.

The family watch as the creature draws near until they can make out its silver-grey fur as the unmistakable hide of a wolf. Gwen looks anxiously towards the kids who remain, mesmerised, in silence.

Terry takes a step forward, scanning the distance behind for any sign of a pack, then looks nervously towards the corral, seeing that one of the three calves that had newly arrived that morning, sensing a shift in the air, has wandered up to the fence and stuck its head enquiringly between the bars. All the while the wolf trots closer and closer, its head bobbing beneath its shoulders until it's barely ten yards away. At least it looks like a wolf, thinks Terry, even if it is twice the size of any that he has ever seen before. Stranger yet is the pale blue electricity of its eyes. A crossbreed perhaps, he wonders.

The creature keeps coming until it's at Attison's legs, close enough for the old man to run his hand through the thick, wet fur.

'Must have come from the reservation,' he says to the others.

The wolf arches its back under Attison's hand, and brushes against his legs with all the playfulness of an old family dog. Gwen waves for the kids to come down from the truck and join in.

'Can we keep it?' asks K.

Before Terry can respond, the wolf is already in motion, heading straight for the corral. A moment later the six-month-old Angus calf is squealing in agony, its snout caught inside the wolf's jaws.

Gwen backs the children away, as Attison pulls a baseball bat from the truck, bringing it down hard on to the wolf's back as Terry tries his best to kick it free from the calf.

'Get the magnum,' screams Terry.

T leaps on to the truck, pulls the magnum from its holster and runs it over to his father. Yelling for his son and Attison to step away, Terry checks the barrel before snapping it back into place and squeezing the trigger. The shot thunders into the animal.

But the wolf doesn't back down.

Gwen does her best to shield K's eyes as Terry takes another step closer and fires a second slug into the wolf's chest but again there's nothing, not even a whimper. The exhausted calf sinks to the ground, its wide eyes rolling back in terror as it waits for death. Terry shoots again seeing the bullet clearly thud into the wolf's stomach this time. Finally, it releases the prey and stumbles back a few yards. The calf collapses backwards, panting heavily as blood pours from his nose. The next bullet enters around the heart. The wolf stands unmoved for one more beat, fixing Terry with its eyes before finally pulling away.

'Fetch the rifle,' says Terry calmly.

T runs into the house, watched closely by Gwen, holding her daughter tight as she cries into her mother's stomach. Seconds later, T returns delivering the .30-06 sniper rifle to Terry. With the wolf now thirty yards away, Terry raises the gun to his eye and pulls the trigger. They all gasp as the bullet rips through the body – but the wolf remains still, staring Terry down with its electric blue eyes.

Terry fires again. This time the bullet visibly tears flesh and fur from the creature's chest. Without as much as a whimper, the wolf eyes the calf one last time before finally turning away and heading off back in the direction from which it had come. Attison, in a state of disbelief, wanders towards the piece of flesh torn off by the bullet. When he bends down to pick it up, he recoils in disgust. The meat is putrid and riddled with the stench of decay. Terry will later attempt to track the wolf and kill it once and for all, following its clear set of footprints for over a mile into the bush before they inexplicably disappear from the land.

That was day one.

For the next few months the Shermans continue to spot a number of large creatures that seem almost to be stalking them from the edges of their fields. Once, Gwen had just got back into her car after closing the entrance gate on her way back from work, when she noticed a shadow fall across the dashboard. Turning to look out the window, she was startled to see a large pair of eyes, more black than pale blue, staring back at her, belonging to what she could only assume was another wolf; it was almost as tall as the car.

Concerned for the rest of their livestock due to arrive in a matter of weeks, the family had no choice but to bring the matter up with the local tribal office. The following day, Gwen made the short trip to the reservation offices located in nearby Fort Duchesne. She requested to speak to someone about the wolves running wild on her land only to be met with a bemused silence. An official politely informed Gwen that there were no such animals anywhere on the reservation. Not only would they not be kept as pets, but wolves had not been indigenous to the region since the 1930s when they had been slaughtered as part of a national extermination campaign.

The Shermans' cattle arrived in mid-November: forty-odd black Simmental heifers along with four prize bulls. The family are also joined by three blue heelers – expert cattle-herding dogs. A short time later Terry and Gwen's nephew D came to stay with the family. Early in the visit, Terry and his son took D with them on an evening check for stray cows when Terry spotted a set of headlights from a truck parked up about half a mile to the west. Assuming they were trespassers, the three of them set off towards the vehicle, but as they drew nearer it started to move away. As Terry broke into a jog to keep up he realised something strange. Any ordinary truck would have been bumping up and down over the rugged terrain flashing its beams of light every-where, and yet the lights on this vehicle were perfectly set. Eventually, with no place to go, the vehicle came to a stop oppo-site a thick clump of trees bordering the western edge of the ranch. While Terry, T and D took a moment to catch their breath, something extraordinary happened. The vehicle, which they could now see was cuboid and no longer than five feet in length, appeared to lift straight up from the ground. Moments later it cleared the tallest of the cottonwoods, flashing red and white lights underneath as it turned smoothly and silently before flying off into the night.

When Terry relayed this story to Gwen he was surprised to hear that she had been seeing strange things too – other flying objects, black and triangular in shape, that seemed to follow her car down the entrance drive; vehicles parked up in the fields that suddenly disappeared, leaving no trace save for sets of human-looking footprints twice the size of any foot she had ever seen.

Then a few weeks later, Terry noticed a weird golden orb in the night sky just above the trees to the western end of the ranch. One night, as Terry watched, the orb seemed to expand, revealing something peculiar inside. Terry couldn't say for sure but it was almost as though he were looking through into another world, to a different place where it was in fact daytime. As he continued to stare at it, a black object seemed to fly out of it, which he lost sight of shortly after.

Though undoubtedly strange, the family were reluctant to draw any wild conclusions from the peculiar events, speculating that some kind of military experimentation might be going on nearby. In any case, the oddities were soon forgotten when a bitter winter drew in that by the turn of the new year had claimed the lives of two of their herd. By the time spring arrived, three more of the Shermans' cattle had succumbed to the harsh conditions and all memory of strange flying objects and gigantic wolves had long been forgotten – but that was about to change.

Terry had been rounding up cattle when he heard his son's cries. He arrived to find him retching by the banks of the canal and pointing to a spot for Terry to go and investigate. Moments later, as a torrential rain lashed down again, Terry was waist deep in the canal tying a thick rope around a dead heifer's back legs and, together with Terry's horse, they hauled the animal from the water. Terry sunk to the ground exhausted as the rain streamed down his face. On the ground before him lay the heifer, minus its rear end, which appeared to have been completely removed with surgical precision. The cow's insides were also gone and there was no sign of blood anywhere. Perhaps it was one of the wolves, suggested T, but Terry wasn't so sure. No, he thought, this was something else entirely, something he had never seen before. It would prove to be only the first of many bizarre cattle mutilations that would plague Terry and Gwen over the next few months.

Towards the end of April, Terry is sitting outside the ranch one evening after another gruelling day, basking in a warm sunset with his trusted blue heelers by his side. At some point one of the dogs begins to growl, causing him to sit up in his chair. It must have been several hundred yards away and roughly about the size of a tennis ball. It looked as if it were made entirely from blue electrical sparks. With the dogs barking manically Terry gives them a nod, at which they tear off instantly in pursuit of the strange blue orb. He soon grows concerned, however, when the dogs chase the thing to the edge of a copse, before following it into the trees and disappearing into the undergrowth. When Terry heads inside later that evening he reassures the children that the dogs will find their way back home.

The following morning, the heelers have not returned, prompting Terry to go and look for them. Stepping through the trees where he saw them last, he detects a distinct smell of burnt flesh mingling with the morning dew and sagebrush. Pushing through to a clearing beyond, Terry soon discovers to his horror, the source of the smell: three circles of dried grass each with their own gooey mess piled up on top.

The loss of the much-loved dogs is devastating for Terry and the rest of the family who are beginning to feel increasingly terrorised by the weird events. For the first time, Terry is thoroughly rattled and worried for his family's safety. With no one else to talk to, he sought help from local resident Junior Hicks who had introduced himself to the family a few months previously after first hearing about the strange events taking place on the ranch. Hicks is a retired high school science teacher from the nearby town of Roosevelt and has spent a lifetime trying to convince people that there's something peculiar happening around the Uintah Basin – but even he isn't sure what to make of the recent happenings at the Sherman ranch.

Hicks's fascination stemmed mostly from a number of local sightings of UFOs in the early 1950s, in particular a sighting recorded in 1952 by a Navy warrant officer named Delbert Newhouse that took place near Tremonton just to the north of Salt Lake City. Whilst driving through Utah on their way to vacation in Portland, Oregon, Newhouse and his wife Norma along with their son Delbert and daughter Anne, spotted twelve saucer-shaped objects identical in size flying in the air above their car. Newhouse estimated the objects to be similar in size to B-29 bomber planes if they had been flying at 10,000ft.[6] After watching the objects for a short time, Newhouse grabbed his film camera from the boot of his car and proceeded to record the objects for a number of minutes. The footage he captured remains to this day one of the most compelling in the annals of Ufology.

For Terry, being able to talk openly with Hicks, without any fear of judgement was a welcome relief; but what Hicks would later tell him after they had inspected the remains of the dogs, was far from reassuring. Hicks had documented over 400 cases of strange sightings within the Uintah region alone, ranging from balls of electricity to black triangular objects flying overhead, just like the ones seen by Gwen. This wasn't the first time that strange things had occurred on the ranch. According to Hicks, the former owner Edith Myers spoke regularly of bizarre goings on at the homestead whenever she ventured into town. Hicks himself, who claimed to have worked at the ranch carrying out small jobs for Edith, had also noticed little oddities such as compasses behaving irregularly.

Hicks has a number of theories for what might be going on but there is one in particular that proves especially unsettling to the Shermans. One afternoon Hicks brings round a map of the local region to better explain the situation. After spreading it out in front of Terry he picks out the position of the ranch, noting how it seems unnaturally snipped out of the surrounding Uintah and Ouray reservation. It wouldn't be the first time a piece of land had been confiscated and sold off but the Sherman ranch is a decidedly different proposition since the local Nūche, as Hicks explains, had never wanted anything to do with it.

While the Nūche were being pressed on each side by newcomers hungry for the land they occupied, they were forced to enter into a series of strategic alliances in a last bid for survival. One such alliance came at a bloody cost for the neighbouring Dinè people, later named Navajo by settlers from Spain. In retaliation, so the story goes, one night the Dinè medicine men gathered under the cover of darkness and, illuminated only by the flickering flames of a ritual fire, danced and chanted a curse upon the Nūche and their land. Ever since, the tribe have considered themselves haunted by the embodiment of this curse: terrifying shapeshifting witches they call *yee naaldlooshii*, otherwise known as Skinwalkers.

The Skinwalker of Diné folklore exists only to bring death or harm to any who come across it. Once it has taken animal form, most often as a wolf or a coyote, it will start to seek out its prey, stalking them at night and occasionally sprinkling the dust of ground children's bones into their victims' homes as a pestilence. According to Junior Hicks, the local Nūche considered the entirety of the tabletop ridge at the north of the Sherman's ranch to be part of the Skinwalkers' domain and as such were terrified to go anywhere near it. In fact, the ridge was even known locally as Skinwalker Ridge. There was one place in particular according to Hicks that was especially feared: a place called Dark Canyon, located just over thirty miles to the north of the ranch. It is thought that many of the ancient petroglyphs – prehistoric rock drawings – found within the canyon, are in fact depictions of these terrifying creatures. It is also there that some believe new Skinwalkers are created; where tribal witches, dressed in masks and beads, gather in caves lined with row upon row of human heads, singing discordant songs around rising fires as they draw pictures in the dirt before spitting and defecating on their markings as they work to summon another Skinwalker into existence.[7]

Petroglyphs drawn on a canyon wall in Utah
dated to sometime around 2500 BCE.

Hicks also explained that to the Nūche the sighting of a wolf or dog in strange circumstances was evidence enough that they had seen a Skinwalker, and any such sighting was deemed a portent of immediate danger to their families. Terry thought back uneasily to that early encounter with the wolf that would not be killed, and the time a huge wolf-like creature had approached Gwen's truck.

Although Terry tried to ignore Hicks's warnings, there was no ignoring the number of dead and mutilated cattle that continued to mount up and the effect it was all having on the family's mental health, not to mention finances. The final straw came late one evening in July after the family had settled down for the night. Terry had noticed the lights in the yard flickering on and off before lights inside started also to dim and flicker. Seconds later, Gwen let out a horrifying scream when she caught sight of another orb gently hovering around the homestead, lingering by the window as if it were watching them. Moments later it would be gone, but the Shermans had had enough.

By the end of that summer in 1996 they had lost a total of four-teen cattle since moving only two years previously and the stress of it all had exerted a heavy toll, with Gwen on the verge of losing her job at the local bank due to all the sleepless nights and missed hours, and the children's grades at school suffering too.

Having decided once and for all to move on, the Shermans were on the verge of putting the ranch up for sale when they received a phone call from someone in Las Vegas calling on behalf of a man named Robert Bigelow. As the caller explained, a few days previously Bigelow had been alerted to an article in Utah's *Deseret News* about the weird happenings at the Sherman ranch.[8] Without even wishing to view the property, Bigelow was willing to make an immediate offer of $200,000 to take the ranch off their hands. The Shermans didn't think twice.

When Robert Bigelow was a young boy he had listened with astonishment as his grandparents recounted a story in matter-of-fact terms about the time an alien spacecraft had once buzzed their car while they made their way down a country road just outside of Vegas. The craft had apparently shot off at an acute angle and disappeared into the distance before they were able to get a proper look at it.

Later Bigelow would become a multimillionaire through his hospitality company Budget Suites of America, but the wonder of hearing his grandparents' story would never leave him. In the early 1990s, with significant financial means, Bigelow began funding a series of fringe science projects through the University of Nevada in Las Vegas. The programmes were designed to cover a wide area of study investigating various phenomena such as 'altered states of consciousness, near-death experiences and extra-sensory perception'.[9] By 1996, he was ready to take his fascination to another level.

Colm Kelleher was a bright, young biochemist working at the national Jewish Center for Immunology in Denver when he came across a job recruitment ad in *Science*, placed by the National

Institute for Discovery Science (NIDS). The institute, set up by Bigelow, sought to bring together PhD-level scientists from across the scientific spectrum to investigate paranormal phenomena and listed as its remit the modest intention to study the 'origin and evolution of consciousness in the universe'. Kelleher was instantly hooked and without hesitation applied for the job. A few weeks later, he was on a plane to Las Vegas to take up his new role as a NIDS research manager.

On his arrival in Vegas, Kelleher found Bigelow to be an engaging, intelligent and ambitious character who was genuinely and deeply committed to the organisation's goals. This commitment was echoed loudly by the team of personnel so far brought to the table, including two of the only twelve humans ever to have walked on the moon, Dr Harrison Schmitt and Dr Edgar Mitchell, as well as retired US Army Colonel John Alexander – a Special Forces A-Team commander during the American/Vietnamese War of 1955–75 who had become a controversial figure due to his particular interest in non-lethal defence and the potential of mind control in warfare.

With the newly assembled NIDS team eager to get out into the field to put their investigative skills to the test, Bigelow suggested the Sherman ranch as their first case study and in September, they moved on to their new homestead. A huge observation trailer was installed opposite the ranch house and loaded with all the latest tech to conduct their investigations, including spectrum and frequency analysers and recording equipment utilising the latest in CD-ROM-based storage. A bank of monitors was assembled, piled up alongside boxes of magnetometers and Geiger counters, useful for recording any radioactive discharges that might be taking place.

Despite their eagerness to leave the property, Terry had not been entirely ready to give in. He had taken it as a personal affront that the family had effectively been run off their land and arranged a deal with Bigelow to not only keep cattle on the ranch, but also to assist the NIDS team as property manager of what would henceforth be known as Bigelow Ranch. Once the team arrived, Terry took Kelleher and the others on a tour of the property to get a sense of what exactly they were up against. As they walked, the team listened enrapt as the rancher recounted the events of the past few years. On that bright September day, as the chirrup of crickets mixed with the lowing of distant cattle and a warm breeze drifted over the pastures, it wasn't hard to see why the Shermans had resisted leaving for so long. Moments later, Terry, Kelleher and another colleague were staring down at the putrid carcass of a cow; one of two from the farm next door that had died in the last few days from mysterious circumstances.

The rugged plains of the Uintah and Ouray Reservation.

The next day the team began compiling witness testimonies from the neighbouring ranch families and reservation residents, which over the following months would reveal a startling number of bizarre and inexplicable experiences occurring over the years. In tandem with these reports, by day the team took electromagnetic readings and tested the land for levels of radiation. Come night, they would take it in turns to sit under the stars and gaze up at the sky in the hope of spotting anything unusual. By December, however, the snows had arrived and there had been little activity of note. As the temperature continued to drop Terry moved most of the cattle to the family's new ranch located twenty or so miles away. The NIDS team brought the first stage of their investigation to a close and returned to their Vegas headquarters.

The cattle returned in February and two weeks later Terry was tagging some of the new arrivals. Having singled one out, he quickly grabbed it by the head and wrestled it to the ground. Its mother watched nervously as Terry calmed the young animal and punched the first tag quickly through its ear. Once it had settled, Terry took the other ear and swiftly punched in a second tag before releasing the calf in a flurry of jerking movements, the animal trying to shake off the pain as it stumbled back to the safety of its mother.

A short time later, an anxious barking caught the attention of Terry and Gwen as they were inspecting the rest of the animals. One of their heelers had wandered off to the west of the pasture and was now yapping at something in the undergrowth on the edge of the field. Without warning she sprinted off into the scrub. Then a strange cry came from within the herd.

It was happening again.

Terry jogged back to the mother whose calf he had just tagged but found no sign of the young animal until he noticed the small leg bone, freshly shorn of meat, left lying on the ground. Taking a few more steps Terry came across the rest of the butchered carcass. It was laid out on the grass with its legs splayed. All its organs had been ripped from the inside and its hide almost completely removed, exposing the ribs underneath. One of its ears had also been sliced off but there wasn't a speck of blood in sight. Terry took a step back in shock before calling out to Gwen.

Five hours later, having flown straight up from Vegas, Dr Kelleher along with a physicist and veterinarian from the NIDS team are standing over the remains. The three men swiftly get to work fishing for magnetic and radioactive anomalies, anxiously eyeing the edges of the pasture as the machines bleep and hiss. It was clear from the way the animals were huddled together that something out there was watching them. Looking closely at the calf's ear the vet remarks on the precision of the incision, and when the necropsy is finished, it is clear that if the culprit was an animal, it isn't something either of them have ever seen before. On the edge of the herd, the calf's mother lolls her head and sniffs at the ground as she waits for a child that would never return.

A few evenings later, Kelleher and a colleague are in the trailer assessing the readings from Monday when they hear the ranch dogs barking manically in the paddock. The men run out of the trailer to find Terry tending to the dogs as he stares off into the distance.

'Out there,' he says, nodding towards the horizon.

Moments later, Kelleher and his colleague are holding on to the back of Terry's pickup as it tears off towards a group of cattle nervously huddled together at the foot of Skinwalker Ridge. The high-powered beams of the truck flash across the pasture as they roll and bump over the rugged terrain. Having drawn close enough, Terry points out a silhouetted shape standing just off from the herd, sheltering by the trees. Assuming it to be one of the cows, Terry drives around in an attempt to corral it back into the pack but when they look again, the shape has gone. Scanning the spaces beyond, they see it again now sitting high up in a tree; its eyes are like two small lights staring straight back at them. Only when they get nearer do they realise just how enormous it is.

Terry hits the brakes and grabs his rifle from the back. In seconds he is leant against the bonnet, his eye peering down the gun sight as he lines up the shot and squeezes the trigger. The gun kicks back and something in the distance falls to the ground. Terry scrambles to the scene, desperately looking for any sign of the creature while the others search the ground under the cottonwood, but find nothing. Terry catches a movement to the left and turns to see something huge, crouching like a dog with thick, taut muscles. It turns to Terry before springing high and away into the air. Kelleher watches with alarm as Terry fires two more shots into the dark before running off into the scrub.

The NIDS colleagues, terrified that something may pounce on them, set off after Terry and find him moments later crouched over a small patch of snow. He directs their torches to the ground where they find an enormous single footprint – it's round at the base and roughly 6 inches wide with what seems like two elongated claws coming off it. It looks like the print of an eagle or a hawk, but at this size what it most resembles is a large dinosaur.

It's now June, and Dr Kelleher, along with three colleagues and two heelers, is setting out to capture a mysterious light that had been spotted a week earlier by another of the NIDS investigators, near the old ranch house. Having set up camp a few hundred yards south of the old cabin, it isn't long before the dogs begin to bristle, alerted to something invisible in the space between them and the house. Kelleher switches on his night-vision goggles and gives a stifled cry. Barely a hundred yards in front of him, invisible to the naked eye but clearly visible through the goggles, is a bright ball of light, hovering 4 metres off the ground. Almost as soon as he sees it, however, it disappears. Kelleher flicks a switch and bathes the pasture in the bright beams of floodlights set up for the task.

'There,' shouts his colleague, M, now also looking through night-vision binoculars. 'There's something in the trees, moving north.'

Kelleher fumbles with his camera and points it towards the tree line. He hurriedly takes a snap, holding the camera in place while he counts to twenty under his breath to give the infrared film time to pick up the image. The dogs, barking louder now, turn all their attention to whatever is lurking beyond the tree line while M scans left to right with the binoculars, tracking the shape through the trees.

'It's still moving,' he says.

Kelleher clicks and counts to twenty again.

'We are watching you.'

Kelleher nearly drops the camera, turning to his colleague in astonishment. The words had come from M's mouth, but the voice had not been his.

'Jesus Christ. It took control of my mind!' says M, recoiling in horror.

The dogs have ceased their barking and all about is still. Kelleher looks on, incredulous, as M struggles to come to terms with what just occurred. Undeterred the pair remain for over an hour in the hope of recording more activity but there is nothing else.

The NIDS team will return to this location on numerous occasions over the next few weeks only to continually be disappointed. That is until one evening in August. Whilst packing up after yet another fruitless six-hour shift under the stars, one of the team noticed something reflective on the dirt track below. It wasn't uncommon for a well-polished surface or even a scrap of foil to pick up moonlight, especially under a vast desert sky with a bright full moon above. Only, the moon had been full over a week ago. What's more, whatever it was appeared to be getting bigger. Before long they realised it wasn't a reflective substance at all, but some kind of light in and of itself. One of the team grabbed a camera and hurriedly stuffed it with a roll of infrared while another colleague pulled out the night-vision binoculars and raised them to his eyes. The pair struggled to focus on the orb of light it as it continued to grow steadily in size, distorting and shifting as it expanded until it suddenly became clear that it wasn't an orb at all.

It was a tunnel.

All of a sudden, one of the men caught sight of something inside, something moving. They watched with horror as a faceless creature, with seemingly distended limbs and dark fur crawled forth from out of an unknown place. Small at first, it appeared to grow in size as it pulled itself forward, scraping closer and closer to the edge of the tunnel before finally slipping out of the light and dropping on to the prairie. The men continued watching, utterly mesmerised as the creature stood up on two legs and sped off into the fields. A moment later the light was gone. The men, feeling suddenly exposed, paused for a moment before hurtling down to the bottom of the ridge and back to the safety of the observation trailer. The following day when the whole roll of infrared film was developed, it revealed nothing.

In fact, despite a number of startling observations the NIDS team had so far failed to capture anything on film after almost a year. Having tried the subtle approach due to an earlier suggestion of Terry's who felt that every time he tried to observe the anomalous activity it would stop, as if it knew it was being watched, by the end of that summer, the team decided to change tack and promptly erect six 24-hour surveillance cameras. All they needed to do now was wait.

A full year passes without incident until late July, when Terry, in his continuing capacity as site manager, is making his routine check of the cameras when he approaches the primary unit: a telegraph pole in the middle of the pasture with three cameras attached to the top. A wry smile breaks out across his face as he gazes up at the equipment. The cables that had previously been threaded so carefully through metres of PVC tubing and held in place with duct tape were now dangling freely in the breeze, the tubing wrenched apart and discarded at the bottom of the pole. As for the duct tape, it had completely vanished. Later that afternoon, having flown straight in from Las Vegas, Kelleher sits in the NIDS trailer working through the footage from the damaged cameras. On the monitor, shots of the pastures play out; the cattle ambling back and forth flicking their tails as they chew on the grass. The images speed forward, flickering and stretching as Kelleher skips the tape onwards, then, releasing the dial, he lets the last few minutes go. When the time code reaches 20:30 the tape completely cuts out. The other tapes are the same, each going dark at precisely 20:30. Kelleher realises with some excitement that whatever had happened must have occurred at that precise point. A moment later one of the team members returns to the trailer carrying another tape taken from a camera that had been pointed directly at the vandalised post. If this tape works they will know exactly what destroyed those cables. Kelleher slips the tape into the deck and runs it back to shortly before 20:30, then hits play.

Another scene flashes up on the screen, full of green pastures and milling cattle like before, only this time, standing right in the middle of the image, is the telegraph pole with the three cameras attached to the top. The team watches transfixed as the time edges ever closer to the 20:30 mark until finally the moment has arrived. 20:29:57 . . . 20:29:58 . . . 20:29:59 and then 20:30:00 . . . but there is nothing. The image remains just as before with no sign of anybody tampering with anything, not even approaching the post. The team skips the footage backwards and forwards watching as the daylight fades to night but still there is nothing. The following morning the footage is taken to NIDS HQ in Las Vegas where it is cleaned up and sharpened, so much so that they are even able to see the tiny red LEDs lit up on the front of each camera as they record. As they play the footage back again, they watch stunned as each LED light is inexplicably snuffed out at precisely 20:30 while all around, the pastures remain empty and still.

For the next two years, Terry will continue to assist the NIDS team hoping desperately for any kind of explanation as to what had terrorised his family and all the animals at the ranch, but the answers would not come. By 1999 the phenomenon, whatever it was, had gradually abated to almost non-existent. There was still the occasional orb or light in places it shouldn't be but something fundamental had changed. Eventually Terry made the decision to leave Bigelow Ranch behind for good and new caretakers were installed with instructions to report on any strange activity that might occur, though to date it is not known if any such activity has taken place. Looking at the various incidents one at a time, the phenomenon might have been explained away as unusual but not necessarily paranormal. When put together, however, it was hard for Terry not to suspect that something extraordinary, unknown and organised had either been observing them, examining them like zoologists to see how they ticked, or had been using the cattle as cannon fodder for devices beyond his knowledge. He could only be thankful that whatever it was, or whoever they were, his family had not been harmed.

By the end of the 20th century with the dissipation of activity on Bigelow Ranch, Robert Bigelow turned his focus to a new company he had founded in 1998 called Bigelow Aerospace. The company was established to develop space destinations, using the latest in expandable technology, with plans to launch the first hotel in space by the year 2022. With interest in Bigelow Ranch beginning to wane, Dr Kelleher and the rest of the investigative team were forced to call it a day and in 2004 The National Institute for Discovery Science was eventually wound down and disbanded. The NIDS team and Sherman family maintain to this day that they had witnessed a variety of extraordinary and anomalous events but concede they have no firm evidence to substantiate or back up any of their claims. In 2016, the Adamantium Real Estate Company whose owners and provenance remain a mystery to this day, took ownership of Bigelow Ranch. Despite no official operations thought to be taking place on the site it is believed to still be watched over by a number of cameras, motion detectors as well as a 24-hour surveillance team of armed, ex-military personnel.

As our understanding of the world and the space around us continues to grow ever more sophisticated, so too do our tools of exploration. Where once our intrepid endeavours were marked by a distinctly two-dimensional, terrestrial curiosity to look only beyond the distant mountain peaks or across the seemingly endless bodies of water that lapped invitingly at our feet, more recently it is to below those oceans and above those mountain peaks that we have turned our imaginations. It is interesting then, as our comprehension of spaces and dimensions evolves, to wonder where our descendants might find themselves venturing to one day. Equally fascinating is how easily our prevailing notions about the space around us can restrict our understanding of what its true properties might actually be.

On 29 May 1919 on the remote island of Principe, off the west coast of Africa, a team of British scientists, led by Secretary of the British Astronomical Society Arthur Eddington, are transfixed by something extraordinary occurring above them in the sky. It's shortly after 13:00 hours when a black disc begins to creep across the face of the sun, drawing a vast blanket of shadow over the land. Further and further it creeps until the light is all but extinguished save for a few bright yellow beads peeking through the vast outer ridges of the jet-black disc. All around the scientists, strange bands of undulating shadows ripple over surfaces as a moment of eerie silence gives way to a crescendo of untimely cricket song. When the last of the solar crest is finally extinguished, a blinding flash of white flares out from behind before receding to reveal the iris hue of the sun's majestic corona, and all around a distant hazy red glows ominously at the horizon of the Earth.

It would be impossible for Eddington's team to ignore one of the most spectacular solar eclipses of the last 500 years, but remarkably it is not the sun that they have come to observe. Instead it is to the giant orange eye of a bull that their attentions are turned, along with the other four brightest stars of the Hyades cluster that make up part of the constellation of Taurus. It is via the light emitted from these gigantic celestial bodies, reaching out to us from 153 years in the past, that Eddington and his team will record the gravitational warping of space predicted by Albert Einstein's General Theory of Relativity. Within six months, when the results of the experiment are finally revealed to the world in a flurry of giddy broadsheet headlines, our fundamental understanding of the universe will be changed forever.

In 1905 Einstein's special theory of relativity had revolutionised the way we think of space and time. No longer would they be considered fixed and immutable but flexible, malleable terms dependent on the relative difference between the motion of the observed and the observer. With his general theory of relativity Einstein had uncovered something perhaps even more profound. Where Isaac Newton before him had envisaged gravity as an attractive force operating within a three-dimensional concept of space, Einstein had uncovered a fourth dimension of space-time, theorising that gravity wasn't a force bringing objects together as such, but rather was the bending of space itself. Although the prevailing laws of Newtonian physics had also predicted the gravitational warping of light as recorded by Eddington's team, they were wrong by roughly a half compared to Einstein's predictions. Prior to Einstein's calculations, Isaac Newton's law of universal gravitation had remained unchallenged for over 200 years, primarily because for all intents and purposes, it worked. Indeed, Newton's laws do a great job predicting the motions of planets, rockets shooting for the moon or the trajectory of a ski jumper, but when applied to the universe that Einstein had discovered, they fundamentally broke down. Einstein's conviction that the speed of light is a constant had lifted a veil to reveal a new universe that had been there all along; we had just been too blinded by prevailing ideas to see it.

In 1923 Georges Lemaitre, a young priest from Belgium studying at Cambridge University under Arthur Eddington's tutelage found something unexpected in Einstein's calculations. At the time, it was generally held that the universe was infinitely old and the various bodies within it completely static. Yet when Lemaitre examined Einstein's calculations he discovered something quite different; the universe wasn't static, it was expanding.[10] In 1927 Lemaitre published his findings with great excitement in the *Annales de la Société Scientifique de Bruxelles.* Unfortunately for Lemaitre nobody paid any attention, except for Einstein who met with him later that year telling him, 'your calculations are correct, but your grasp of physics is abominable.'[11]

What was most troubling about the implications of Lemaitre's idea, and what had so upset Einstein, was that if everything was moving further away, it must have at one point been a lot closer together. Lemaitre called his discovery his 'hypothesis of the primeval atom'[12] – we might know this better today as the Big Bang theory. This theory was given greater credence when astronomer Edwin Hubble announced in 1929 that distant galaxies were moving further away from us faster than those closest to us,[13] and with the discovery in 1964 by Arno Penzias and Robert Wilson, with the guidance of Robert Dicke, of the cosmic microwave background, a signal of residual radiation pervading all of the known universe that many consider to be the best evidence to date for a big bang.

Realising his mistake, Einstein proclaimed Lemaitre's theory the most 'beautiful and satisfactory explanation of creation to which I have ever listened',[14] demonstrating that what counts ultimately is the data, not the ideology, but what can't be overlooked is the reason Einstein had missed what was already apparent in his calculations. It wasn't because he didn't understand it but rather it was because he was effectively blind to it. Einstein was so convinced that such a universe wasn't possible (even creating an additional component to account for it called the cosmological constant, that he later admitted was his greatest mistake) that he missed the proof of expansion already inherent in his calculations.[15] Just as Einstein had been prepared to look beyond conventional wisdom to reassess the work of Isaac Newton, so too had Lemaitre disregarded pervading convictions of the day in order to 'see' the universe anew.

Although it is of course one thing to reinterpret calculations that have already been demonstrated to work, it is quite another to speculate on something with no hard evidence whatsoever. Lest we forget, it is less than a hundred years ago since, as far as we understood it, the universe existed without finitude, static in its composition, three dimensional and consisting entirely of the Milky Way. Today many leading scientists are beginning to consider the possibility that our universe is only one of many universes existing within a much broader region of space-time than we had previously imagined. With our ever-advancing understanding of the quantum realm we find ourselves taking seriously notions such as the Many Worlds Interpretation (MWI), first proposed by physicist Hugh Everett III in the 1950s for which he was widely ridiculed at the time, which poses the possibility of an infinite number of universes branching out from ours, providing an alternative universe at every conceivable moment. Such an idea has some quite startling implications, not least the possibility that everything that could have ever happened or could ever happen, already has. Having barely had a moment to wrap our heads around Einstein's four-dimensional universe, advocates of the branch of physics known as string theory have proposed space might actually consist of eleven or even twenty-six dimensions.[16]

There are some, however, who would discourage our intrepid ventures, who aren't so keen on the prospect of uncovering new worlds and whatever else we might encounter along the way. As Stephen Hawking pointed out, the history of humankind is littered with the debris of civilisations destroyed at the hands of those who considered themselves superior.[17] If we struggle to see the world in the same way within our own species – let alone how irrelevant we consider the opinions of the millions of other species with whom we share the planet – what complications might arise should we be confronted with something more advanced?

If, in our search for hidden worlds, we find a gateway to access one, what price might we pay for opening it?

Perhaps sticking to our own patch is best, lest we suffer the fate of Frank Cotton from Clive Barker's darkly erotic paean to human flesh, *The Hellbound Heart*. In Barker's novella, the hedonistically curious Frank, in his quest for ever more sensual pleasure, is introduced to a mystical puzzle box known as the Lemarchand Configuration. It is said that the box opens a portal to an extra-dimensional realm of unfathomable pleasure administered by a race of powerful entities known as Cenobites. It is only when Frank successfully unlocks the portal that he realises to his horror that the sadomasochistic Cenobites, 'demons to some, angels to others', have an understanding of pleasure that is somewhat different to ours. Frank's reward for accessing their world is to have the skin ripped from his body before spending an eternity in torture. From most human perspectives, the Cenobites are monstrous, from theirs they are merely Cenobites . . .

For now at least, we need not worry about such horrors, but it is worth bearing in mind just how often, and significantly, extraordinary theories drawn from the maths can predate our ability to empirically prove them. Although those multiverse and MWI theories are only presently speculation, they might one day prove to be places we will not only communicate with, but visit too. As unfathomable as some ideas may at first appear, sometimes it isn't until our perceptions of what is possible have shifted that previously unseen layers of the universe, or indeed universes, can be peeled back to reveal their true nature underneath, even if the evidence was in front of us all along. To paraphrase philosopher Roger Scruton: the consolation of the imagination often turns out not to be imaginary consolation.[18]

Ultimately, no matter how much further or deeper we look, perhaps there will always be something that we don't know, hidden away from the beaming light of human endeavour. One thing seems certain: as long as we are around to do so, we will never stop searching for whatever 'that' is.

Chapter Nine

THE NOUS FEAR

'This is a terror of the world's edge, is the vertigo of an accelerated culture. Out beyond the lights of every city, every town and every century, this is the abyss that abides.'

Alan Moore – 'Coal Memory'

In *Le phénomène humain*, written in 1938, the idealist philosopher and Jesuit priest Pierre Teilhard de Chardin makes the claim that evolution is a process that gives rise to increasingly complex organisms which in turn leads to expanded consciousness. At the book's core is the theory that as humans evolve and society becomes more elaborate, a collective space is formed that allows us to hold and share our ideas in order to better communicate with one another. Although an abstraction, Teilhard de Chardin imagined this 'thinking layer',[1] much like the atmosphere and the biosphere, to be as integral and real as any material aspect of the planet. Borrowing a term from the pioneering biochemist Vladimir Vernadsky, Teilhard de Chardin called this space the 'noosphere', taken from the Greek νοῦς (*nous*) meaning 'mind'. He believed that through this 'organised web of thought'[2] our disparate cultural knowledge and perspectives would become so diffused and universally understood that they would effectively converge into one singular point of human awareness.

Late October 1969, in the University of California's computer lab, twenty-one-year-old UCLA student and programmer Charley

Kline sat, on the phone, in front of a keyboard connected to a computer so large it would barely fit inside a garage. Shortly before 9.30 p.m., Kline pressed the letter 'L' on the keyboard and waited. A moment later, the voice of fellow programmer Bill Duval came down the line from his base at the Stanford Research Institute letting Kline know that the 'L' had been received. Next, Kline typed the letter 'O'. After a moment's pause, Bill came back on the line to confirm it too had been received. The following attempt to send a letter resulted in a complete system meltdown, but by now the test had been a success.

Kline and Duval had been drafted in to help with a project set up by the US Department of Defense's Advanced Research Projects Agency to help build a digital communication network that could accommodate more than two computer terminals at one time and transmit across large distances. They had been attempting to send the word LOGIN before the computer crashed as it tried to process the third letter. Like a biblical proclamation, the resultant 'LO' became the first communication across what would later be known as ARPANET, the foundation for what we know today as the Internet.[3]

29 OCT 69	2100	LOADED OP. PROGRAM FOR BEN BARKER BBN	CSK
	22:30	Talked to SRI Host to Host	CSK
		Left op. imp program running after sending a host dead message to imp.	CSK

The first ARPANET Interface Message Processor
(IMP) Log recorded by Charles S. Kline (CSK).

It shouldn't surprise us that, like many of our most advanced technologies, the Internet began as a military project. However, it is fairly certain that the Pentagon had not envisaged opening up their secretive systems of communication to the wider world. So although we have them to thank (or blame) for developing the structural underpinnings of the Net, the spirit that gave rise to the Internet, as we broadly understand it today, is more closely related to the utopian ideals of Pierre Teilhard de Chardin. Emerging out of the fertile corridors of the European Strategy for Particle Physics' CERN laboratory, the World Wide Web was first proposed by Tim Berners Lee as an open system, whereby we could all store and share information freely and globally without interference. On 6 August 1991 Berners Lee launched the world's first website at http://info.cern.ch which explained the concept of the Web as an open invitation to all, even providing instructions on how you might get started on building your own site.

Though Teilhard de Chardin has been criticised for his erroneous reading of evolution as a process which leads inevitably to a singular point of higher intelligence,[4] it is hard not to see something of his 'thinking layer' at least in the functionality of the Internet, this networked repository of data, from which we now store, share and receive so much of our information. Our personal lives and minds become increasingly merged and atomised into this space, our records, thoughts and experiences backed up on clouds, shared and available for all to see. Furthermore, with the rise of Web 2.0, a term coined by web pioneer Dale Dougherty that describes platforms such as YouTube, Twitter and Reddit, which facilitate user-generated content, it has never been so easy to share that information. Never before as a species have we been so interconnected and exposed to each other. In an echo of the noosphere concept, tech writer Tim O'Reilly describes the leading Web 2.0 companies as those that embrace 'the power of the web to harness collective intelligence'.[5]

Visionary, utopian thinking, as media scholar Ethan Zuckerman notes, drawing on the work of historian Langdon Winner, is often catalysed by the emergence of major new technologies, never more so than when those technologies promise to make the world more connected.[6] Today the Internet stands alone as the fundamental component at the heart of most of 'our visions for a world made better through connection.'[7] Such cyber-utopianism can be seen in mission statements like that of Facebook, an archetypal platform of Web 2.0, which reads simply, 'bring people closer together.' Much in the manner of the noosphere, the cyber-utopian sees the Internet as the medium through which we will globally combine as one, no longer restricted by 'status, class, power, wealth and geography';[8] a promised land where all our oppressive, arbitrary social barriers will finally be transcended.

However, as our lives become evermore entangled with this digital realm some have been left fearing that rather than providing us with the tools for our next evolutionary step forward, the Internet is in fact ensnaring us in an evolutionary cul-de-sac; a trap from which we might struggle to escape. Amplified by the accelerated nature of technological development, many have become unnerved at the way the tools of the Internet seem to be undermining the old, more 'stable' ways, fearing that the familiar, 'solid' world they once knew is disintegrating before their eyes and ushering in a much less certain one, governed by processes that are out of our control and beyond comprehension for most.

It is as if from that laboratory at the University of California in 1969, a portal to an abyss was opened, and from its depths the siren call of a hopeless future has been growing steadily louder ever since. That feeling of uncertainty is the horror of the unknown, the fear of chaos and a fear of the monsters that lurk in the shadows, waiting for that chaos to descend.

In 2009, something monstrous did materialise on the Internet that might yet prove our worst fears about where this new world is taking us. He is the personification of the unknown; a messenger of the medium, at once new but strangely, archaically, familiar. Some say he appeared one night centuries ago in Germany's

Black Forest of Baden-Württemberg; others that he lives in a mansion deep in the heart of Chequamegon-Nicolet National Forest, Wisconsin. He is unnaturally tall, dressed in a dark suit, with distended limbs and, in some cases, grotesque, cthulhuesque tentacles emanating from his back. The face is blank, but some claim it appears differently depending on the observer. It isn't clear exactly what he wants, but the triggering of profound nausea and nosebleeds when he is near suggests whatever it is, it isn't good. Some also believe it is only possible to see him for the brief moment before he takes your life. His name is The Slender Man, and one way or another, he is coming for us all.

The first evidence of Slender came in the form of two deeply unsettling low-resolution, black-and-white photographs posted to a forum thread on the Something Awful website on 10 June 2009.[9] The first picture showed what at first seemed to be a group of twelve anguished children walking towards an unknown destination. But it wasn't the disturbed look on their faces that was so unsettling – it was the creepy wraith-like figure standing at the back of the group in a black suit with strangely distended limbs and a faceless head, which appeared to be shepherding them on their way. A caption below declared: 'We didn't want to go, we didn't want to kill them, but its persistent silence and outstretched arms horrified and comforted us at the same time.'[10] The photo was marked 1983 and accredited to 'photographer unknown, presumed dead'.

The second photo, which again appeared innocuous at first glance, showed a young girl climbing to the top of a slide in a small park in Stirling, Australia, while other children play happily around her. An authentic-looking watermark for the 'City of Stirling Libraries, Local Studies Collection' is printed in the corner. Looking closer, you'll find a mysterious shape, shrouded in darkness, standing under the trees at the back of the shot. Once more the figure, who appears to be keeping a watchful eye on the children, is oddly elongated and dressed in a black suit but here there is something else – a set of cephalopodan arms reaching out from behind his back. This time the caption comes with a little more detail:

> One of two recovered photographs from the Stirling City Library blaze. Notable for being taken the day when fourteen children vanished and for what is referred to as "The Slender Man". Deformities cited as film defects by officials. Fire at library occurred one week later. Actual photograph confiscated as evidence. Photographer: Mary Thomas, missing since June 13th, 1986.[11]

As much as they may have looked like unearthed pieces of a peculiar lost history, the pictures were in fact the work of regular SA forum user Victor Surge (birth name Eric Knudsen) who had posted them as part of a 'paranormal pictures' contest set up by another SA user named Gerogerigegege under the thread 'Create Paranormal Images'. The caption for the second photo marks the first direct mention of the terrifying entity that was soon to become a global phenomenon. For the next few days, Surge continued to post further images and allusions to the entity from hysterical police reports to an archive newspaper article about a young boy from Wichita who had apparently gone missing in 2004. Within hours Surge's creation started to draw attention from other forum users and before long the legend had spread. Other SA members suggested modifications and refinements to the physiognomy while others made changes themselves or chimed in with their own 'experiences' and found-pieces of evidence.

Throughout all this, something extraordinary was taking place. Although this creature had only come into existence a few days previously, through the rapidity of proliferation enabled by the Internet, as more people began to add to the mythology with every passing day it was as if it were being inserted into pockets of history stretching back centuries. One particularly striking image, posted a few days after the original by SA member 'Gyvermac', showed a bizarre 16th-century woodcutting print titled 'Der Ritter' said to have been unearthed at 'Halstberg Castle' in 1883. Purportedly made by famed artist of the day, 'Hans Freckenberg', the picture appeared to show a knight doing battle against the skeleton of a mysterious creature with distended limbs similar to those of Slender Man.[12] Over the next few months, the Slender Man universe expanded way beyond the SA forums on to various social media and content-sharing networks in all digital mediums from photoshopped images, to text, to videos and online games.

Slender lives in the public consciousness . . . Anonymous graffiti of the enigmatic entity appears one morning on a London street.

Today the breadth of the tentacle-like reach of the Slender Man mythos has left many, including Slender's original creator Eric Knudsen and academics like folklorist Jeffrey Tolbert, suggesting that the Slender universe could reasonably be considered the first genuine example of digital folklore, a myth that has been realised almost entirely through the utility of the Internet.[13] Certainly if you ask any of the children and young adults who have heard of Slender Man to explain what he is, and there will be many, they would describe something much like any other folk legend: his origins vague and timeless, the story mutating as it is passed from person to person, sometimes wildly or maybe just in subtle ways, but always with the central figure remaining consistent. Much like tales of the Slavic witch, Baba Yaga, who sometimes flies in a pestle and mortar, other times on a broom; one moment she is benign, the next monstrously wicked. To think of her today it might feel, like Slender Man, that she has always been there, lurking in the darkest peripheries of our nightmares.

Many academics have baulked at the idea of something so recently conceived being considered folklore. Despite their apparent timelessness, even the most ancient tales had an origin, but traditionally this ageless sense of time is significant. A term thought to have been first coined by writer William Thoms in 1846, 'folklore' is broadly considered to encompass the 'traditional beliefs, customs, and stories of a community, passed through the generations by word of mouth.'[14] Such stories can be weighted in old superstitions, serving to impart useful life lessons, or merely the passing on of rituals, customs and traditions shared through a common ancestry. As the term denotes, it is quintessentially about the folk, the people, but more specifically about the passing down of the shared histories of specific cultures through oral transmission. In the traditional mode of thinking, folklore is passed down vertically through generations. How then might the myth of Slender Man, conceived as recently as 2009, possibly constitute such a thing? Two academics from the University of Southern Denmark have proposed an extraordinary theory that, although not specific to the Slender Man mythos, goes some way to explaining how we might consider it a true example of folklore in the digital age. Their idea has profound, unsettling and for some, truly terrifying implications.

In May 2007, Thomas Pettitt, associate Professor of English at the University of Southern Denmark, presented a paper at an MIT media conference titled, 'Before the Gutenberg Parenthesis: Elizabethan-American Compatibilities'. Pettit's paper marked the first formal outing for the 'Gutenberg Parenthesis', a controversial and radical understanding of the digital age. The phrase, coined by Pettitt's colleague Professor Lars Ole Sauerberg, encapsulates the idea that the 500-year period following the 15th-century invention of Johannes Gutenberg's printing press was not the beginning of a change in the way we share information but was in fact an anomalous blip. Inherent in this neat phrase is the idea that if we imagine the history of communication as a sentence, everything leading up to the invention of the printing press comes before the parenthesis, the 500 years or so following its invention is the interruption within the parenthesis, and anything since the emergence of the Internet comes after – in effect continuing the 'sentence' from before.

Much has happened in the years since we adopted the tools of mass-print media production, and considering the many advanced ways we have to communicate and share technology at our disposal today, we might be right to question Pettitt and Sauerberg's proposal. What Pettitt and Sauerberg recognised, however, is how the digital age, albeit in a far more rapid and advanced manner, through its various mediums – the mechanisms through which information is shared, i.e. through social media and content-sharing websites – has returned us to the fluid, mutable way in which information used to be shared before mass print and the supremacy of fixed, authoritative texts. The digital world therefore has not led us into the future, but is returning us to a more medieval and unstable past.

As Pettitt noted in his 2007 talk, prior to the printing press, most knowledge was shared orally, it was sampled, remixed, borrowed, reshaped, appropriated and continually re-contextualised.[15] There were the authorial texts of religious institutions and, for a select minority, access to authoritative academic texts, but broadly speaking for most people, from the plays to the songs we wrote, to the sharing of news and life events, knowledge was communal with no fixed origin, and subject to mutation.

The expansion of the Slender Man mythos was fuelled in part by our copy-and-paste meme-sharing culture, which epitomises the way in which information is often shared online, in particular through the phenomenon of Creepypasta,[16] which emerged in the early 2000s. Creepypasta is the sharing and proliferation of short-form horror stories, usually in the tone of an urban legend, written as if true events are being recounted. Creepypasta can take the form of anything from prose to multi-part video, but serves only one purpose: to freak you out. One famous example is a video titled 'The Scariest Picture on the Internet (REAL)' uploaded to YouTube sometime around 2010. The video depicted a painting of a young woman with long brown hair and azure blue eyes that was purportedly drawn and then uploaded by a teenage girl from Japan, shortly before she committed suicide. Viewers of the video, which runs at just over five minutes, are warned that 'it is hard for a person to stare into the girl's eyes for longer than 5 minutes . . . there are reports that some people have taken their own lives after doing so.'[17] Through websites such as creepypasta.com, created in 2008, and later creepypasta.wikia, users are encouraged to make their own contributions, create mashups of other stories or extend the universe of someone else's original idea. Creepypasta thrives on the fluidity of information, unofficiated, unverified and passed around from person to person in the manner of the oral tradition where the story is free to mutate, expand and contract with no discernible author.

Key to the fluid transference of information in the digital age has been the dominance of Web 2.0 platforms that facilitate user-generated content. Platforms such as Twitter, Facebook and YouTube have for many been a liberating tool that allows thoughts and ideas to be heard regardless of financial means or the necessity of having to satisfy the gate-keepers of old, be they publishing companies, record companies, TV executives or stringent ethical codes of conduct which might otherwise have dictated what content can be seen or heard. Some, however, have voiced concern over the way in which Web 2.0, rather than broadening our awareness and understanding of the world is in fact making us more stupid and diluting culture. In *The Cult of The Amateur: How*

Today's Internet is Killing Our Culture Internet critic Andrew Keen, argues that rather than enabling us to pool our intelligence, the explosion of amateur, user-generated content has given us a world in which sketchy Wikipedia entries are given prominence over the perceived erudite authority of the *Encyclopaedia Britannica*, which Keen believes is leading to 'superficial observations of the world around us rather than deep analysis'.[18]

What the Gutenberg Parenthesis theory suggests, and what Keen is alluding to, is that prior to the rise of the Internet, information came with a degree of 'permanence and "containment"',[19] the information was set, allowing the receiver to hold it to account and interrogate its veracity. Words became 'unalterable and thus given a new authority, whether it was deserved or not, that oral communication didn't have.'[20] The printing press in a way was democratising and egalitarian too: fuelling literacy and empowering people by allowing for a wider access to the words that had previously been controlled by the authorities of the day. For the first time many people who hadn't had a voice could spread their ideas and be heard. This in turn allowed for more solid foundations from which to build our collective knowledge, which, as media critic Dean Starkman suggests, led directly to the Enlightenment, the foundations for democracy and a rapid explosion of scientific advancement,[21] as well as allowing for challenges to the authority of the religious and feudal orthodoxies of the period.

A post-Guttenberg Parenthesis world, it is argued, is one in which, through the manner in which information is exchanged on the Internet, the authoritative, immutable word is untethered. It is a return to a world in which there is virtually no way of confirming a story's origin, or its *truth*. It is a world in which the 'stable' reassuring authority of the old established orders is being undermined and replaced by gut feeling and entrenched tribalism, a place where things might feel a little less certain than they did before. A world, you might say, in which the spectre of the Slender Man can be felt pushing in from the shadows.

*   *   *

In February 2018, as part of an ongoing investigation into Russian governmental interference into the United States election, thirteen Russian nationals were indicted by the FBI due to their alleged involvement in 'information warfare against the United States, with the stated goal of spreading distrust towards the candidates and the political system in general.'[22] As part of their campaign the defendants were accused of making fake social media accounts, posing as US citizens in order to spread 'derogatory information about a number of candidates.'[23] The indictment points the finger squarely at companies such as Facebook and Twitter that are now routinely accused of allowing fake news to spread, giving credibility to false stories through a complicated system of algorithms that enables some stories to be promoted above others on account of how popular they are regardless of whether they are true or not. In March 2017, Google, the world's most popular search engine[24] was accused of spreading fake news by promoting stories through its 'featured snippets in search function' which finds short answers to common queries and forms the basis of quick answers performed by its speaker device, Google Home. If users of this device were to ask, 'is (President Barack) Obama planning a coup' they would be treated to the answer: 'According to details exposed in Western Center for Journalism's exclusive video, not only could Obama be in bed with the communist Chinese, but Obama may in fact be planning a communist coup d'état at the end of his term in 2016!'[25]

Over an eighteen-month period, ex-Google engineer Guillaume Chaslot used a computer programme he had built to investigate bias in YouTube content. Talking to Paul Lewis for the *Guardian*, Chaslot concluded that 'on YouTube, fiction is outperforming reality,'[26] that the company's algorithmic preferences frequently pushed 'videos that are divisive, sensational and conspiratorial.'[27] One example was a search for 'Who is Michelle Obama' which resulted in most of the 'up next' videos in the search's chain being videos claiming she is a man.[28] A YouTube spokesperson responded to the findings by rightly making the point that the results were not a confirmation of bias in the system's algorithm, but merely a reflection of 'viewer interest'.[29] However, in what has become a feature of online interaction, it does perhaps suggest that users are more interested in watching or reading content that mimics or justifies their world view regardless of whether it is factually correct or not. Our instinct to forge social groups with like-minded people only helps to service this further, resulting in the online experience being little more than an echo chamber that makes us less likely to scrutinise the veracity of the information we receive and engage in. Add to this a mechanism that allows us to copy and share stories at the click of a button, open to image, video and sound manipulation, and a completely bogus conspiracy theory can be trending within seconds, appearing as real and legitimate as any other story.

Throughout the world, governments are being urged to clamp down on platforms that are deemed to be undermining democracy or might be detrimental to the health of society.[30] In doing so governments would be imposing the same real-world restrictions on the online space that we have become accustomed to in the offline space. It is a clash of two polarising ideas of what the Internet should be: open-source, unregulated and libertarian versus something which is more controlled and stable but less egalitarian, governed by elite (and I don't necessarily use that term pejoratively) gatekeepers who decide what should or shouldn't be published.

As the old authorities appear increasingly undermined, when 'citizen journalists' with no obligation to ethical standards can become as popular and trusted as long-standing media institutions, it can often feel that rather than offering utopia, the Internet has delivered chaos. A place where nothing is stable and where it no longer matters what is true, only what people believe or want to be true. It is a world where fact and fiction become progressively blurred; and as our offline and online worlds become increasingly merged, those online fictions don't stay online.

They bleed into the real world, with real-world consequences.

*   *   *

One bright spring morning in 2014, in the quiet leafy city of Waukesha, Wisconsin, Greg Steinberg sets out for his usual weekend cycle ride. A short time later, approaching the back of David's Park, he spots what looks like a young girl crawling out of a nearby wood. As he draws closer, he finds to his horror that she is covered in blood.

'Please help me!' she cries, reaching out in pained desperation.

Greg leaps from his bike and rushes to help the girl as she collapses to the ground. Calling 911, Gregg does his best to comfort her as he relays the necessary information to the operator. The girl gives her name as Bella but is reluctant to say who exactly has attacked her until the Waukesha Fire and Police Department arrive moments later and she eventually gives up the information. Bella, whose birth name is Peyton Lautner, is rushed straight to Waukesha Memorial Hospital and immediately operated on where she is found to have nineteen stab wounds in total, with two entering major organs and one missing a major artery by a matter of millimetres. With the name and description of the suspect, the Waukesha police, along with the help of the County Sheriff's department and an emergency helicopter mount an immediate search of the area but fail to find the perpetrator.

Later that afternoon, a Waukesha County Sheriff deputy spots two young girls, no more than twelve years old, sitting on a grass verge by the I-94 highway. Stepping out of the car he asks what they're doing out there. The pair, giving their names as Morgan and Anissa, calmly explain that they have just stopped for a rest as they make their way towards the Nicolet Forest located some 200 miles away. Not quite sure what to make of it all, the deputy orders the pair to stand up and hand over their bags for inspection, which is when he notices the blood spatterings on Morgan's hands and sleeves. The girls pass him an old purse and a large rucksack they have been carrying and watch blankly, making no attempt to flee, as the deputy opens the purse to find a 5-inch steak knife inside, sticky with blood. The girls are immediately arrested and taken into custody where a further search of their bags reveals items of clothing, granola bars, bottles of water and photos of family members.

If things weren't already askew on that warm Saturday afternoon in that ordinarily quiet upper-middle-class Milwaukee suburb, they are about to get very strange indeed. As Morgan and Anissa are grilled over a combined total of nine hours, both will confess their involvement in Bella's stabbing, and after taking the detectives through the events of the last twenty-four hours will reveal a motivation for the attack that is nothing that any of the officers could possibly have imagined.

The three girls, it turns out, are best friends. Only the day before the incident they had celebrated Morgan's twelfth birthday together at the local ice-rink, before returning to her house for a sleepover. The following morning, they had eaten breakfast together before heading out to play at David's Park, a neatly kept playing field on the corner of S. East Avenue and Garfield. After messing about for a while on the swings, Anissa had suggested they head into a small patch of nearby woodland to play hide and seek. With the other two in agreement, the three of them made their way past the row of large houses on Big Bend and across the road into the small pocket of trees on the other side.

As they stepped through the tree line, Anissa and Morgan looked around, making sure that the three of them were totally alone. When Bella turned to see what they were doing, Anissa shouted for Morgan to 'do it', at which point twelve-year-old Morgan pulled a knife from under her plaid jacket and plunged it into the chest, arms and legs of her best friend before she had time to react.

Bella screams in agony and begs for their help as she tries to stand, before falling in a bloody heap on the ground. Anissa calmly asks her friend to try and keep quiet and stop screaming. Bella has little choice as she struggles to breathe and her vision starts to blur; her body is getting colder. She tries once more to stand, and this time manages to plant her feet. Morgan and Anissa watch for a moment as Bella stumbles towards the edge of the forest before falling back down. She begs again for their help, and Morgan and Anissa eventually pull her to her feet again, only to turn her round and walk her deeper into the woods. A few moments later, Morgan and Anissa order their friend to lie down on the ground, before turning their backs on her once and for all and heading home, leaving her there to die.

Back in their separate interview rooms at the Waukesha County Sheriff's Department, having detailed the circumstances of the brutal attack, Morgan and Anissa are each asked why they had done such a thing. The answer was simple, they said; they had done it to please the Slender Man.

When asked later where it was they were heading when the deputy picked them up, their response was even more astonishing: the girls believed that buried deep within the 700,000 acres of Nicolet Forest, they would find Slender Man's mansion where he would be waiting for them with open arms.

Morgan and Anissa discovered Slender independently through reading Creepypasta Wiki, which had become a major repository for the mythos. Most Slender-based Creepypasta tended to adopt the style of reported 'sightings' or 'true-life' encounters that people claimed to have had with the entity. Before long, the two young friends were adopting a similar approach with each other, insisting that they had both seen the figure a number of times throughout their lives. Reinforcing each other's delusion, the pair decided they wanted to gain his approval and in order to do so they would have to murder their best friend. Morgan later insisted they had no particular ill will towards Bella – she was just the most convenient means to an end in their efforts to prove themselves worthy of Slender. As journalist Alex Mar noted in an essay she wrote for *VQR*, the girls had convinced themselves that the very act of killing their friend would also be the thing that conjured Slender Man into existence.[31]

Mercifully Bella survived the ordeal and Morgan and Anissa were both arrested and charged with her attempted murder and placed in separate areas of the Washington County Jail for juveniles. Morgan was adjudged to have been the instigator of the attack and in an effort to determine her capacity to stand trial she was moved to Winnebago Mental Health Institute in the autumn of 2014, to be kept under observation. After completing a twenty-four-hour psychiatric test, it was determined that she was suffering from early-onset schizophrenia and ordered to remain at the institute until her trial. In December 2014, however, the case judge perversely found her fit to stand trial, while simultaneously ordering her to return to the Winnebago Mental Health Institute for further treatment. Having been declared fit for trial, the institute were not legally obliged to take her, resulting in the Catch-22 situation that saw Morgan moved back to the Washington County Jail for juveniles. By late 2015, despite being diagnosed with early-onset schizophrenia over a year ago, Morgan had yet to receive any treatment for it.

At first, Anissa was not judged to have suffered from any type of delusional psychiatric disorder, but was instead thought to have become complicit in Morgan's delusions through a process of 'shared delusional beliefs'.[32] This was said to have been enabled through the unique and intense feelings of loneliness and alienation that Morgan and Anissa shared with each other, which in Anissa's case was considered to have been exacerbated by her parents' divorce and bullying at school. As Alex Mar also noted, it was believed that these shared feelings had contributed to Morgan and Anissa developing a shared perception of the world that only the pair of them could understand, which in turn served to reinforce their unique perspective. In September 2017 Anissa Weier was judged 'not guilty by mental disease or defect' and sentenced to a minimum of three years in a psychiatric hospital, which was later extended to twenty-five at her final sentencing on 21 December of the same year. In October 2017, Morgan Geyser pleaded guilty to attempted first-degree murder but was found not guilty by reason of mental disease or defect. In February 2018 she was sentenced to spend her next forty years in a psychiatric hospital.

Without wanting to justify or conflate the experiences of the three girls, or dilute the severity of the crime, it is possible to see in twelve-year-old Morgan's and Anissa's obsession with Slender Man a desperate desire to be accepted and understood in a world that seemed increasingly to be leaving them behind. For many of us the transition from childhood to adulthood is a perilous and treacherous journey, one that can often leave us feeling dangerously cut adrift as the illusory permanence of childhood is lifted to reveal a world far less fixed and certain than we had once believed it to be. Most of us will find our way back to a world that many hold in common, some will forge their own paths, imagining new worlds into which others can follow and belong, but some of us are fated never to find either.

After news broke of Peyton 'Bella' Lautner's stabbing, an almost inevitable moral panic ensued; the desperate human urge to find a reason for how and why something so terrible could happen, followed by the all too predictable pointing of the finger at the first bogeyman that could be found. Waukesha police chief Russell Jack urged parents to 'restrict and monitor their children's Internet usage',[33] with one Australian news agency declaring Creepypasta an 'Internet horror cult that almost caused a killing'.[34] Many other media outlets were quick to join in the hype, only helping to fuel the legend even further. What they found in Slender Man was not the perpetrator, merely a personification of their fear of the Internet. He was the faceless entity of the faceless technology that has come to dominate our lives, the haunting spectre of a world rapidly evolving and changing from the one we thought we once understood.

Maybe the police were right to urge parents to limit their children's Internet usage if indeed it is leading us toward a disastrous end point. Or as some contemporary thinkers argue, if such is our fate, better yet to harness the speed of technological change to bring about this end even sooner, arguing that only when we get to this moment will we be able to start again and realise a better future.

It was critical theorist Benjamin Noys who coined the term 'accelerationism' in 2010, taking it from Roger Zelazny's 1967 novel *Lord of Light*.[35] The novel, drawing heavily on the mythology of Hinduism and Buddhism, tells the story of a planet colonised by the last survivors of Earth who have gained control over its inhabitants by using technology to turn themselves into gods based on Hindu mythology. In this guise the earthlings/gods hoard technology to suppress the planet's indigenous races. One former earthling, known as Sam, 'the last accelerationist', effectively plays out the role of Buddha by rejecting the status quo and rebelling against his compatriots, securing technology for the masses so they can escape the subjugation of the gods.

Although there are a number of approaches to the idea, the roots of accelerationism can be traced back to the early 1990s, to an extraordinary academic group known as the Cybernetic Culture Research Unit (CCRU). The collective saw the capitalist model specifically as inseparable from self-propelling technology, arguing that the two should be accelerated since they were already unstoppable. Like the Bill Hicks joke admonishing advertisers to kill themselves only for them to become excited at the prospect of being able to market his angry anti-marketing persona, they believed that the Internet was a slave to capitalism and all its worst, most destructive features were a direct result of this.

CCRU was spawned in Warwick University's philosophy department, sometime in October 1995. Primarily led by renegade philosophers Sadie Plant and Nick Land (a leading proponent of the concept of hyperstitions as mentioned in Chapter Two), they were described in a 1998 article by music journalist Simon Reynolds as occupying an 'uncanny interzone between science and superstition'.[36] Their intellectual aesthetic owed as much to Land's deep fascination with the occult and H. P. Lovecraft's Cthulhu mythos as it did to the work of pioneering post-structuralists Gilles Deleuze and Felix Guattari.[37]

To their detractors, operating beyond the normative expectations of academic practice, their work was too thin in research and amounted to little more than a highly intellectualised game of cultural pattern recognition, too in thrall to pop culture and Aleister Crowley, they said. Yet for the five manic years that CCRU was active, they produced a vast emporium of works and ideas that today form the bedrock of some of the most radical, challenging and terrifying ideas in philosophy and cultural theory, with much of it being dispersed through their now defunct website http://www.ccru.net/index.htm.

To the uninitiated, such as myself, stumbling upon ccru.net (sadly taken offline in early 2018) was akin to being a crewmember of the *Nostromo* from Ridley Scott's *Alien*, stepping into the strange abandoned ship of the enigmatic engineers for the first time. Like many forgotten websites, cut off from the present bloodline of the active Net, there was a sense of stumbling upon an ancient relic. The text was an impenetrable loose circuitry of cryptic phrases and insider references, which felt at once both arcane and as if delivered to us from the future. Often these words were dark warnings of an apocalyptic future giving the sense that they had been hermetically sealed away because they weren't supposed to get out. Only having found it did I realise with horror that the place wasn't a tomb; the words were alive and something *had* got out, the true horror being the realisation that we may already be living through that exact apocalypse they were trying to warn us about. Take just the following passage for example, from a piece titled 'Cybehype-6: Dark Side of the Wave':

> In the depths of the economic darkside the world becomes a puppet for things yet to come. It is here that future-positive 'disruptive technologies' are spawned, where labor, capital, and markets are cheap to acquire.[38]

Where others might have heralded the digital age as ushering in a bright utopian future, arriving just in time to fix humanity's greatest problems, CCRU saw something far more disturbing. To them, the digital age amounted to the final phase of a capitalistic death drive speeding us ever nearer to an inevitable cataclysmic end, a system that, rather than offering us ways out, was accelerating the process of diminution to a final end point.

For some the process of accelerationism is at its most unnerving when modern technologies threaten to disrupt or make entirely redundant many of our traditional institutions; from the role of the media, law and order, and politics, down to the ways in which we receive and prioritise information. Although it is important to remember that none of these traditions are old in the grand scheme of things, their destabilisation is for some of us nonetheless deeply unsettling. It may then be even more alarming to discover that the language of the Internet itself might leave us unable to imagine a way out of our current predicaments. In his 2015 book *You Are Not A Gadget*, theorist and tech pioneer Jaron Lanier details the paradox of how Web 2.0 platforms on the one hand make it easier to share our expressions and ideas, but on the other, through their readily assembled, easy to navigate interfaces, actually limit us by removing the possibility for altering and playing with the medium of expression itself.[39] As Marshall McLuhan famously stated, 'the medium is the message'[40] by which he meant that it isn't only the content of an idea that influences us but also the mechanism with which that content is delivered. In this sense, if you imagine the tools we use to communicate online as a language in themselves, influencing the way we think and formulate ideas, if that language becomes restricted so too will it restrict our creativity.

An obvious example of this would be Twitter's 140-character format (doubled to 280 in 2017). Enforcing a tweet to be brief can have positive consequences; it encourages us to think more carefully about precisely what it is we are trying to say. On the other hand, it can also lead to the propensity of sharing only small snippets of information, in which the true scope and depth of ideas are lost and reduced to at best a superficial rendering, and at worst a complete misappropriation. To engage with others on Twitter means having to communicate within these parameters. There are of course many other online tools with which to share information, and who's to say that communicating in only 140 characters might not in fact invigorate our creative potential or lead to more and better ways to be creative. Either way, if Twitter is where the conversation is taking place, if you want to get involved you must do so on the company's terms.

Lanier also highlights the emergence of the advertising business model as one of a handful of viable ways to make money from creative industries which are increasingly dependent on the digital sphere (possibly all of them, one day) as another way in which our imaginations are being shackled. The impact is twofold. If receiving money from advertising is the only way to make significant earnings for the things we create, as Lanier argues, we will be coerced into creating in ways that satisfy that model;[41] musicians will make music that is more likely to appeal to those sections of the market that are streaming music more regularly; journalism becomes an industry more focused on clickbait headlines and articles that grab the audience's attention, and bring eyeballs to their sponsors' adverts, rather than one that delivers something useful. If algorithms decide which content deserves to be more visible than others, it stands to reason that people will also create content that serves the algorithm rather than look to create something innovative.

Such a model also leads to an explosion of advertising in our personal space, as anyone who has ever tried to read an article online while having to contend with tropical sunsets emerging out of the third paragraph, or the sudden appearance of the latest Škoda speeding across the top of the page will attest. As we become enveloped by advertising, even our creative freedom to choose the things we want to buy becomes restricted thanks to the clever use of algorithms to decide what you need, based on your previous search history or something you might have liked on a friend's Facebook page. There are few things that unsettle me more than the terrifying scene in Stephen Spielberg's adaptation of *Minority Report* where the central character John Anderson is bombarded by targeted adverts that pop up on every adjacent surface as he strides through a building on his way to work. What unsettles is how preposterous that seemed in 2002, and how commonplace it feels now.

It could be argued that as long as this model dominates we might find innovative ways to do things within it, but we will always in some way be constrained by it. In a sense it would be as if we have become trapped inside a Zeno's Paradox of false progress. Where once the Internet appeared to offer us an infinite potential of creative possibilities, we discover it isn't the infinity of an ascending whole-number scale, merely one moving eternally upwards from 0 through the decimal numbers, fated never to get higher than 1.

The late Mark Fisher, cultural theorist and early member of CCRU who tragically committed suicide in 2017, similarly became increasingly concerned that we might never escape the trap of what is termed 'capitalist realism',[42] and that – especially since its hijacking of the digital sphere – we are becoming increasingly entombed by it. Fisher examined this through the concept of hauntology. The term, a portmanteau of haunting and ontology – the philosophical study of the nature of being – was coined by French Philosopher Jacques Derrida in his 1993 book, *Spectres of Marx: The state of the debt, the work of mourning and the new international.* For Derrida, the term is a play on the temporality of ideas, or more precisely the impossibility of eradicating knowledge or ideas (in this case pertaining to Marxist philosophy) once they have been conceived. From the moment they exist, they remain forever a part of our collective knowledge, haunting our perception of both the past and the future. Much like in the way something new is discovered, learning the Earth revolves around the sun for example, it is no longer possible to conceive of a time when this idea was not understood. The implication is that only by returning to before the idea was conceived could we hope to imagine an alternate and 'better' future unshaped by it. It is through concepts such as hauntology that we might better understand, if not support, the despotic fixation for burning books or ISIL's strategy of destroying ancient cultural artefacts. Such practices form the practical reality of attempts to expunge the past in the hope of creating a different future.

In the noughties, Fisher, and a number of other cultural theorists, found evidence that in sociocultural terms at least, we were approaching an evolutionary cul-de-sac, by applying the idea to emergent trends in art and pop culture – in particular with regards to the growing sense that 'westernised' music, especially electronic music, had already reached this creative dead-end. If electronic music was supposed to evince a sense of the future, it seemed only now to evince a sense of nostalgia: 'There was no leading edge of innovation any more.'[43] In the accelerationist interpretation, the Internet can be viewed as a mechanism in service to our restrictive social and economic models hastening our arrival at the end of this cul-de-sac. Consider the way in which the television drama *Stranger Things* was universally received, for example. As much a fan of the series as I am, it's hard not to see it as symptomatic of a cultural dead-end – a sort of televisual backwash of almost every trope and idea from the genre of horror and science fiction imaginable, reassuring in its nostalgia but trapped by the limits of its language.

If we choose to see Slender Man as the Internet's own monster, something that embodies all that is to be feared about where the Internet and digital technology is taking us as a species, it is little surprise that he is associated with luring us, and, particularly, children to their doom – a perfect metaphor for a damned future. As we become ever more tightly wound up in a feedback loop of diminishing imagination, the Slender Man stands in the shadows, waiting to smother us with his tentacle embrace.

Slender Man's association with children has often seen him compared to the Pied Piper of Hamelin. In the German folktale, thought to date back to the 1300s, the people from the town of Hamelin are struggling to rid themselves of a troublesome rat infestation when a mysterious stranger arrives promising to take care of it in return for a modest fee. The townspeople accept his help and the following day the stranger, using his skills as a pipe player, leads the rats away. However, when he returns for his fee the citizens refuse to pay him. In retaliation the piper lures all the children from the village to a mountain from which they will never return. It is easy to see the comparison with the Slender Man since both characters are considered monstrous unknown others who are said to commit the most heinous crime imaginable: stealing our children away.

If Slender Man is to be compared to the Pied Piper, we might as well read this as symptomatic of our wider concerns about 'the Internet'. Where once we saw it as a magic technology that we hoped would improve our lives, like the Piper with his mysterious pipe, now suddenly it has turned on us, corrupting our children and robbing us of all hope for our future. Not an unfair analogy if indeed Slender Man embodies the worst of the Net.

But is there another way to look at it?

Something frequently overlooked in Slender's comparison to the Piper is that it isn't the Piper who is the villain, but the townspeople. Not only do they double-cross him and refuse to pay for his services, we could just as easily say that in the Piper's final act he isn't stealing the children away, but merely protecting them from the 'rat-infested' world their forebears have created. In other words, the problem is not 'the Internet': the problem is us.

If I may be allowed to add my own Creepypasta entry to the myth of Slender Man,[44] it would be to portray him not as an emblem of the terror of the unknown that lurks on the horizon of an uncertain digital future but rather as a messenger from that future sent back to guide us. How fitting that it would be the younger generations, the children, who are most aware of the Slender Man; not only are they the ones who will be most harmed by a failure to correct a doomed future, but it will be them who will save us from it.

That being said, for all the fear of how the Internet might be damaging us, it is important to remember just how young it is. We've barely got the Internet out of the box, let alone plugged it in. Should we not expect a few teething issues? The simple fact may be that as a species we just haven't yet figured out how to best work it to our advantage (although of course, 'best to our advantage' is a wholly subjective phrase). We shouldn't be panicked by online behaviour that we don't understand or feel threatened by, but see it as part of a process of an entire species learning to use a new tool. Humanity has always fought with itself in the offline world, establishing laws and rules to create societies; why should we expect it to be any different in the online world? As these online battles play out over how we might best use our latest tool, it is worth examining what it is exactly that scares us about it. Where once the Internet was thought to offer something akin to a beneficial noosphere, a place to pool our best ideas, it has left some fearing it has merely opened a door to chaos, disrupting established orders and threatening all the 'progress' that such order has contributed to. Is this fear warranted or is it born from the inconvenience of hearing other voices and perspectives that aren't like ours, voices that have been made louder and more potent thanks to the Internet? For all the uncertainty of a 'post-truth', more fluid world, could something like the #metoo movement have been successful in a pre-Internet age? For all those who talk about a return to a more stable, simpler time, do they mean a time where they don't have to be confronted by ideas such as white privilege? That sense of fear and uncertainty could simply be the feeling of being inside the paradigm shift of a changing world.

Indeed, for many, despite the disruptiveness, the immediate consequences of a digitally accelerated culture remain profoundly appealing. The feminist philosopher Donna Harraway was an early accelerationist before the term had been adopted. Her 1984 seminal essay *The Cyborg Manifesto* provides an idea of what a post-accelerated world, in which our bodies and minds become more and more entwined with the digital sphere, might look like. Harraway's essay invites us to imagine the human evolving into cyborg – a 'hybrid of machine and organism'[45] – ushering in a post-gender world. Since the cyborg is not human in the traditional sense, it is transcendent of restricting social conventions to do with perceptions of gender, a transcendence which by extension could be applied to all restrictive perceptions – for example of race, disability and sexuality.

What cyber-utopians had hoped was that the Internet and the virtual space would help us escape the worst aspects of ourselves, yet this virtual space is nothing if not an extension of ourselves. It was always going to be subject to the same stresses and complications we experience in real-world societies. And like those real-world societies, it will always be evolving through the ongoing processes of different ideas and perspectives rubbing up against each other. As unsettling as it may be, there are positive reasons to challenge stable established orders. Take one recent example: in 1991 as speaker of the United States House of Representatives, Newt Gingrich gave an interview to the influential *Broadcasting and Cable* magazine telling advertisers not to sponsor radio stations that played 'Rap music'.

Gingrich's stance was one adopted by many US government officials that sought to demonise a growing trend that they didn't understand. Concerned that hip hop was a threat to the country's moral values, instead of seeking to understand it, they tried to destroy it. In 2017, R&B/hip hop surpassed rock music to become the biggest selling music genre in the United States and one of its leading cultural exports. Although as a genre it was already well on its way there, its dominance owes much to the free-spirited sharing and streaming culture of the Internet. Interestingly, as Thomas Pettitt acknowledges in his Gutenberg Parenthesis theory, hip hop as a genre, much like the orality of pre-printing press culture, is a medium that thrives on the mutability of ideas and the fluidity of sampling. Once dismissed and often maligned as an inferior art form, hip hop and its myriad offshoots are now widely regarded as superior modes of innovative, creative expression.

As for concerns over Web 2.0 platforms, 'the cult of the noble amateur' and the drift toward thinking which prioritises the wisdom of the crowd over the authority of individual experts, it seems often that the primary concern is not the diminishing quality of creative content but more to do with the fear that people won't be individually rewarded and recognised for their creative ideas. Yet, in the grand scheme of things, what does it matter who has an idea exactly? Is it not more important that the idea exists in the first place, that it is used well and propagated widely, so that it can be better understood and improved upon? As for questioning the quality of work that might emerge from a culture no longer chained to the obsession with authorship and ownership, we might consider the work of one of literature's greatest pilferers: William Shakespeare. Routinely regarded as the finest writer of the English-speaking world, unlikely ever to be surpassed, Shakespeare is a pure product of the pre-printing-press age, his work pulling liberally from 'Plutarch's *Lives* and Holinshed's *Chronicles* to Montaigne's *Essays*'.[46]

In 2018, a book, written by self-taught Shakespeare scholar Dennis McCarthy and Professor of English June Schlueter revealed that one manuscript in particular had proved a source of inspiration for up to eleven of Shakespeare's plays. McCarthy and Schlueter made the discovery after applying the plagiarism software WCopyfind to a late 16th-century text titled *A Brief Discourse of Rebellion and Rebels*. The unpublished manuscript, written by a minor courtier of Queen Elizabeth I called George North was found to include source material for plays including *King Lear*, *Macbeth* and *Henry V*. Not only did Shakespeare use 'the same words as North, but often (used) them in scenes about similar themes, and even the same historical character.'[47]

There is no reason to assume our digital fate is sealed, that we are a species hurtling towards a destruction of our own making, locked in by the tools we have made. It is far more likely that in a thousand years time we will be discussing the problems of a new technology that will make the Internet look like two cups joined together by a piece of string. Whether by considered choice, survival instinct or by pre-determined genetic compulsion we are a species of explorers, primed always to be looking for new ways and new ideas, never more productive than when confronted with a problem that threatens our existence. If ever we should fear that we might be losing our way, bear in mind the words of historian Aaron Sachs that I came across in Rebecca Solnit's *A Field Guide to Getting Lost*. In responding to a query of Solnit's on the subject of exploration, Sachs replied, 'Explorers were always lost because they'd never been to these places before. They never expected to know exactly where they were . . . In my opinion their most important skill was simply a sense of optimism about surviving and finding their way.'[48]

Chapter Ten

EVERY STORY IS A GHOST STORY

'He was not staring at her anymore. He was still. He had gone. The moment of truth had vanished forever, and she would never know. What had happened was Then, was already past, in some other dimension of time, and the present was Now, part of a future he could not share.'

Daphne Du Maurier – 'A Border-Line Case'

The ghost holds a unique place in the world of the supernatural. As capable of scaring us senseless as they are of inflicting us with the deepest of melancholies, they also come in many forms: the ghosts that we carry with us in our daily lives, memories of those we have loved and lost or perhaps even wronged; thoughts that sit in the deepest parts of the psyche, straining to become manifest. But what of the apparitions that seem not to have been brought forth from the subconscious? Those that have no connection to the observer but instead seem to be reaching out to us from a seemingly timeless space?

For some, to witness a ghost, particularly that of a relative, might bring a certain comfort: the reassuring glimpse of a life beyond death. Almost without exception, however, dating back to our earliest cultures from those of the Igbo in West Africa to the Bengali of South Asia, the sighting of a ghost was rarely something to celebrate. Commonly the appearance of a ghost would speak of something unsettled, the result of a body not properly buried perhaps, or one that had been lost at sea, or it might be a sign that the cause of death was suspicious and required avenging. Failure to rectify the situation could condemn the ghost to an eternity of restlessness.

For the ancient Sumerians, death was an act from which there was ordinarily no coming back, the souls of the dead left to dwell in Kur, the 'Land of No Return'. It was a place where all men and women were equal regardless of their actions in life, no matter how rich or poor; a place where they would remain for the rest of eternity in dreary un-light watched over by Ereshkigal, the dark queen of the Netherworld. The oppressive conditions of Kur were said to be alleviated for the dead if their surviving family continued to make offerings of food and drink once they were gone. Failure to do so would see the ghost of the deceased return to punish their callous relatives with misfortune and ill health.

In ancient Japan the appearance of a ghost, or yūrie, was especially ominous. Yūrie were sometimes said to transform from souls – or reikon – in fits of explosive emotion often motivated by vengeance. Violent murder or suicide would almost always presage the arrival of a yūrie intent on retribution. Until the disturbance had been settled they would be fated to haunt the living indefinitely. Yūrie are traditionally portrayed as woman with long black hair, wearing white burial robes with hands hanging loosely from the wrists, an image that fans of the character Sadako Yamamura might recognise from author Kôji Suzuki's petrifying Ringu series. Yamamura's portrayal as a traditional yūrie with a penchant for climbing out of TVs and video monitors, as realised to devastating effect in Hideo Nakata's terrifying 1998 adaptation of the first book in the series, is for me the most nightmarish portrayal of a ghost in cinematic history.

Often, a ghost or apparition is said to be inexorably linked to a specific location. For those of us living in the United Kingdom there are many such ghosts, two of our tourist boards claiming the Great Tower of London and Edinburgh Castle as their respective country's most haunted destinations. However, I have always found such a notion problematic, in a very literal sense at least, for reasons laid out with a great mournful and affecting beauty in *A Ghost Story*. In this striking 2017 film, written and directed by David Lowery, the eponymous ghost of the title, having chosen to remain behind on Earth, is fated to drift through time as all the world changes around him. Although Lowery slips the ghost back into his original corporeal timeline, I have always wondered where such a ghost might end up were it not so easy to escape the seemingly ceaseless arrow of time; just where might a ghost be left to haunt tens of billions of years from now when the planet has long since been obliterated by the sun?

When it comes to the sheer terror of the supernatural, for me there are few more disturbing notions than the poltergeist; malignant spirits of wrathful agency dead-set on singling you out for inexplicable – and therefore, deeply frightening – reasons. Though some consider supposed poltergeist activity to be the result of the extra-sensory projections of troubled teenage minds, it is surely in the portrayal as an active spirit that the notion is most potent.

I have always felt a little haunted by this idea.

Doubtless there are many of my generation whose first experiences of the fabled 'knocking-ghost' came through Tobe Hooper's mesmeric 1982 film *Poltergeist* (which many forget was written by Stephen Spielberg). Perhaps it is simply nostalgia that draws me back to this masterful movie, hypnotic in its alluring fusion of slick Hollywood with a less familiar place that seems to call out silently to us from somewhere between the frames.

But there is something else.

Although there is little telling which was cause and which effect, for as long as I can remember since seeing this film, I have had a recurring, terrifying poltergeist nightmare. Always occurring in that liminal lucid space shortly before waking, it begins with me standing at the top of the stairs of an old childhood home while friends or members of my family are gathered at the bottom. But as I walk down to join them, something has caught me in its grip. Something of unfathomable malignance from which I know I cannot escape. As I kick and scream, it continues to pull me back further and further and then ... I wake up. Every time it is the same.

I understand this to be a common dream trope and was once advised that the way to do away with it might be to try to turn around and face this unseen, manifest fear. I've not yet been able to achieve this, though I'm sure there's a good lesson in there somewhere ...

So it always fills me with a particular sense of caution, and no little excitement when I learn of new alleged poltergeist events, particularly ones that invoke the work of Nigel Kneale involving learned men and women on the hunt for ghosts ...

At thirty-three years old, Tony Cornell was by no means the most senior member of the Cambridge University Society for Psychical Research, but he was certainly one of the more proactive, always on the look-out for a new site to investigate. Like most members of CUSPR, he was a proud rationalist with little time for superstition or spiritual nonsense, whose interest in supposed paranormal and supernatural events began from a thoroughly sceptical point of view. He did, however, maintain a healthy fascination with the strange due to a peculiar event he had experienced ten years previously.

As a young naval officer during the Second World War, Tony had been stationed in southern India, close to the Nilgiri Mountains, where he became enthralled by stories of the local Fakirs – holy men and women without any possessions or relations who are believed to possess mystical powers. It was said that a Fakir could perform miracles, with many people travelling for miles to seek their wisdom and guidance. One such Fakir was said to be living in the hills not far from where Tony was billeted, and although thoroughly dubious, Tony was nonetheless intrigued enough to try to find the man in the hope of witnessing these 'miracles' for himself.

After a number of hours trekking through rolling tree-capped hills, across treacherous paths flanked by steep jagged cliffs, Tony had made it to about 6,000ft above sea level when he came across an old man in simple clothes standing at the end of a small plateau, as if he had been waiting for him. To the side of the plateau lay a steep drop into a gulley with a stream gushing through it.

Without acknowledging the young Navy officer, the Fakir asked what it was that Tony wanted.

'I hear you can perform miracles,' replied a startled Tony.

'You're too materialistic,' said the old man, 'but I'll give you what you want.'

There was a pause as the Fakir thought for a moment. Tony smiled awkwardly, suddenly self-conscious at this clash of cultures.

'Look towards those hills, my son,' the Fakir said finally.

Tony was not quite sure what to expect.

'Those hills?' Tony said, pointing towards some prominent peaks in the east.

The Fakir gestured yes with a gentle nod of the head and Tony duly turned back to inspect them.

'Do you see?' he asked.

Tony looked confused, scratching his head before turning back to the man.

'I'm sorry I don't . . .'

But the man wasn't there.

'Well, my son,' shouted the Fakir from the far side of the stream. 'Did that entertain you?'

Tony stood for a moment trying to fathom how a seventy-year-old man could have dropped into the gulley and raced to the other side of the fast-flowing waters in only a matter of seconds. Smiling now to himself, he watched as the Fakir slowly picked his way along the rocky bank before disappearing into the bush.

The Society of Psychical Research, of which Tony's CUSPR group was an affiliate, had been established in 1882 largely in response to a peculiar craze that had been gripping the nation, which had its origins in a small wooden house in the tiny hamlet of Hydesville, New York. It was there that in 1848 two sisters – Kate and Margaret Fox – claimed to have made contact with the spirit of a dead man who had communicated with them through a series of knocks and bangs. In other words, they had allegedly made contact with a 'poltergeist' and in doing so had inadvertently created a movement that would come to be known as Spiritualism. As news of the Fox sisters' incredible claims spread through the UK, it wasn't long before everybody from scullery staff, to Queen Victoria was conducting séances in an attempt to communicate with the dead.

As the movement grew in popularity throughout the world, so too did the stories of strange paranormal happenings that seemed suddenly to be breaking out everywhere. For those caught up in the scientific fervour of the Enlightenment age, the emergence of such stories was a horrifying riposte to the increasingly rationalist and atheistic principles catalysing academia at the time. However, although many in the scientific community dismissed paranormal claims out of hand, a small number of academics led by Henry and Eleanor Sidgwick, William Barrett and Edmund Gurney amongst others, decided instead to 'approach these varied problems without prejudice or prepossession of any kind . . . in the same spirit of exact and unimpassioned enquiry which has enabled science to solve so many problems, once not less obscure nor less hotly debated.'[1] And so the SPR was born: the world's first Ghostbusters.

The Cambridge branch of the society had been founded in 1906, and fifty years later existed mostly as an organisation for like-minded people to get together and share stories regarding the latest papers and theories they had read. But sometimes, if they were lucky, the chance for something more hands-on would crop up like that which Tony brought to the group one evening in November 1957. The curious case had presented itself a few days earlier when a young journalist based out of Wisbech, some forty miles north of Cambridge, had contacted him.

At the beginning of October, Anthony Wilmot, who worked for the *Wisbech Advertiser*, had overheard a conversation about some mysterious goings-on at an old manor house known as Hannath Hall, situated out in the Fens not far from where he lived. The house, he would later discover, had been plagued by hauntings for years. Wilmot didn't care much for silly ghost stories but after learning one of the current tenants was the local Labour candidate, Derek Page, he couldn't resist following up on the story.

Having arranged to interview Derek and his wife Audrey, as well as Audrey's mother Rose who lived with the family, Wilmot had arrived with tongue firmly in cheek only to find them in a state of some distress. For the next hour, he was treated to a variety of extraordinary tales outlining their experiences since they had arrived from Cheshire two months previously.

They had only been there a matter of days, as Audrey explained, when she was first awoken in the early hours of the morning by the sound of a very clear and insistent tapping that seemed to be coming from just outside her bedroom. Thinking she had only imagined it she turned to go back to sleep only for it to come again, this time a little louder. Sitting up in bed, knowing it couldn't have been Derek since he stayed in Ipswich during the week for work, she had assumed it was one of the children or perhaps her mother who slept in the bedroom opposite.

'Yes?' Audrey had whispered in the dark. 'Hello?'

Knock, knock, came the reply.

Audrey bolted upright and hurriedly switched on the bedside light.

'Hello?' she asked again.

But there was no reply.

Collecting herself, she stepped out of bed and made her way cautiously towards the door. With a trembling hand, she took hold of the handle and eased the door open a fraction, peering through the gap into the corridor beyond.

There was nobody there.

Ever since that night the family had been hearing similar knocks and taps throughout the house. Audrey was certain that, on a separate occasion, she had heard footsteps descending the stairs with a clearly defined shifting of weight from one foot to another. She had been alone in the house at the time.

A few weeks later, Audrey's mother Rose had woken up after feeling a violent jolt against her bed, and not long after, despite being partially deaf, she had been woken in the middle of the night by an inexplicably loud crashing sound just outside the door, as if the door itself were being smashed in.

Derek had not heard these noises himself and joked that it was probably the old Tories who used to own the house turning in their graves at the thought of him living there. He did recount one rather strange story of his own, however. Not long after they'd moved in, his mother had travelled down from Manchester with a view to staying with the family for a few weeks. After a couple of nights sleeping in the spare bedroom she began to experience a recurring set of bizarre and terrifying nightmares. A couple of times she had found herself floating out of her body and looking down at herself as she slept with the very vivid sense that something profoundly malignant was trying to pull her away, and that if she didn't return to her body she would never wake up. Other times she found herself trapped under the legs of a horse as it kicked violently at her face. After less than a week, having also started to hear the noises, she made a hasty retreat back to Manchester.

Audrey and Rose told the young journalist that the knocking sounds had become worse over the last few weeks, and that, increasingly, they seemed to be coming from one room. Located at the north end of the first floor, the room was assumed by the family to have been a bedroom at some point owing to its size, but was currently being used for storage. Since, unlike every other room in the property, it had never been rigged up to the mains, the Pages were happy to keep it that way and rarely had cause to go in there. After leaving Hannath Hall that afternoon, Wilmot determined to do some further digging of his own. And that, as he explained to Tony over the phone a few weeks later, was when things started to get really interesting.

The house, as he discovered, had been built sometime in the 16th century, and was thought originally to have belonged to a Richard Sparrow, earning it the nickname Sparrow's Nest. Over the years it had been passed through a number of owners, gaining its current name after being purchased by Joseph Hannath in 1812. The house was sold again to George Williams in 1899 who elected to keep the name Hannath Hall. Wilmot got in touch with the building's current owner, Hugh Williams, George's grandson, to find out more. Much to his surprise, Hugh and his family – who had lived in the house for forty years before deciding to rent it out to Audrey and Derek – were more than familiar with the spooky goings on there. Hugh went on to describe an incident a few years back involving his brother Peter, who, while staying alone in the house, had witnessed a door handle turning of its own accord. Another time, Hugh's nieces had suffered vivid nightmares while sleeping in the now disused room at the far end of the property, and had also awakened one night to find a pair of blood-stained hands floating in the room with them.

'That wouldn't be the bedroom on the north side would it, by any chance?' Wilmot had asked.

'You mean the haunted bedroom?' replied Hugh.

As it turned out, Hugh's family had taken to calling it this on account of a morbid story they had heard about one of the previous owners.

Long before the house had been wired for electricity, the 'haunted room' had in fact been the sole master bedroom. As the story went, it was in this room that the wife of former owner Joseph Hannath, who bought the property from his father in 1812, had died young. The death had left Joseph so bereft he couldn't bear to release the body for burial, deciding instead to have it interred in an open coffin which he kept at the end of the marital bed. For six weeks, an increasingly unhinged Joseph continued to order his servants to bring his wife three meals a day as her body steadily putrefied. Eventually, with the stench becoming unbearable, Joseph was brought to his senses just long enough to take the body into the front garden where he is said to have buried it under a large horse chestnut tree.

As Wilmot continued to explain over the phone to Tony, since the first article had been well received, and with Halloween drawing near, he approached Derek and Audrey about the possibility of spending a night in the house with a view to publishing another article about it. Since the couple were eager to prove they weren't making anything up, they welcomed Wilmot – joined this time by a senior colleague from the paper as well as a local friend, and his pet Labrador Simba – back to Hannath Hall on 31 October to conduct an investigation.

Later that night, as the Devil's hour approached, and with Audrey, Rose and the children fast asleep, Derek, Wilmot and his colleague took up positions on the landing while the friend and Simba kept watch in the old master bedroom. Despite some initial nervous joshing, it hadn't taken long for a pervasive eeriness to descend. When from somewhere in the house a clock struck twelve, Simba began to whimper mournfully. A noise was heard from inside a spare bedroom off to the side but not one of the men had the courage to investigate. A moment later they all sensed a significant drop in temperature followed by the smell of sandalwood that seemed to be sweeping back and forth along the corridor.

Although little else occurred that evening, whether it had been the charge of the occasion or merely the atmosphere of the evocative old building, when the men finally called it a night at 2.30 a.m., it was with the distinct impression that they had experienced *something*. It was a few days later, unable to shake the weight of the evening from his mind that Wilmot decided to get in touch with the Society of Psychical Research.

*   *   *

It's just after 8 p.m. on the evening of 17 November, with only the barest sliver of a waning moon in the sky, when Tony and fellow CUSPR members Alan Gauld, David Murray and Michael Brotherton assemble briefly outside Tony's apartment before getting into his car and heading out towards Wisbech. With the university towers and spires of the city receding behind them, they soon slip out beyond the city's edge and into the darkness of the East Anglian countryside. Making their way northwards along winding country roads, with eyes adjusting, a broad menagerie of stars is slowly beginning to emerge from above, while below, the strange flatlands of rich black earth and shimmering waterways of the Fens are encroaching.

It has just gone 10 p.m. when the team eventually arrive at the pretty market town of Wisbech, located on the banks of the River Nene. The town, known as the capital of the Fens, is a rare fixture in an otherwise ever-changing landscape. Four hundred years ago, the region was a mass of treacherous peaty swamps and quicksilver surfaces, a perilous place for unsuspecting travellers foolish enough to go chasing the many will-o-wisps that regularly danced

Mist descends over the Fens.

across its transitory planes. They may appear tamed for now but the Fens remain a border country where the firm and fluid mingle, of histories washed from the land and an ever-shifting reminder of the illusion of solidity.

Turning into the town centre, the team find the short and bespectacled Wilmot waiting for them outside the Rose and Crown along with two friends he has unexpectedly brought along for the evening. The appearance of the two men, who introduce themselves as Mr Trumpess and Mr Perryman, immediately raises Alan's suspicions, concerned that they might be under instruction from the journalist to guarantee some 'strange' goings-on later.

'We should keep an eye on them,' he warns the others as they drive off again.

The group continue in convoy behind Wilmot's car and it's not long before they're back among the fields and waterways staring out at the edge of fenland flats that seem to merge with the night, when the temperature takes a sudden plunge. The men watch with concern as a thick fog starts to sweep across the fields, until finally it has all but engulfed the cars. Tony works hard to keep Wilmot's rear lights in view as Alan struggles to locate their position on the map. After another ten minutes or so, Tony catches Wilmot making a sharp left turn, which according to Alan has them heading in the direction of the small hamlet of Tydd St Mary. With Wilmot's car having disappeared into the fog, they have little option but to continue straight along the road. After half a mile or so, the fog finally begins to clear, revealing the journalist's car parked up ahead at the entrance to a driveway. And in a space some fifty yards beyond, obscured by darkness and a dense row of tall trees, they can just make out the imposing presence of Hannath Hall. As Tony turns into the drive, moving through the line of trees, the large red-brick pile looms out of the darkness.

There is something of the dark fairy-tale about the five-bedroom Elizabethan manor, flanked by two prominent gable roofs and shrouded by trees that seem unusually tall for these parts; its stately symmetry oddly offset by the peculiar placement of the building's central windows. That all the windows appear so small for such a large façade – and with only one presently lit from within – does little to dispel the ominous air of the building's brooding visage. Seeing the place now up close, how its lines have warped and buckled with age, and how thirstily the creeping vines of ivy seem to be claiming it for their own, it feels as much a natural part of the landscape as any surrounding birch or alder.

As the men exit their car, making sure to remember their notebooks, they are struck by the stillness. A strained animal cry from the dark of the field opposite breaks the silence.

'Impressive isn't it,' says Wilmot as he walks round to the front. 'Come on, I'll introduce you.'

With Derek and Audrey out at the cinema, and the children tucked up in bed, Audrey's mother Rose steps out to welcome the men, inviting them to come inside and sit down in the living room, a comparatively small space at the front of the house. Rose disappears to make teas and coffees as the men take seats around the table and, with a warm fire licking and crackling at the back of the room, Wilmot takes the opportunity to recount the details of his last visit. It isn't long before talk turns to the haunted bedroom.

'Yes, that's where I hear it coming from too,' says Rose as she brings the drinks into the room, barely audible above the growing chatter of the men.

'What was that?' asks Tony, as Rose quietly takes her seat beside him at the table.

'The dreadful knockings,' she replies, bringing a sudden hush to the room.

'Have you heard them recently, Mrs Halls?' asks Alan as they all move in closer to listen.

'Oh, yes, I heard them only two hours ago,' she replies.

At that moment the sound of the opening front door is followed by the entrance of Derek and Audrey who, after apologising for their lateness, quickly set about introducing themselves to Tony and the rest of the group.

No more than ten minutes later, Audrey is leading them on a tour of the house; first to the large washroom at the north end, then back to the living room, pointing out the pantry and the kitchen to the side, before taking them through to an impressive dining room at the back of the southern end and on into the equally impressive lounge at the front. They continue up the red-carpeted stairs and on to the landing. It was on these stairs, Audrey explains, that she had heard the sound of footsteps not long after they had moved in. The landing is illuminated with a single bulb, which flickers weakly as it struggles to keep the shadows at bay. Along the walls are a number of antique military artefacts that have belonged to the Williams family for many generations.

Continuing the tour, Audrey points out her mother's bedroom at the back followed by the master bedroom where she and Derek sleep, directly opposite. Moving quietly over the thickly carpeted hall, past the antique swords and flintlocks, Audrey stops the men outside the children's room and gives the door a gentle push to reveal the two small bodies of her three-year-old son and five-year-old daughter, lying sound asleep in their beds. Continuing on, just past the children's room to the right is the spare bedroom where Derek's mother had experienced her unsettling dreams; and then, finally, they come to the large disused room at the northern end.

'The haunted bedroom,' says Wilmot from the back.

'Let's call this Bedroom A, shall we?' says Alan, eager to keep things professional.

'May I?' asks Tony, looking to Audrey.

'Please. But mind there's no light, so you'll need to switch on your torches.'

Tony eases open the door, and, assisted by Alan and Michael's torchlight, leads the group inside.

Moving the beams around they find a number of packing cases stacked up against the inside left corner, with further piles of books and chairs placed up on top of them; three chairs and a dressing table are lined up against the back and in the far left corner, pieces of a dismantled brass bed leaning against the wall. A few other bits are dotted about including two mattresses on the floor lying end to end under the front window. Wilmot explains they had been placed there on his last visit to the house when he and his friends had kept their late night vigil. Alan and Tony agree it will be useful to keep them as they are for sitting on later.

Next, Derek leads the group outside to make a quick inspection of the exterior, but they find nothing of note. Once back inside, after a quick synchronising of watches, Alan makes his way upstairs on to the landing to start preliminary observations while Tony, David and Michael gather everyone else into the living room so they can get their measure.

'I thought we might begin with a séance,' says Tony, taking a wine glass from a nearby cabinet and placing it upside down in the middle of the table. A ripple of excitement circles the room but Trumpess looks uneasy.

What Tony doesn't tell them is that he and the rest of his group have devised the séance gambit as a way to keep an eye on the others while they initiate their investigations.

With them all finally seated, Tony takes a set of cards from his pocket – letters of the alphabet, numbers zero to nine and the words 'YES' and 'NO' – and lays them out in a wide circle around the glass.

'I take it you're all familiar with spirit boards?'

All nod enthusiastically and draw closer together.

Tony takes a candle from the mantelpiece and places it on the table, lighting it with a single strike of a match.

Meanwhile, upstairs along the dimly lit landing, having made his way to the northern end, Alan closes the door to Bedroom A, and positions a small table just outside with a thermometer placed on top. He marks the reading as 60°F in his notebook then heads back downstairs.

'All set,' he says to Tony, poking his head into the living room.

'Great,' says Tony. 'Let's begin. Derek would you mind turning off the lights?'

Derek switches off the main lights and returns to his seat as Alan clicks on his torch and returns to the landing upstairs.

With everyone seated, basked in the yellow flickering light of the candle and the dying embers of the fire, Tony instructs the Pages, Wilmot and his friends as well as Rose, Michael and David, to all place their fingers on top of the upturned glass.

'Is there anybody there?' asks Tony.

There is no response.

A scattering of nervous laughter breaks out before Tony asks again, 'Is there anybody there?'

'Look, it's moving!' says Rose.

All attention is fixed on the glass, as it clearly begins to shift along the table.

'Is there anybody there?' repeats Tony.

Upstairs, in the pitch black of the hall, from the top of the stairs Alan is trying to ignore the voices coming up from the kitchen when he hears a loud snap. Although he can't be sure, it sounded like it came from inside Bedroom A. He points the flashlight down the hall, and is surprised to see that the door is slightly ajar. Momentarily unsettled he holds the light on the gap in the door and slowly starts to move towards the room, stopping to check the children are still in bed, before continuing on his way to the bottom of the corridor. He stops outside Bedroom A and listens again for any sound coming from inside.

Wilmot lets out a gasp as the glass begins to shift across the surface of the table stopping just in front of the card labelled YES.

'Now come on, who's doing that?'

'Really it could be any of us,' says Tony.

'Well it isn't me, I'm hardly touching it, look!' says Derek.

'Shhh,' says Audrey, 'we need to concentrate.'

'Thank you, Audrey. Perhaps you'd like to ask the next question?'

Audrey looks nervously to Tony and pauses for effect before finally asking, 'Who are you?'

Back upstairs, having heard no repeat of the snapping sound, Alan has just returned to the middle of the hall and turned off the torch when he feels the temperature drop suddenly. Then from the southern end of the hall, he hears the unmistakable sound of footsteps, ascending the stairs.

'T . . .' says Tony, as the glass continues its way around the alphabet, 'and . . . H. Hannath? Was that Hannath?'
    The others watch in stunned silence as the glass moves back towards the YES card.

With the sound of the footsteps getting louder Alan keeps the torch pointed down the corridor as he makes his way to the top of the stairs, but when he shines his torch to the bottom there is no one to be seen.

When Alan returns shortly after to the living room, the séance is brought to a close and the CUSPR team retire to the lounge to discuss their findings. Alan fills them in on the sounds he heard but suspects the noises were little more than the creakings of an old house. In return, the others discuss the Ouija session, speculating that either Wilmot or his friend Perryman might have been orchestrating the movements of the glass. After a quick break for tea and sandwiches back in the living room, Tony and Alan head off to begin their observations in Bedroom A while David and Michael initiate another séance to keep an eye on everyone else and to make sure nobody is carrying out a hoax.
    Shortly after 01:30, with the others back round the living-room table, Tony and Alan switch on their torches and make their way toward Bedroom A. As they pass the children's bedroom, Tony makes a quick check inside and finds the children both still fast asleep in their beds. Alan checks the thermometer he left outside

the room, surprised to see the mercury has sunk a full 10 degrees. With the distant sound of voices coming from the kitchen the two men push open the door to the bedroom and head inside.

Back in the living room, Michael rearranges the alphanumerical circle and places the wine glass back in the centre as David lights the candle and switches off the main lights again before returning to the table.

'Let's see what we can get this time', says Michael, placing his finger on the top of the glass. As the others do the same a sudden hush descends, and all eyes fix on the empty vessel.

'Is there anybody there?' asks David.

Upstairs, Alan and Tony point their torches around, finding it unchanged from their earlier inspection. Tony notices part of the far corner appears to have been covered up for some reason and heads over to inspect it. It seems to be some sort of asbestos boarding which Tony takes care to prise a little from the wall only to find nothing but a small empty space behind. Satisfied there is nobody hiding in the room with them Alan closes the door and bolts it shut. They take a mattress each, sitting down face to face with the soles of their feet touching so as to make sure neither is able to fool the other. Alan lays a blanket over them both as a second precautionary measure and having both settled into place they push the switches on their torches, plunging themselves into complete and utter darkness.

'Perhaps it's gone for the night,' says a despondent Derek.

The group take a collective breath and take their fingers away from the glass, which hasn't moved an inch since they started. Michael suggests Rose try the next question.

Rose pauses for a moment before asking, 'Is there anybody there?'

For a moment there is nothing. But then, almost imperceptibly at first, the glass starts to move.

'What was that?' says Tony, throwing torchlight into the corner of the room.

Alan does the same.

'Forget it, it was nothing,' Tony says, settling back into place.

'Christ you nearly gave me a heart attack.'

'Wait – over there! Listen!'

Alan turns on his torch and points it round the room.

'No, keep it off. Just listen . . .' says Tony.

'Is your name Hannath, can you please confirm?' asks Rose.

The group watches enrapt as the glass slides across the table to the YES card before returning to the centre of the circle.

'Why are you here?'

Quicker now, the glass moves across from one letter to the other as it hastily spells out the words: 'Looking for someone.'

Rose looks nervously to her daughter.

'Who . . . who are you looking for?' she asks.

But the glass doesn't move.

'Will you give us a sign of your presence?' she tries again.

After a moment's pause, the glass moves again to the YES card . . .

'There! Did you hear it, just to your left,' says Tony excitedly.

It comes again, clear and unmistakable this time: three knocks on the floor just to Alan's left.

'Good God—'

'Hello? Can you knock again three times?'

Knock, knock, knock.

'I don't believe it,' says Alan before adding hurriedly, 'knock once for yes and two knocks for no. Do you understand?'

Knock . . .

'You don't really think it's going to be able to make its presence known do you?' says Audrey.

'Try something else,' insists Derek.

'Where are you now?' asks Rose.

Again the glass begins to move, but slowly this time, much more deliberately. It stops beside the letter G, then left to the letter E, then back to H and around the circle until the word GEHENNA is spelt out and the glass returns to the centre of the circle.

'Ge . . . *henna*? Is that what it said? That isn't even a word.'

'It must be a mistake, try it again,' says Wilmot.

'Wait, nobody knows that word?' says David looking across at all the bemused faces. He takes his finger suddenly from the glass.

'What is it?' asks Rose.

'I'm not sure I should . . .'

'Just tell us,' insists Wilmot.

David proceeds to explain that Gehenna, a Hebrew word meaning 'Valley of Hinnom', describes a place just south of Mt Zion in Jerusalem; the place where the kings of Judah are said to have sacrificed their children by burning them alive. It's also another word for Hell.

'Are you male?' asks Tony.

Knock knock, comes the reply.

'Did you die in the house?'

Knock.

'Did you die a natural death?'

Knock, knock . . .

Downstairs, the group, now thoroughly unsettled by David's revelation, have brought the séance to an abrupt end. Perryman and Trumpess decide to call it a night and despite Wilmot's pleas that they might stay a while longer, he eventually agrees to join them in heading home. Wilmot is disappointed that he won't get the chance to confer with Tony and Alan before leaving but David promises to be in touch as soon as their reports are formally written up. Soon after, the three friends head off back to Wisbech leaving the Pages with the men from CUSPR to continue with the evening.

* * *

With the others gone, Michael and David head upstairs to let Alan and Tony know and are staggered when they catch the sound of knocks coming from inside the bedroom responding to Tony and Alan's questions. Alan explains from behind the door that they have just spent the last ten minutes communicating with some kind of female entity claiming to have been murdered in the house in 1906. Alan tells David and Michael to check the room below to make sure no one is making the noises. The pair quickly make a trap outside the bedroom, tying a length of cotton string around two music stands in case anyone plans to sneak around the corridor while they're gone, then head down to the room below. The family remain sitting in the living room as Michael and David continue through into the washroom, confirming that there is no one messing about inside it.

Back inside Bedroom A, the knocks are growing louder and more insistent as Tony and Alan continue to quiz the entity.

'How old were you when you died?' asks Alan.

There is a pause before a loud BANG, BANG, BANG rings out from opposite sides of the room, each one getting closer to Tony until finally a fourth raps against the brass bedstand beside his head. Tony launches himself from the mattress.

'That's too close! Why don't we check on the others downstairs?'

Growing deeply unnerved, Alan is only too happy to take a break. He grabs his torch from the bed and hurriedly makes his way to the door. At the sound of yet another loud knock, Alan flings the door open and charges straight into David and Michael's trap, bringing the stands clattering to the floor and sending him stumbling back into the bedroom. With Tony following close behind the pair are forced back for a moment when they hear a strange rumbling from inside. Tony points the torch just in time to catch one of the chairs being flung through the air and on to the mattress where he had just been sitting. A stunned Tony holds the chair in the beam of light, staring at it for what seems like hours. Satisfied it won't move again, he picks it up and places it back on the pile of boxes, only for it to slip back down on to the floor, making both men jump again. Cursing himself, Tony picks it up one more time, placing it firmly back on to the boxes.

'Tony's had a chair thrown at him, and we're getting clear messages,' says Alan, running into the washroom, adrenaline almost visibly coursing through him. Michael and David agree to keep watch on the family as Alan and Tony, having gathered themselves, return to Bedroom A to finish their questioning.

Stepping back into the bedroom Tony gasps when he catches sight of another chair that seems to have been placed on the floor, blocking the path from the door, while a cardboard box has also been left on one of the mattresses. Undeterred, the men move the items to the side, and return to their makeshift beds to begin their questions anew, starting again by asking how old the entity was when she died.

A few minutes later, David and Michael hear a commotion in the living room. David heads in to investigate and finds that Wilmot and his two friends have returned to the house. Their car broke down half a mile away so they are back in the hope of securing a lift into Wisbech. With the family having filled them in on the events of the last few minutes, Wilmot asks if they can be of any assistance, but David suggests it might be best if they leave them to it. Derek offers to drive the three men back and they head off together soon after, with the time just gone 2.20 a.m. Having overheard the exchange, Michael can't help but wonder if the men had indeed broken down or if they hadn't in fact spent the last twenty minutes fooling around outside. This time he watches the car all the way as it drives off the property before disappearing down the road and into the night.

'What month did you die?' asks Tony.

Eleven knocks comes the reply.

'And what day was that?'

Again the knocks come, seeming to emerge from a space just to the right of Tony. But as the knocks continue, now up to fourteen, they begin slowly to draw nearer to him. In a panic he shines his torch at the spot, bringing the knocks to an abrupt stop, much to Alan's frustration.

'Sorry, that was too close,' says Tony. He takes a moment to recompose himself before switching the light off again and repeating the question. The knocks return almost instantly and stop at eighteen.

'18th November 1906, is that correct?'

Knock, comes the reply.

Just to make sure that neither are fabricating the exchanges, Tony suggests they hold hands for the next question. Now with the soles of their feet planted against each other's and their hands clasped tightly together, Tony asks again, 'Are you still there?'

Knock, comes the reply.

With only Rose and Audrey left downstairs, Michael remains in the living room to keep watch over Rose while David and Audrey, eager to hear the noises for themselves, move into the washroom to listen from underneath. For the next twenty minutes, the pair stand in the pitch black together, listening silently as Tony and Alan can be heard from above. Each time they ask a question the knocks come back without fail. It is not until 2.45 a.m. that the raps finally begin to peter out, with Tony and Alan concluding the entity's age of death to have been either thirty-eight or eighty-three.

Nearly an hour later, Derek has returned and with the men from CUSPR having taken a break to write preliminary reports, they are ready to restart the investigation. With David wanting to experience the haunted bedroom first hand, Michael agrees to keep the Pages and Rose company downstairs while the other three head up to Bedroom A. With Alan leading the way, the men once again pause outside the children's bedroom to make a quick check on the pair, and find the young boy and girl asleep in their beds. Shining the torch towards the end of the corridor, Alan gives a start. Bedroom A's door is slightly ajar.

'What is it?' asks Tony.

'I closed that when we came downstairs.'

Undeterred, Alan leads the other two into the room. Tony has just shut the door behind them when a strange metallic clattering is heard. He swiftly points his torch towards the internal bolt lock, where a large brass toasting fork has been thoroughly jammed in its place, locking them inside. The men quickly flash their torches about the room but no one is there and all is still and silent. Taking a breath, Tony removes the fork from the lock and places it to the side and the three of them take up places on the mattress nearest the middle of the room.

Arranging themselves into a circle, the men plant their feet, one against each other, and switch off their torches. Then in the complete darkness, they reach out and take hold of each other's hands.

'Is anybody there?' asks Tony.

Silence.

Then something very gentle, like a soft rustling, is heard. As they listen, the noise intensifies, now sounding like scratching.

'Perhaps it's the ivy dragging across the wall outside, or an animal?' suggests Alan.

But Tony isn't so sure. He listens more intently now, focusing his mind on nothing but the sound coming from somewhere out of the dark to his right. As he stares towards the back wall it feels as though that same dark is collapsing into itself and then it is pulling him in from somewhere far away.

A cold breeze drifts through the room when suddenly David and Alan sense something tugging at their hands. Tony's body has gone limp.

'Go away, go away!' he shouts, startling himself awake before leaning forward suddenly with his head in his hands.

'Sorry, I must have fallen asleep.'

Alan quickly feels for his pulse and finds it racing at over two beats a second.

'What happened?'

'Something was attacking me; a horse I think. All I could see were the hooves kicking down on to my head.' It was as Derek's mother had experienced during her brief stay in the same room.

David and Alan wait a moment for Tony to calm, then, satisfied he is happy to carry on, they begin again. For more than an hour the men sit holding hands in the dark asking questions into the air, but there will be no more replies. At 5 a.m. the men decide to call it a night, gather their things together and make their way downstairs for a final cup of tea and debrief, where Tony shows the brass fork to the family: each claims to have never seen it before. A short time later, the men of the Cambridge University Society for Psychical Research thank Rose and the Pages for their time and make their way back to the car.

It is still dark outside as Tony pulls up to the edge of the driveway, taking in the looming presence of Hannath Hall one last time before slowly easing out into the road and heading back home.

Neither man will ever be entirely sure quite what it was they had experienced that night and as they make their way south, it isn't long before the waterways, vast open skies and ploughed black earths of the Fens have been replaced by more familiar and solid surrounds. As they cross the border into the city of Cambridge proper, a pale winter sun is just creeping up over the horizon while in the sky above, the many stars have all but completely vanished under the cover of daylight.

Though Michael never returned to the house and David only once, Tony and Alan between them would return on ten further occasions over the course of the next two years as they continued their investigation to varying degrees of success. Although no audio or visual proof of the poltergeist activity was ever recorded, of the 800 cases of supposed paranormal activity that Tony Cornell would eventually go on to investigate, he only considered a handful to be as genuine as you might ever hope to find; Hannath Hall was one of them.

*   *   *

The imposing Hannath Hall, 2018.

Whether you're one of the 34 per cent of the British public who believe in ghosts,[2] or one of the thousands in Southern China so concerned by the superstitions of Ghost Month that their heightened sense of caution in going about their daily dealings actively brings the area's death rate down, as a species we are thoroughly preoccupied by the idea of them. Though it is often poetic to talk about ghosts in the sense of being haunted by others or in the sense of existing alongside multiple other worlds theoretically present but forever impossible to reach, for me, the idea that ghosts might exist has always and only ever been about one thing: the possibility of life beyond death. Not for me the Stone Tape repetitions of a moment captured in time or the artificially, atomically perfect replication of my person to a digital cloud – if it isn't *me* who is aware of my continuing existence, then I'm not interested. Although it would remain to be seen just how enjoyable an infinite existence might be, since my fear of death remains as strong today as it was when I woke screaming into the night at six years old with the sudden and inescapable epiphany of my own mortality, an eternal life still seems preferable.

Failing the likelihood of achieving infinite life, I often find myself searching for new ideas with which to reposition my understanding of just how such a thing might be possible. And what better place to start than with our strangely simplistic notions of 'time'? When we think of time, we tend to picture a clock or a set of numbers with which to reference our day. We may say that time is the ageing of things, or talk about the passing of time. We once counted it by the rising and setting of the sun, becoming in turn the revolutions of the Earth and its orbit around the sun. Yet, this isn't time in any independent sense, but rather a convenient way to structure the world around us. Not only would two separate inhabitants of two different planets have completely different understandings of how long a 'day' would be, even if they both understood the same principle of an earthly hour, neither would experience it as the same length of time unless by some freak coincidence both their planets were orbiting, spinning and stretching across space-time at exactly the same rate. In other words, time, as discovered by Albert Einstein, is entirely relative to the observer – it is not an objectively quantifiable unit.

Since the early 20th century, scientists have been searching for the Theory of Everything – a framework to unify the seeming incompatibility of Einstein's theory of general relativity with the laws of quantum mechanics. Einstein's theory, which centres on the function of gravity and describes processes on large scales such as the orbits of planets, prefigures a deterministic universe in which it is possible in theory to calculate the cause of any event. Processes in the quantum realm, however, which govern the universe on the minute, sub-atomic level, are considered non-deterministic. Due to Heisenberg's uncertainty principle, which states it is impossible to know a sub-atomic particle's position and momentum at the same time, calculations in the quantum realm are measured as probabilities as opposed to definitive answers. While each method gives extraordinarily accurate predictions at their respective scales, they completely break down when applied to the other's, which makes the two 'worlds' fundamentally incompatible.

In the mid 1960s John Wheeler and Bryce DeWitt, two theoretical physicists from Princeton and the University of North Carolina, devised a way to combine the two processes. Wheeler and DeWitt's radical approach was to ignore the rules of the larger-scale laws and treat the entire universe as a quantum system, applying the laws of quantum mechanics to the function of gravity and space-time. Or more precisely, assuming the universe to be a closed system, they imagined it as one single quantum object. If the universe is a closed system (as mentioned in Chapter One), mathematically, the sum total of all the information within it is constant, which in effect means that ultimately the universe doesn't change. Of course we see change all the time – flowers blossom, trees bloom and birds fly, but what the Wheeler–DeWitt Equation, as it came to be known, implies is that there is no external time reference to measure this change.[3] If such a thing were to be true, on paper at least, the linear notion of past, present, and future is nothing but an illusory process within a much larger system that ultimately doesn't recognise it. The only thing that is fundamentally demonstrable is the whole of it, existing together constantly. Although many scientists have rejected this consequence of the Wheeler–DeWitt Equation, it is widely considered a useful step towards understanding decoherence,[4] the process that occurs at the border where the rules of the larger-scale world of classical physics begin to conflict with the laws of the quantum level.

One suggestion as to why we don't perceive time as it truly is, is that the language we use to describe it prohibits us from 'seeing' its true state. As the saying goes, 'time is what keeps everything from happening at once,'[5] which is to say that its appearance as something that flows from the past to the present, which in turn helps define movement, emerges solely because we describe it in that way. Ted Chiang draws on this idea to startling effect in his 1998 novella 'Story of Your Life' (later adapted as the 2016 film *Arrival* directed by Denis Villeneuve). Chiang's poetic and revelatory story opens with the sudden appearance of 112 monolithic structures suspended in the air in various locations across the globe. When the structures are found to be audio-visual links to a highly advanced species recently arrived in Earth's orbit, linguistics specialist Dr Louise Banks is tasked with deciphering their language in order to communicate with them. What Banks eventually discovers is that the written language of the aliens – called Heptapods due to their seven-limbed appearance – is essentially without linear structure, their sentences a collection of ideograms that appear simultaneously. Banks makes the startling realisation that rather than experiencing time in a sequential, linear fashion, the Heptapods experience it all at once. As Banks becomes more adept at the Heptopods' use of language she finds herself becoming untethered from her human-constructed sense of time until finally she too begins to see her past, present and future as one.

Without for a moment suggesting the Wheeler–DeWitt Equation is right to remove time as a quantifiable variable, and much less that it proves the existence of ghosts, I find myself oddly reassured by the non-linear interpretation of time. Perhaps, if we were so blessed (or cursed), we might too imagine ourselves, like Chiang's Heptapods, or indeed Kurt Vonnegut's Tralfamadorians, as creatures that have evolved to see not just the present but the entirety of everything that has been and will ever be; that ghosts become, not the spirits of the dead, but instead the bodies of the very much alive existing alongside us in perpetuity.

In a quote tentatively attributed to the Australian author Christina Stead, it is said that every love story is a ghost story. But might it be more correct to say that *every* story is a ghost story? That every tale we tell is something that has once passed yet somehow remains, kept alive, or in existence, within us. Isn't all of life just a story that we tell each other, whether it be shared by memory or through the very genetic imprint of our blood? And when, or if, all stories were to finally disappear, we might hope that somewhere still a ghostly imprint will remain. But if there really is no such thing as time, and nothing ever truly dies, then really there would be no ghosts, only us, and everything else, existing together forever.

NOTES

INTRODUCTION

1. Albert and Ian Smith, *Mosquito Pathfinder: A Navigator's 90 WWII Bomber Operations*, Crécy Publishing, 2011.
2. Mark Fisher, *The Weird and the Eerie*, Repeater Books, 2016, p. 8.
3. Max Tegmark, 'The Multiverse & You (& You & You & You)', podcast transcript, 20 April 2016, *Waking Up Podcast,* www.samharris.org/blog/item/the-multiverse-you-you-you-you
4. Arie Kruglanski and Donna Webster, 'Motivated Closing of the Mind: "Seizing" and "Freezing"', *Psychological Review*, Vol. 103, No. 2, 1996, p. 264.
5. Takeo Watanabe, Masako Tamaki, Ji Won Bang, Yuka Sasaki, 'Night Watch in One Brain Hemisphere during Sleep Associated with the First-Night Effect in Humans', *Current Biology*, Vol. 26, Issue 9, 9 May 2016, pp. 1190–94.

CHAPTER 1

1. A 2011 poll conducted by Ipsos Social Research Institute involving 18,000 people across 23 countries found that 51 per cent of participants believed in an afterlife.
2. Ernest Hemingway, *Death in the Afternoon,* Simon and Schuster, 2002, p.100.
3. Aaron J. Atsma, 'Kerberos', *Theoi*, 2017, www.theoi.com/Ther /KuonKerberos.html

4. John H. Taylor, *Journey Through the Afterlife: Ancient Egyptian Book of the Dead*, Harvard University Press, 2010, p. 215.

5. Jim Tucker, *Return to Life: Extraordinary Cases of Children who Remember Past Lives*, St Martin's Press, 2013, p. 89.

6. Humphrey Jennings, *Pandemonium 1660–1886: The Coming of the Machine as Seen by Contemporary Observers*, Icon Books, 2012, p. xvii.

7. H. G. Reid, quoted by David Simpson, 'Middlesbrough and Surrounds', *England's North East*, 2015, http://englandsnorth-east.co.uk/Middlesbrough.html.

8. Peter and Mary Harrison, *The Children That Time Forgot*, pp. 45–46

9. William Bernet, 'Children Who Remember Previous Lives: A Question of Reincarnation, Revised Edition', *Journal of the American Academy of Child & Adolescent Psychiatry*, Vol. 41, Issue 8, August 2002, pp. 1022–23.

10. *Ian Stevenson, Reincarnation and Biology: A Contribution to the Etiology of Birthmarks and Birth Defects*, Praeger Publishers, 1997, pp. 728–45.

11. Ian Stevenson, *European Cases of the Reincarnation Type*, McFarland & Company, 2003, p. 74.

12. Robert Macfarlane, *Landmarks*, Penguin, 2016, p. 232.

13. Bill Norman, *South Bank Dornier: South Bank, Cleveland, 15 January 1942*, Bill Norman, 2008.

14. Raymond J. St. Leger (2018), *Genomic Imprinting* [Video file]. Retrieved from https://www.coursera.org/learn/genes/lecture/B8ilo/genomic-imprinting

15. Brian G. Dias, and Kerry J. Ressler, 'Parental olfactory experience influences behavior and neural structure in subsequent generations', *Nature Neuroscience*, 17 (2014), pp. 89–96.

16. Ray Kurzweil, *The Singularity Is Near*, Gerald Duckworth & Co. Ltd, 2006.

17. It can also be asserted that, since we are natural, anything we consider 'technological', being an extension of us, is also natural, meaning that theoretically technological developments

are in themselves organic and natural developments and therefore can be considered a natural process of evolution.

18. H. H. Ehrsson, C. Spence and R. E. Passingham, 'That's my hand! Activity in premotor cortex reflects feeling of ownership of a limb', *Science*, 305 (5685), 6 August 2004.

19. We could argue that Sully's process of transformation has awakened an entirely new version of 'Jake Sully' but since the transformed Sully retains the agency and access to past memories that the previous Jake Sully had, we can in the broad sense be satisfied that these different versions, at root, constitute the same person.

20. Explored in more detail in Chapter Nine.

CHAPTER 2

1. Rob Sheffield, '100 Greatest TV Shows of All Time', *Rolling Stone*, 21 September 2016. Retrieved from: www.rollingstone.com/tv/lists/100-greatest-tv-shows-of-all-time-w439520/lost-w439598

2. J. J. Abrams (2007), 'The Mystery Box' [Video file]. Retrieved from www.ted.com/talks/j_j_abrams_mystery_box/transcript?language=en

3. The producers of *Lost* withheld the central conceit of the show until the final episodes of its sixth season.

4. For a truly mind-bending introduction to this phenomenon seek out Professor Jim Al-Khalili's explanation of the Double Slit Experiment presented as part of a lecture for the Royal Institution in 2013, available to watch via The Royal Institution YouTube page: www.youtube.com/watch?v=A9tKncAdlHQ

5. Although Schrödinger had in fact intended the experiment as a refutation of the Copenhagen Interpretation it leaves us with a neat way to visualise one of its principal ideas.

6. It must be stressed that no cats are harmed in this thought experiment since the cat is really just a metaphor for sub-atomic particles . . .

7. Kevin Mannis, Dibbuk Box original Ebay listing, cited in Jason Haxton, *The Dibbuk Box*, Truman State University Press, 2012, p. 6.

8. Ibid. p. 13.

9. Jason Haxton, *The Dibbuk Box*, Truman State University Press, 2012, p. 19.

10. Due to the misspelling, the specific box bought by Kevin Mannis is known as the 'Dibbuk Box'.

11. Haxton, *The Dibbuk Box*, p. 20.

12. Ioseph's original Ebay listing, cited in Haxton, *The Dibbuk Box*, p. 26.

13. Kevin Mannis, Dibbuk Box original Ebay listing, cited in Haxton, *The Dibbuk Box*, p. 27.

14. Jessica Lussenhop, 'Devil's Wine Box: Missouri's tie to *The Possession*,' *Riverfront Times*, 30 August 2012. Retrieved from: www.riverfronttimes.com/stlouis/devils-wine-box-missouris-tie-to-the-possession/Content?oid=2500991

15. Paulo Coelho, 'Mysteries of Aleph', Paulo Coelho Blog, 3 January 2012. Retrieved from: http://paulocoelhoblog.com/2012/01/03/misteries-of-aleph

16. Hearthstone, *In Praise of Olympus: Prayers to the Greek Gods*, lulu.com, 2012, p. 224.

17. Haxton, *Dibbuk Box*, p. 117.

18. Ibid.

19. Haxton, *Dibbuk Box*, p. 142.

20. Regardless of the veracity of Kevin's story, what is beyond doubt is that the Jewish population of Poland would suffer the greatest losses as a direct result of the Holocaust and anti-Semitic polices. Even leaving aside the myriad and quotidian forms of discrimination, it has been estimated that the population of Polish Jews in 1939 was roughly 3,474,000. Of these, an estimated 3,000,000 were murdered during the Holocaust.

21. http://www.dibbukbox.com

22. Alan C. Kerchoff, 'Analyzing a Case of Mass Psychogenic Illness', *Mass Psychogenic Illness: A Social Psychological*

Analysis, ed. Colligan *et al.*, L. Erlbaum Associates, 1982, pp. 5–19.

23. Nocebo (2018), *Merriam-Webster's dictionary online*. Retrieved from: https://www.merriam-webster.com/diction-ary/nocebo,

24. Mary Caffrey, '*Lancet* Study Highlights "Nocebo" Effect of Statins', *AJMC*, 3 May 2017. Retrieved from: http://www.ajmc.com/newsroom/no-rise-in-side-effects-from-statins-when-patients-dont-know-theyre-taking-them-lancet-finds

25. For those interested in learning more, the film *Hyperstition* (2015) by Christopher Roth in collaboration with Armen Avanession is a good place to start. Available to rent at hyper-stition.org.

26. Delphi Carstens, 'Hyperstition', *Xenopraxis*, 2010. Retrieved from: http://xenopraxis.net/readings/carstens_hyperstition.pdf

CHAPTER 3

1. The coining of the term 'Unidentified Flying Object' has been attributed to both aviator and writer Donald Keyhoe (1953) and USAF officer Edward Ruppelt (1956) by the Oxford English Dictionary.

2. B. J. Booth, 'Before the Wright Brothers . . . There Were UFOs', *American Chronicle*, 8 December 2006. Retrieved from: https://web.archive.org/web/20120819213938/http://www.americanchronicle.com/articles/view/17732

3. Curtis Fuller, *Proceedings of the First International UFO Congress,* Warner Books, 1980.

4. You can hear more about this incident in Season 1, Episode 3: *Do You See What I See* of *Unexplained*.

5. W. G. Sebald, *The Rings of Saturn*, Vintage, 2002, p.229.

6. This and the dialogue that follows is taken from the actual recording of the incident made by Lieutenant Colonel Charles

Halt, available to listen to at www.charleshalt.com

7. Greg Grewell, 'Colonizing the Universe: Science Fictions Then, Now, and in the (Imagined) Future', *Rocky Mountain Review of Language and Literature*, Vol. 55, No. 2 (2001), pp. 25–47.

8. A. Frank and W. T. Sullivan, 'A New Empirical Constraint on the Prevalence of Technological Species in the Universe', *Astrobiology*, Vol, No. 5, 13 May 2016.

9. Eric M. Jones, 'Where is Everybody?' An Account of Fermi's Question, March 1985. Retrieved from: https://fas.org/sgp/othergov/doe/lanl/la-10311-ms.pdf

10. Elizabeth Tasker, *The Planet Factory: Exoplanets and the Search for a Second Earth*, Bloomsbury Publishing, 2017, p. 8.

11. Mike Wall, 'No Alien Megastructure: Star's Weird Dimming Likely Caused By Dust', Space.com, 3 January 2018. Retrieved from: https://www.space.com/39263-alien-megastructure-tabbys-star-dust.html.

12. Sean Carey (2017), *7 Exo Planets Discovered on Trappist 1 – NASA Press Conference* [Video file]. Retrieved from: https://www.youtube.com/watch?v=x5lMRwBForE

13. Thomas Zurbuchen (2017), *7 Exo Planets Discovered on Trappist 1 – NASA Press Conference* [Video file]. Retreived from: https://www.youtube.com/watch?v=x5lMRwBForE

14. Jonathan Leake, 'Cox's theory on missing aliens', *The Times*, 9 October 2016.

15. George Knapp, 'I-Team: new film claims UFOs monitored nuclear weapons', *Las Vegas Now*, 6 July 2016. Retrieved from: http://www.lasvegasnow.com/news/i-team-new-film-claims-ufos-monitored-nuclear-weapons/500671865

CHAPTER 4

1. John Gray, *Straw Dogs: Thoughts on Humans and Other Animals*, Granta Books, 2003, p. 69.

2. An electroencephalogram records brain activity via electrodes placed on the scalp, which measure communication between brain cells.

3. Benjamin Libet, 'Unconscious cerebral initiative and the role of conscious will in voluntary action', *The Behavioral and Brain Sciences*, 8 (1985), pp. 529–556.

4. Perhaps a little unnerved by the results himself, Professor Haynes was quick to leave the door open for free will, declaring that it remained to be seen if such decisions could also be reversed or deliberately not acted on. Research News, 'Unconscious decisions in the brain: A team of scientists has unravelled how the brain unconsciously prepares our decisions', Max-Planck-Gesellschaft, 14 April 2008. Retrieved from: https://www.mpg.de/research/unconscious-decisions-in-the-brain

5. Much of the technology and techniques developed in the implementation of Aktion T4 would later become instrumental in the perpetration of the Holocaust.

6. Felicitas D. Goodman, *Exorcism of Anneliese Michel*, Resource Publications, 1981, p. 175.

7. Ibid., p. 178.

8. Eric Hansen, 'What in God's Name', *The Washington Post*, 4 September 2005, http://www.washingtonpost.com/wp-dyn/content/article/2005/09/02/AR2005090200559.html

9. Goodman, *Exorcism of Anneliese Michel*, 1981, p. 62.

10. Zoë Corbyn, 'Hungry judges dispense rough justice', *Nature*, 11 April 2011. Retrieved from: https://www.nature.com/news/2011/110411/full/news.2011.227.html

11. D. L. Olds, H. Kitzman, R. Cole *et al.*, 'Effects of nurse home visiting on maternal life-course and child development: age-six follow-up of a randomized trial', *Pediatrics*, 114 (2004), pp. 1550–59.

12. H. J. Kitzman, D. L. Olds, R. E. Cole *et al.*, 'Enduring Effects of Prenatal and Infancy Home Visiting by Nurses on Children – Follow up of a Randomized Trial Among Children at Age 12,' *Arch Pediatr Adolesc Med*, 164 (5) (2010), pp. 412–418.

13. Reanalysis of D. L. Olds, C. R. Henderson, R. Cole *et al.*, 'Long-term effects of nurse home visitation on children's criminal and antisocial behavior: 15-year follow-up of a randomized controlled trial', *JAMA: The Journal of the American Medical Association*, 280 (14) (1998), pp. 1238–44.

14. Raymond J. St. Leger, (2018), *Epigenetics and You* [Video file]. Retrieved from https://www.coursera.org/learn/genes/lecture/5A5Bg/epigenetics-and-you

15. Kathleen D. Vohs, Nicole L. Mead, Miranda R. Goode, 'The Psychological Consequences of Money', *Science*, Vol. 314, Issue 5802 (17 Nov. 2006), pp. 1154–6.

16. Daniel C. Dennett, *Elbow Room: The Varieties of Free Will Worth Wanting,* MIT Press, 1984.

17. Sean Carroll, 'Free Will is as Real as Baseball', *Preposterous Universe*, 13 July 2011. Retrieved from: http://www.preposterousuniverse.com/blog/2011/07/13/free-will-is-as-real-as-baseball.

18. http://www.open.edu/openlearn/ocw/mod/oucontent/view.php?printable=1&id=18956

19. Michael Mosley, 'The Uncomfortable Truth About Mind Control: Is Free Will Simply A Myth?', *Independent*, 6 January 2011. Retrieved from: https://www.independent.co.uk/lifestyle/health-and-families/features/the-uncomfortable-truth-about-mind-control-is-free-will-simply-a-myth-2177014.html.

20. Stanley Milgram, 'Behavioral study of obedience', *Journal of Abnormal and Social Psychology*, 67 (1963), pp. 371–378.

21. Stanley Milgram (Director) 1962, *Obedience* [Video file]. Retrieved from https://www.youtube.com/watch?v=wdUu3u9Web4

22. Milgram, 'Behavioral study of obedience', pp. 371–378.

23. Shaun Nichols, 'Free Will versus the Programmed brain', *Scientific American,* 19 August 2008, https://www.scientificamerican.com/article/free-will-vs-programmed-brain/

24. *True Detective*, HBO, New York, US, 2014.

CHAPTER 5

1. William Atkins, 'The mystery of Saddleworth Moor: who was Neil Dovestone?' *The Guardian*, 14 May 2016.

2. Robert Krulwich, 'Who's the First Person in History Whose Name We Know?', *National Geographic*, 19 August 2015, http://phenomena.nationalgeographic.com/2015/08/19/whos-the-first-person-in-history-whose-name-we-know/

3. Yuval Noah Harari, *Sapiens: A Brief History of Humankind*, Random House, 2014, p. 137.

4. Omar Khayyám & Edward Fitzgerald, *The Rubáiyát of Omar Khayyám*, Collins, 1947, p. 66.

5. Ibid., p. 89.

6. G. M. Feltus, *The Unknown Man: A Suspicious Death at Somerton Beach*, Port Campbell Press, 2017, location 1100 of 4916.

7. *The Rubáiyát of Omar Khayyám* was a series of quatrains attributed to Omar Khayyám, a mathematician and astronomer who lived in Persia in the 11th and 12th centuries CE, which were loosely compiled and translated by the poet Edward FitzGerald. First published in 1859, the book initially failed to sell until a fashion for Orientalism in the English-speaking world saw its popularity increase markedly. The *Rubáiyát* became even more popular during the First and Second World Wars, offering solace to many with its themes of accepting fate and embracing the virtues of living life by the day. Today over 1,330 versions of the *Rubáiyát* have been published. https://news.utexas.edu/2008/12/19/hrc_rubáiyát

8. Renato Castello, 'New twist in Somerton Man mystery as fresh claim emerges', Adelaide Now, 23 November 2013, http://www.adelaidenow.com.au/news/south-australia/new-twist-in-somerton-man-mystery-as-fresh-claims-emerge/news-story/18b3fe551a0b50d1adad4b42646a1748?nk=392ac697c93839c-6c1feb79ccb8b6c94-1520941080

9. Arthur Miller, *The Crucible*, Heinemann, 1992, p. 115.

10. William Shakespeare, *Romeo and Juliet*, J. B. Lippincott, 1913, p. 98.
11. Alexandra Sims, 'Muhammad Ali: why did the boxing legend change his name from Cassius Clay,' *Independent*, 4 June 2016.

CHAPTER 6

1. Barry Evans, 'Myth of the Invisible Ships', *North Coast Journal*, 23 June 2009, https://www.northcoastjournal.com/humboldt/myth-of-the-invisible-ships/Content?oid=2129921
2. Bob Ralph, 'Forum: Now you see it now you don't – a problem that may as well be invisible', *New Scientist*, 17 June 1989, https://www.newscientist.com/article/mg12216695.700-forum-now-you-see-it-now-you-dont--a-problem-that-might-as-well-be-invisible/
3. Ibid.
4. Arien Mack and Irvin Rock, *Inattentional Blindness*. MIT Press, 1998.
5. Daniel Simon and Christopher Chabris, *The Invisible Gorilla: And Other Ways Our Intuition Decieves Us*, HarperCollins, 2011.
6. Sarah Iles Johnston, *Ancient Greek Divination*, Wiley-Blackwell, 2008, p. 43.
7. Sarah Iles Johnston & Peter T. Struck (eds.), *Mantikê: Studies in Ancient Divination*, BRILL, 2005, p. 132.
8. Sarah Iles Johnston, 'Charming Children: the Use of the child in Ancient Divination,' *Arethusa*, Volume 34, Number 1, 2001, pp. 97–117.
9. BBC, *Broad Haven UFO sightings marked 40 years on*, BBC.co.uk, 4 February 2017, http://www.bbc.co.uk/news/uk-wales-south-west-wales-38723643
10. Jerome Clark, *The UFO Book: Encyclopedia of the Extraterrestrial*, Visible Ink Press, 1998.
11. Cynthia Hind, 'UFO Flap in Zimbabwe: Case No. 95', *Afrinews*, No. 11, February 1995, p. 12.

12. Ibid., p. 14.

13. Ibid., p. 12.

14. This and the subsequent exchanges with Cynthia Hind are taken verbatim from Cynthia's interview of the Ariel School pupils as filmed by Tim Leach, retrieved from https://www.youtube.com/watch?v=eBqKJHSrYZg

15. Van Hunks, 'The Tokoloshi (Tokolosh, Tokoloshe, Tokoloshie, Tikaloshe)', Vanhunks.com, 2002, http://www.vanhunks.com/tokoloshi1.html

16. John E. Mack, *Passport to the Cosmos: Human Transformation and Alien Encounters*, Three Rivers Press, 2000, p. 9.

17. This and the subsequent exchanges with Dr Mack are taken verbatim from Mack's interview of the Ariel School pupils, retrieved from https://www.youtube.com/watch?v=TBiMzxdco90&t=89s

18. John E. Mack, *Passport to the Cosmos: Human Transformation and Alien Encounters*, Three Rivers Press, 2000, p. 94.

19. Jennifer Bayot, 'Dr. John. E. Mack, Psychiatrist, Dies at 74', *The New York Times*, 30 September 2004.

20. Susana Martinez-Conde, 'What Babies See That You No Longer Can', *Scientific American*, 1 February 2016, https://blogs.scientificamerican.com/illusion-chasers/what-little-babies-see-that-you-no-longer-can/

21. Ibid.

22. Susana Martinez-Conde (2016), *The Dance of Life* [Video file]. Retrieved from: https://iai.tv/video/the-dance-of-life

23. Hilary Lawson (2017), *The Strangeness of Things* [Video file]. Retrieved from: https://iai.tv/video/the-strangeness-of-things

24. Timothy Morton, *Dark Ecology: For a Logic of Future Coexistence*, Columbia University Press, 6 May 2016.

25. Ibid.

26. Ibid., p. 6.

27. Oliver Moody, 'Why dolphins and whales are even cleverer than we thought', *The Times*, 16 October 2017.

CHAPTER 7

1. Robert Macfarlane, 'The word-hoard: Robert Macfarlane on rewilding our language of landscape', *The Guardian*, 27 February 2015.

2. Edgar Allan Poe, *The Fall of House of Usher: And Other Writings*, Penguin, 2008 p90

3. Ibid., p. 109.

4. John J. Miller, 'Chilling Fiction', *The Wall Street Journal*, 29 October 2009, https://www.wsj.com/articles/SB10001424052 748703298004574455551864001062

5. Shirley Jackson, *The Haunting of Hill House*, Penguin, 2009, p. 82.

6. Both locations represent two of the UKs most celebrated sites of 'poltergeist' hauntings. You can find out more about the The Pontefract Ghost in Unexplained Season 01 Episode 04: 'Where Darkness Plays'.

7. Alfred Hitchcock credited the inspiration for the Bates Mansion to Edward Hopper's *House by the Railroad*.

8. Jill Levoy, *Ghettoside: A True Story of Murder in America*, Random House, 2015, p. 116.

9. Having gone on the run after committing the murders in Los Angeles, Unterweger was eventually caught and arrested in Miami in February 1992 when it would transpire that he had in fact killed at least eight women since his release in 1990.

10. Kimjoy24, 'Dad's stay at the haunted Cecil Hotel', The Memories Project, 23 February 2012, https://memoriesproject.com/2012/02/23/dads-stay-at-the-haunted-hotel/

11. *Haunted Encounters: Face to Face*, Biography Channel, 2012.

12. Eyewitness News, 'Ghost' photo captured outside Cecil Hotel in downtown Los Angeles, 27 January 2014, http://abc7.com/archive/9409571/

13. Stephen King, 'The Shining: Inspiration', StephenKing.com,

2000–2018, https://www.stephenking.com/library/novel/shining_the_inspiration.html

14. John Reppion, *Spirits of Place*, Daily Grail Publishing, 2016, back cover.

15. Tim Edensor, *Industrial Ruins: Spaces, Aesthetics and Materiality*, Berg, 2005, p. 11.

16. Ibid.

17. Ibid

18. Tim Edensor, 'Artist Statement', Topographies of the Obsolete, 2013, http://topographies.khib.no/participants/tim-edensor-mmu/

19. Edensor, *Industrial Ruins: Spaces, Aesthetics and Materiality*, 2005, p. 152.

20. Ibid

CHAPTER 8

1. Incidentally, Wes Craven is thought to have drawn partial inspiration for *A Nightmare on Elm Street* from the crudely labelled 'Asian Death Syndrome' of the late 70s and 80s. During this period, over 110 Hmong men, who had fled to America from Laos in the 70s to escape the newly installed Communist government, are thought to have fallen victim to this syndrome, having died following unexplained seizures in their sleep.

2. Capt. James Cook was killed on 14 February 1779 on the island of Hawaii during his third exploratory voyage of the globe; the exact circumstances of his death remain a mystery.

3. Mark Twain, *Roughing It*, American Publishing Co., 1872, p. 514.

4. Abu Bakr II never returned after setting out on his voyage of intrigue, however Malian writer and historian, Prof. Gaoussou Diawara, writing in his 2010 book *Abubakari II Explorateur Mandingue* has suggested that he reached as far as present-day Brazil.

5. In many ways the hard-science search for 'truth' is not too dissimilar to the Gnostic or religious search for 'truth'. Both are founded on the belief that there is more to reality than what we know; both are striving to peer behind the wizard's curtain. Where they differ is in their approach: Gnostics start with the absolute conviction that there is something more to it all, some guiding hand. Their search cannot stop until this manufacturer is revealed. This approach often leaves me wondering what would prevent this search from continuing *ad infinitum*? What if we did discover one day that there was an omnipotent creator after all? How soon before this God would be assimilated into a regular mundane picture of existence? How long then before the next movement of Gnostics, having decided that this God doesn't quite satisfy, begin a new quest for knowledge and enlightenment in order to reveal the true hidden world behind this just-discovered God . . . Scientists on the other hand tend not to start with an end point. Although they are more than happy to acknowledge there are things not yet known that may yet be discovered, they get there one step at a time through trial and error and the slow, methodical accumulation of empirical data – they might occasionally take a leap of faith for an idea, but if the data doesn't correlate the idea is discarded.

6. Kevin Randle, 'Delbert Newhouse and the Utah Movie', A Different Perspective, 7 December 2013, http://kevinrandle. blogspot.co.uk/2013/12/delbert-newhouse-and-utah-movie. html

7. Margaret Brady, *Some Kind of Power: Navajo Children and Skinwalker Narratives*, University of Utah Press, 1984, p. 22.

8. Zack Van Eyack, 'Frequent Flyers', Deseret News, 30 June 1996, https://www.deseretnews.com/article/498676/ FREQUENT-FLIERS.html

9. Ken Layne, 'The Strange History of Robert Bigelow, Who Just Sold NASA Inflatable Space Station Modules', The Awl, 17 January 2013, https://www.theawl.com/2013/01/the-strange

-history-of-robert-bigelow-who-just-sold-nasa-inflatable-space
-station-modules/

10. Russian cosmologist and mathematician Alexander Friedmann had also hit upon the idea as early as 1922 when he provided calculations for both an expansion and steady-state model of the universe. Friedman would never live to see the proof of his theory, however, as he died tragically of typhoid in 1925 at the age of 37.

11. Einstein is thought to have said this to Lemaitre at the Solvoy Conference on physics in 1927.

12. Georges Lemaître, *The primeval atom: An essay on cosmogony*, Van Nostrand Company, 1950. Retrieved at https://philpapers.org/rec/LEMTPA-3

13. In spite of his own observations Hubble remained sceptical for the rest of his life about Lemaitre's theory of space expansion.

14. Simon Singh, 'Even Einstein Had His Off Days', *The New York Times*, 2 January 2005, http://www.nytimes.com/2005/01/02/opinion/even-einstein-had-his-off-days.html

15. Of course, with Einstein being the genius that he was, it turns out that the cosmological constant might have a function after all with some linking it to the unknown quantity often referred to as dark energy.

16. As Margaret Wertheim notes in a 2018 essay for Aeon, most recently, scientists such as cosmologist Sean Caroll, have even suggested that space, much like the way in which individual water molecules are not in themselves *wet*, is merely an emergent property derived from things at a quantum level. For a better understanding, read Margaret Wertheim's fantastic introduction to all things multi-dimensional here: https://aeon.co/essays/how-many-dimensions-are-there-and-what-do-they-do-to-reality

17. Stephen Hawking (2016), *Stephen Hawking's Favourite Places* [Video file], Retrieved from: https://app.curiositystream.com/video/1697

18. Roger Scrutton, *News From Somewhere: On settling*, Continuum, 2006, p. 10.

CHAPTER 9

1. Pierre Teilhard de Chardin, *The Phenomenon of Man*, Harper Perennial, p. 182.

2. Ibid., p. 17.

3. Mike McDowall, 'How a simple "hello" became the first message sent via the Internet', PBS, 9 February 2015, https://www.pbs.org/newshour/science/internet-got-started-simple-hello

4. The process of evolution is often wildly misunderstood. In Teilhard de Chardin's case, there is no guarantee that evolution will make an organism intellectually smarter, merely that, through the process of mutation, the variants of a species that are best suited to their environment will come to dominate.

5. Tim O'Reilly, '2. Harnessing Collective Intelligence', oreilly.com, 2018, http://www.oreilly.com/pub/a/web2/archive/what-is-web-20.html?page=2

6. Ethan Zuckerman, *Digital Cosmopolitans: Why We Think the Internet Connects Us, How it Doesn't and How to Rewire it*, W. W. Norton & Company, 2015, p. 29.

7. Ibid.

8. Heather Brooke, *The Revolution Will be Digitised: Dispatches From the Information War*, Random House, 2012, p. ix.

9. Something Awful (SA) was created in 1999 by Richard Kyanka, best known by his screen name Lowtax. SA began life as little more than a website for Kyanka to share his comedic and irreverent take on the world primarily through the lens of Internet cultures and video games. As the site grew in popularity, its forums became a breeding ground for irreverent, in-jokey Internet humour. Long before Twitter and Facebook, SA forum

users, self-described as 'Goons', pioneered for want of a better word, the caustic, irreverent and mocking humour that has come to define much of online culture. Regardless of whether you find the material on Something Awful funny, the website, whose motto is 'the internet makes you stupid' has been described by dailydot.com as 'one of the single most important websites in the history of internet humour.' https://www.daily-dot.com/unclick/something-awful-history/

10. Victor Surge/Eric Knudsen, 'Comedy Goldmine – Create Paranormal Images', somethingawful.com, 10 June 2009, https://forums.somethingawful.com/showthread.php?threadid=3150591

11. Ibid.

12. In truth the image was a re-working of a print taken from a woodcutting made by Hans Holbein the Younger of a knight doing battle with death: https://forums.somethingawful.com/showthread.php?threadid=3150591&userid=0&perpage=40&pagenumber=8

13. *The Digital Human, Tales*, Series 2 Episode 5, 30 September 2015 [Audio file]. Retrieved at http://www.bbc.co.uk/programmes/b01nl671

14. 'Folklore', The Oxford English Dictionary, https://en.oxforddictionaries.com/definition/folklore

15. Tom Pettitt, 'Before The Gutenberg Parenthesis: Elizabethan-American Compatibilities', presented at 'Media in Transition 5: creativity, ownership and collaboration in the digital age', 27–29 April 2007, https://www.academia.edu/2946207/Before_the_Gutenberg_Parenthesis_Elizabethan-American_Compatibilities

16. The term is a derivation of the online term copypasta, used to describe the process of information sharing which requires little more work from the sharer than simply copy and pasting something.

17. Austin Considine, 'Bored at Work? Try Creepypasta, or Web Scares', *The New York Times*, 12 November 2010.

18. Andrew Keen, *Cult of the Amateur: How Today's Internet is Killing Our Culture*, Doubleday, 2007, p. 16.

19. Deak Starkman, 'The future is medieval', *Columbia Journalism Review*, 7 June 2013, https://archives.cjr.org/the_audit/the_future_is_medieval.php

20. Ibid.

21. Ibid.

22. Kara Scannell, David Shortell and Veronica Stracqualursi, 'Mueller indicts 13 Russian nationals over 2016 election interference', CNN, 17 February 2018, https://edition.cnn.com/2018/02/16/politics/mueller-russia-indictments-election-interference/index.html

23. Ibid.

24. Konrad Krawcyk, 'Google is easily the most popular search engine, but have you heard who's in second?', Digital Trends, 3 July 2014, https://www.digitaltrends.com/web/google-baidu-are-the-worlds-most-popular-search-engines/

25. Alex Hern, 'Google accused of spreading fake news', *The Guardian*, 6 March 2017.

26. Paul Lewis, '"Fiction is outperforming reality": how YouTube's algorithm distorts truth', *The Guardian*, 2 February 2018.

27. Ibid.

28. Ibid.

29. Ibid.

30. Governments also crack down on platforms for the exact opposite reason. Most Google services for example have been blocked in China since 2010.

31. Alex Mar, 'Out Came the Girls: Adolescent Girlhood, the Occult and the Slender Man Phenomenon', VQR, Fall 2017, http://www.vqronline.org/essays-articles/2017/10/out-came-girls

32. Ibid.

33. abc7, 'Girls, 12, stab Wis. Friend 19 times in planned attack, cops say', abc7 Eyewitness News, 2 June 2014, http://abc7chicago.com/news/girls-12-allegedly-stabbed-friend-in-planned-attack/89632/

34. Jamie Seidel, 'A brutal stabbing attack by pre-teens obsessed with the Slenderman puts spotlight back on the popular culture of horror stories', news.com.au, 4 June 2014, http://www.news.com.au/technology/online/a-brutal-stabbing-attack-by-preteens-obsessed-with-the-slenderman-puts-spotlight-back-on-the-popular-culture-of-horror-stories/news-story/bc875cbcf8f27e8767462d176c8c126a

35. Andy Beckett, 'Accelerationism: how a fringe philosophy predicted the future we live in', *The Guardian*, 11 May 2017.

36. Simon Reynolds, 'Renegade Academia', Springerin Magazine, 20 January 2005, Retrieved from: http://k-punk.abstractdynamics.org/archives/004807.html

37. Andy Beckett, 'Accelerationism: how a fringe philosophy predicted the future we live in', *The Guardian*, 11 May 2017.

38. CCRU, 'Cyberhype V1: The Darkside of the Wave', *Mute*, 10 March 2002, http://www.metamute.org/editorial/articles/cyberhype-vi-darkside-wave

39. Jaron Lanier, *You Are Not A Gadget: A Manifesto*, Penguin, 2011.

40. Marshall McLuhan, *Understanding Media: The Extensions of Man*, Gingko Press, 2003, p. 25.

41. Lanier, *You Are Not A Gadget: A Manifesto*, 2011, p. 99.

42. Mark Fisher, *Capitalist Realism: Is There No Alternative*, o books, 2009.

43. Mark Fisher, 'What Is Hauntology?', *Film Quarterly*, Vol. 66, No. 1 (Fall 2012), pp. 16–24

44. Fully aware of the irony that I am doing so within the rigidity of a fixed text . . .

45. Donna Harraway, *A Cyborg Manifesto*, University of Minnesota Press, 2016.

46. Isaac Butler, 'Plagiarism Software's New Discovery About Shakespeare Is an Opportunity to Rethink His Genius', Slate, February 2018, https://slate.com/culture/2018/02/shakespeare-was-no-plagiarist-but-genius-isnt-born-in-a-vacuum.html

47. Michael Blanding, 'Plagiarism Software Unveils a New Source

for 11 of Shakespeare's Plays', *The New York Times*, February 2018, https://www.nytimes.com/2018/02/07/books/plagiarism -software-unveils-a-new-source-for-11-of-shakespeares-plays. html

48. Aaron Sachs, quoted by Rebecca Solnit, *A Field Guide to Getting Lost*, Canongate Books, 2017, p. 14.

CHAPTER 10

1. University of Cambridge, 'Society for Psychical Research', Cambridge University Library, 2018, http://www.lib.cam. ac.uk/collections/departments/manuscripts-university-archives/significant-archival-collections/society

2. Will Dahlgreen, 'Ghosts exist say 1 in 3 Brits', YouGov, 31 October 2014, https://yougov.co.uk/news/2014/10/31/ghosts-exist-say-1-3-brits/

3. The University of Massachusetts, 'The Cosmic Universe', The University of Massachusetts, http://www.faculty.umb.edu/gary _zabel/Courses/Parallel%20Universes/Texts/Cosmology,%20 Quantum%20Gravity,%20and%20the%20Arrow%20of%20 Time.htm

4. Nick Stockton, 'Time might only exist in your head and every-one else's,' *Wired*, 26 September 2016, https://www.wired. com/2016/09/arrow-of-time/

5. Ray Cummings, *The Girl in the Golden Atom*, Gateway 2015, ebook p. 86.9/606.

I'd also like to acknowledge the following resources for informing me during the writing process of this book: www.therendelshamfor-restincident.com; www.ianridpath.com/ufo/rendelsham.htm; David Clarke, 'New light on Rendelshame', www.drdavidclarke.co.uk/secret-files/secret-files-G1, 2012; LVCIFER, 'The Entire Case History of Anneliese Michel – The Real "Emily Rose", *Diabolical Confusions*, https://diabolicalconfusions.wordpress.com/2011/03/14/the-entire-case-history-of-anneliese-michel-the-real-emily-rose-warning-shocking-content/, 2011; Colm A Kehell, Ph.D., and George Knapp, *Hunt for the Skinwalker*, Paraview Pocket Books, 2005; Alan Gauld, Anthony Cornell, Michael Brotherton, David Murray, original Hannath Hall case notes, The Society of Physical Research Archive at Cambridge University Library, 1957.

Whilst the events and people in this book are all real, some dialogue has been fictionalised for the purpose of the narrative.

ACKNOWLEDGEMENTS

Musician Kathleen Hanna, when asked why she wanted to be a singer, said it was because she had so many things to say but nobody was listening to her. I started *Unexplained* out of a similar frustration and I owe a gratitude to every person whose work made it possible for me to speak into a microphone, edit it into a show, and upload it without impediment for anybody, anywhere, to be able to find it. My second gratitude is to all those people who have taken the time to listen.

What I certainly never imagined was being here two years later, on the verge of publishing *Unexplained* the book. For all the benefits of the digital world, nothing can quite match the thrill of being given this opportunity and for that I am eternally grateful to my fantastic editor Emma Herdman, for all the brilliant notes and support but mostly for completely understanding the essence of *Unexplained* from day one, not always an easy thing to put into words. And of course, thanks also to the rest of the amazing team at Sceptre for all their hard work: Lily Cooper, Fleur Clarke and Louise Court. Thanks also to my excellent agent Richard Pike for all the same reasons and for putting everything in motion.

I want to say a special thanks to all those who have given me their time in helping me get a better sense of the stories featured in the book, to the ever-accommodating Jason Haxton, Kevin Mannis and Alan Gauld, and to Oliver Williams for welcoming a random stranger lurking about outside into his home, Hannath Hall.

A special mention to Ryan Skinner for letting me use his picture of Skinwalker Ranch; he has a phenomenal treasure trove of information on the subject at skinwalkerranch.org if you care to look.

Thanks to the Society of Psychical Research for keeping such a great archive of material and to all the staff at the British Library – especially the very patient and reassuring lost-and-found department.

Huge thanks to my Dad and Adam Heal for reading some early drafts and for their vital comments. Huge thanks also to my Mum for her support and keeping me focused. A big apology to my sisters Lucie and Alice, and my nephew Marwood, for not having more time while putting this book together. Big shout out to my other nephew Cohen also, sorry we live so far away.

Unending thanks to my beloved and beautiful fiancée, soon to be wife, Donna for her endless support and advice, and for putting up with far more than should be expected of anybody.

Finally I want to dedicate this book to all the people I have written about that I have never met in particular, to those whose lives and tragic deaths I have encroached on, I hope I have been respectful, to Elisa Lam, Carl Edon, Anneliese Michel and the unknown man.

QUOTE ACKNOWLEDGEMENTS

The lines from *A Field Guide to Getting Lost* by Rebecca Solnit published by Canongate Books 2006. © Canongate Books. reproduced by permission of The Random House Group.

The lines from 'The Lady of the House of Love' from *Burning Your Boats* by Angela Carter, published by Chatto & Windus, 1995. Copyright © Angela Carter. Reproduced by permission of the estate of the author c/o Rogers, Coleridge & White Ltd., 20 Powis Mews, London W11 1JN.

The lines from *Cyclonopedia: Complicity with Anonyous Materials* by Reza Negarastani, published by re.press, 2008. Copyright © re.press and Reza Negarestani 2008. Reproduced by permission of re.press.

The lines from *The Blind Assassin* by Margaret Atwood. Reproduced with permission from Curtis Brown Group Ltd, London, on behalf of Margaret Atwood copyright © O. W. toad Ltd, 2000.

The lines from Kendrick Lamar in conversation with Amos Barshad for Vulture.com. Reproduced by permission of Vulture. com.

The lines from *Dark Ecology* by Timothy Morton, published by Columbia University Press, 2016. Copyright © Columbia University Press. Reproduced by permission of Columbia University Press.

The lines from 'Coal Memory' from *Spirits of Place* by Alan Moore, published by Daily Grail Publishing, 2016. Copyright © Daily Grail Publishing. Reproduced by permission of Daily Grail Publishing.

PICTURE
ACKNOWLEDGEMENTS